Straight Talk About Reading

Straight Talk About Reading

How Parents Can Make a Difference During the Early Years

Susan L. Hall and Louisa C. Moats, Ed.D.

Foreword by G. Reid Lyon, Ph.D.
Chief, Child Development and Behavior Branch,
National Institutes of Health

CB
CONTEMPORARY BOOKS

Library of Congress Cataloging-in-Publication Data

Hall, Susan L. (Susan Long)
Straight talk about reading : how parents can make a difference during the early years / Susan L. Hall and Louisa C. Moats ; foreword by G. Reid Lyon.
p. cm.
Includes bibliographical references.
ISBN 0-8092-2857-2
1. Reading (Early childhood)—United States. 2. Reading—Parent participation—United States. 3. Reading—Remedial teaching—United States. 4. Reading disability—United States. I. Moats, Louisa Cook. II. Title.
LB1139.5.R43H35 1999
372.41—DC21 98-36002
CIP

Cover design by Scott Rattray

Interior design by NK Graphics
Interior illustrations by Cindy Weil

Published by Contemporary Books
A division of NTC/Contemporary Publishing Group, Inc.
4255 West Touhy Avenue, Lincolnwood (Chicago), Illinois 60712-1975 U.S.A.

Printed in the United States of America
International Standard Book Number: 0-8092-2857-2

04 MV 20 19 18 17 16 15 14 13 12 11 10 9 8 7

To my parents, Dwight and Blanche,
who gave me a solid foundation in life.
To David, my husband, and Sally Myers, my friend,
who encouraged me to follow my passion.
To Brandon and Lauren, who are the reason I became passionate
about children and reading.
And to the parents, who not only told me their stories,
but shared my vision that others behind us
might find the journey easier from knowing our stories.

Susan L. Hall

To Charlotte, who taught her parent so much about the joy and
power of reading.

Louisa C. Moats

Credits

Page 3: "How Johnny Should Read." *Time Magazine* (October 27, 1997). Copyright Time, Inc., 1997. Reprinted with permission.

Pages 4, 10, 29, 37–38, 50, 64, 98, 125, 135, 136, 140: *Beginning to Read: Thinking and Learning About Print* by Marilyn Jager Adams. MIT Press, Cambridge, MA, 1990. Reprinted with permission.

Pages 8, 23: "Reading Wars: Endless Squabbles Keep Kids from Getting the Help They Need" by Bonnie Miller Rubin. *Chicago Tribune* (March 2, 1997), Perspective section, page 1. Reprinted with permission.

Pages 9, 77, 96: "How Whole Language Became a Hot Potato In and Out of Academia" by Christina Duff. *Wall Street Journal* (Oct. 30, 1996), 1. Copyright © Dow Jones & Company, Inc. All rights reserved. Reprinted with permission.

Page 11: "In Blast from Past, California Schools Plan to Re-Embrace Phonics" by V. Dion Haynes. *Chicago Tribune* (May 10, 1996). Reprinted with permission.

Page 13: "Reading Scores Tumble: Steep Decline in Test Results Reported in Schools Statewide" by Rosalind Rossi. *Chicago Sun Times* (Sept. 8, 1997). Reprinted with permission.

Page 15: "Romance and Reality" by Keith E. Stanovich. *The Reading Teacher* (December, 1993/January, 1994), vol. 47, no. 4, page 285, 286. Reprinted with permission.

Page 38: "Your Home is Your Child's First School." International Reading Association. Reprinted with permission.

Pages 48–49: *Raising a Reader* by Paul Kropp. New York: Doubleday, 1993. Reprinted with permission.

Pages 56–61: Excerpts from *Curious George Gets a Medal* by H. A. Rey. Copyright © 1957 and © renewed 1985 by Margret E. Rey. Copyright assigned to Houghton Mifflin Company in 1993. Reprinted by permission of Houghton Mifflin Company. All rights reserved.

Page 61: *Becoming Literate: The Construction of Inner Control* by Marie M. Clay. Heinemann Education, 1991. Reprinted with permission.

Page 63: *The Read-Aloud Handbook* by Jim Trelease. Penguin Books, 1995. Reprinted with permission

Pages 77, 99, 113, 115–16, 217: *Teaching Our Children to Read: The Role of Skills in a Comprehensive Reading Program* by Bill Honig. Corwin Press, 1996. Reprinted with permission.

Pages 83, 93, 94, 95–96: *What's Whole About Whole Language?* by Kenneth Goodman. Copyright © 1986 by Kenneth Goodman. All rights reserved. Scholastic Canada Ltd., 123 Newkirk Road, Richmond Hill, Ontario, Canada. Reprinted with permission.

Pages 90–91: Halford, J. M. (September, 1997). "Reading Instruction: A Historical Timeline." *Infobrief* 10, pages 4–5. Used by permission of the Association for Supervision and Curriculum Development. Copyright © 1997 by ASCD. All rights reserved. Reprinted with permission.

Page 92: *The Schools We Need and Why We Don't Have Them* by E. D. Hirsch, Jr. Reprinted with permission of Bantam Books, a division of Bantam Doubleday Dell Publishing Group, Inc.

Page 92–93: *The Troubled Crusade: American Education* 1945–1980 by Diane Ravitch. HarperCollins Publishers, Inc., 1983. Reprinted with permission.

Page 118: *Every Child a Reader: The Report of the California Reading Task Force.* California Department of Education, 1995. Reprinted with permission.

Pages 120–21, 220: *Teaching Reading: A Balanced, Comprehensive Approach to Teaching Reading in Prekindergarten Through Grade Three.* California Department of Education, 1996. Adapted with permission.

Page 152: *Stages of Reading Development* by Jeanne S. Chall. McGraw-Hill, 1983, Harcourt Press, 1996. Reprinted with permission.

Page 160: "How to Build a Baby's Brain" by Sharon Begley. *Newsweek* Special Issue, Your Child: From Birth to Three (Spring/Summer 1997), 31. Reprinted with permission.

Pages 168–71, 176–78, 186, 233–35: *Reading Readiness* by Suzanne Carreker. Neuhaus Education Center, Bellaire, TX, 1992. Reprinted with permission.

Page 173–75: *Phonological Awareness: A Critical Factor in Dyslexia* by Joseph K. Torgesen, Ph.D. A brochure from the Orton Emeritus Series, The International Dyslexia Association. Reprinted with permission.

Pages 179, 182, 236–40, 250, 252–54, 264–65: *Words Their Way: Word Study for Phonics, Vocabulary, and Spelling Instruction* by Bear/Invernizzi/Templeton/Johnston, © 1996. Adapted by permission of Prentice-Hall, Inc., Upper Saddle River, NJ.

Pages 181, 183–85, 187: Excerpts from Yopp, Hallie Kay (May, 1992). "Developing Phonemic Awareness in Young Children." *The Reading Teacher*, 45(9), 696–703. Reprinted with permission of Hallie K. Yopp and the International Reading Association.

Page 198: *Do You Like Cats?* (Bank Street Ready to Read) by Joanne Oppenheim. Copyright © 1993 by Bank Street College of Education. Reprinted with permission.

Page 198: *My Pal Al* by Marcia Leonard. The Millbrook Press, 1998, Brookfield, CT. Reprinted with permission.

Page 206: *The Sunset Pond* by Laura Smith. Flyleaf Publishing, 1997, Lyme, NH. Reprinted with permission.

Pages 226–29: *Preventing Reading Difficulties in Young Children* by Catherine Snow, Susan Burns, and Peg Griffin. Copyright © 1998 by the National Academy of Sciences. Courtesy of the National Academy Press, Washington, D.C. Reprinted with permission.

Page 251: Hopping Frog game created by Janet Bloodgood, Appalachian State University.

Pages 263–4: Apple and Bushel Game created by Charlotte Tucker.

Page 272: *Basic Facts About Dyslexia: What Everyone Ought to Know* by Angela Wilkins, Alice Garside, and Mary Lee Enfield, Ph.D. "B" book of the Orton Emeritus Series, International Dyslexia Association. Reprinted with permission.

Page 273: *Doctors Ask Questions About Dyslexia: A Review of Medical Research* by Sylvia O. Richardson, M.D. "D" book of the Orton Emeritus Series, International Dyslexia Association. Reprinted with permission.

Page 276: "Defining Disability Down," by Ruth Shalit. *The New Republic* (Aug. 25, 1997), 22. Reprinted with permission.

Pages 288–89: *Testing: Critical Components in the Clinical Identification of Dyslexia.* Adapted from booklet from the Orton Emeritus Series written by Jane Fell Greene, Ed.D. and Louisa Cook Moats, Ed.D. Distributed by the International Dyslexia Association, 1995. Reprinted with permission.

Page 306: "Reading Recovery: An Evaluation of Benefits and Cost," by Bonnie Grossen and Gail Coulter. National Right to Read Foundation, 1997. Reprinted with permission.

Page 311: *About Dyslexia: Unraveling the Myth* by Priscilla L. Vail. Programs for Education, Inc., 1990. Reprinted with permission.

Contents

Part Two
What You Can Do to Help Your Child

Part Three
What to Do When Reading Is Difficult for Your Child

Foreword

A Word from an Expert

It is unusual that a book about reading written for parents can be informative, understandable, and true to the scientific basis for understanding reading. To my knowledge, this book is the first of its kind. The scientific research in reading has progressed to the level that dissemination of critical findings to a child's most important teacher—the parents—is not only possible but imperative. As I travel the country talking with parents and teachers about reading, I have found that parents are literally on their own as they attempt to understand a child's frustrations or to help their child learn. Susan Hall and Louisa Moats have also observed the needs of parents and have responded to them by providing the gift of this book. Mrs. Hall, whose own child experienced reading difficulty in first grade, and Dr. Moats, a reading scientist and teacher educator, combine their wisdom and knowledge to produce a readable, informative, accurate, and, above all, practical resource for parents.

G. Reid Lyon, Ph.D.
Chief, Child Development and Behavior Branch
National Institutes of Health
Bethesda, Maryland

INTRODUCTION

Why We Write This Book

Millions of capable children are not learning to read well in America's schools today. The causes and cures are well known in the research community, but classroom practice has been slow to change. Because reading is critical for success in school and in the world of work, the reality of reading failure is alarming, especially to parents. It is critical for parents to understand why some children fail to learn to read well with the instructional methods often used today to teach reading. Your child may or may not learn to read well in school, but you, the parent, will be the first one who recognizes that your child is struggling too much and falling behind. Time and time again it is the parent who first sees the problem and persists with determination to get the right kind of help for the child.

While the news about reading failure is almost overwhelming, straightforward information about reading can provide guidance and hope. For instance, you, the parent, *can* make a considerable difference in how well your child learns. By picking up this book, you are becoming a proactive parent ready to help your child read.

A few simple things in your daily life can make a difference in your child's achievement. Some facts about reading can help you talk to school personnel, who may not know or do what is needed to prevent reading problems. Deciding to be an informed and proactive parent is step number one—and you have taken it by picking up this book. It is written for you.

Almost all children can learn to read well if taught with appropriate methods. But not all children in today's classrooms are receiving the type of instruction that will equip them to be good readers. Parents are frequently told by educators not to worry when their child is struggling, or problems are passed off to developmental lags or learning style differences. Yet research shows that if we wait beyond first grade to give a child appropriate help, that child is likely to remain behind unless intensive, well-designed instruction is given. If a child is behind in third grade, the odds are strong that the child will remain behind for the rest of his schooling. Early identification of problems helps a great deal, and we know that there are certain activities in school as early as kindergarten that make the difference between reading success and reading difficulty in first grade and beyond. We also know that orthodox "whole language" methods, if used without instruction in sounding words out and spelling them correctly, are not effective for many children. Explicit teaching of reading skills is possible and effective even while children are enjoying literature. A majority of any class will learn to read well if the instructional program is complete and well taught with phonics included.

We wrote this book because we believe that parents want a reliable source of information about reading and that it was not readily available in a format that makes it accessible to them. We believe that parents can play a critical role in helping prepare their child for reading instruction, in monitoring instruction, in observing progress, and in advocacy if their child is struggling with reading. Parents armed with the information in this book may help turn their children into avid readers and avoid pitfalls of misinformed teaching.

This book was written collaboratively by a parent and an educator. The parent (Susan L. Hall) has two children, one of whom struggled in learning to read. She has lived through the experience as a parent and shares her family's story of searching for why her child found learning to read to be so difficult. She has spent hours talking with fellow parents to understand their questions and concerns. Her goal was to share what she had learned on her journey, converting educational jargon into language just right for parents.

The educator member of the team (Louisa C. Moats) has faced issues in reading instruction throughout her career. Her early experiences included teaching children with learning disabilities and reading problems, testing children, and consulting extensively with teachers and schools. She has spoken with thousands of parents in her role as a school psychologist and reading specialist. In the 1996–1997 school year she promoted reading reform in California by preparing materials for the State Board of Education and holding seminars for teachers and teacher trainers. The California Reading Initiative is an attempt to reform reading instruction and bring it in line with the best practices supported by research. Through her consultations with the National Institute of Child Health and Human Development (one of the branches of the National Institutes of Health), she is closely affiliated with the reading research community. Her goal in this book is to ensure that the information is accurate, current, and understandable, and that the advice offered to parents is consistent with the best practices known in the field today.

This book has three sections. Part One (Chapters 1–5) gives background information, whereas Part Two (Chapters 6–9) emphasizes activities for each grade starting with preschool through third grade. Part Three (Chapter 10) gives information about what to do if your child is having a reading problem. This book tells you:

- what you need to know about the whole language and phonics controversy
- what activities you can do at home to give your preschooler the best preparation for reading
- how you can tell which approach to teaching reading is used in your child's classroom

- how you can measure your child's reading progress against objective benchmarks to assess if he is on track
- what steps to take if you suspect your child is struggling in learning to read
- how to coach and monitor your child's reading progress throughout the elementary grades (preschool through third grade)

If anything, we have erred on the side of providing you more explanation and detail than you may need. Some of you will read voraciously the first few chapters to make sense of the reading "wars" that are written about in newspapers and magazines. Others will skim the beginning and focus on the practical activities offered in the latter chapters of the book. The book is structured in a question format to enable you to find what you want easily.

We need to inform you about the "voice" in our book. Throughout we have addressed parents as "you." The chapters alternate reference to individual children as "he" or "she." Whenever you see a personal segment that uses "I," it is a story told by Susan. We wrote these stories in her personal voice because she knew that other parents would readily identify with her puzzlement and worry when her son developed reading difficulties. We knew that parents would find comfort in her straight talk about reading.

This is a book about how to help parents raise a reader. We provide you with reliable, realistic, and useful information that should give you confidence in nurturing your child's reading development. We'll take you out of the middle of reading politics and methods arguments to the essentials that will help. If you are looking for more information, visit our Web site:

www.proactiveparent.com

Enjoy *Straight Talk About Reading.*

Straight Talk About Reading

Part One

Background Information You Need to Know

Chapter One

America's Reading Crisis

> The disputes have been dubbed the Reading Wars, and the participants call them "vicious." The passion is fueled in part by a simple fact: reading achievement in the U.S. is low. According to the most recent National Assessment of Educational Progress, 44% of U.S. students in elementary and high school read below the "basic level," meaning they exhibit "little or no mastery of the knowledge and skills necessary to perform work at each grade level." Seventy-two percent of blacks scored below basic; 32% of fourth-graders whose parents both had college degrees also failed to reach the basic level.[1]
>
> Time *magazine, cover article "How Johnny Should Read" October 27, 1997*

Proof of America's Reading Crisis

Is There a Reading Crisis in the United States?

America's reading problem is no secret: the President, the press, the business community, and parents are all concerned. Reading achievement scores in the United States have declined in many states. Too many children do not read well enough to succeed later at basic jobs. Learning disabilities are on the rise. Illiteracy in adults and declining verbal skills in college students are a national concern. The federal government and many state governments have initiated laws or advisories to improve reading instruction. Are these concerns legitimate? Is there truly a crisis in American reading education?

Hard facts say yes. The National Assessment of Educational Progress, the only national test to which states can subscribe voluntarily, showed 44 percent of our nation's fourth-grade children reading below a basic level of proficiency in 1994. In California, which was last in the nation next to Louisiana and Guam,

59 percent of fourth-graders read below the basic level and scores had declined from 1992. Our country's reading levels are average among our industrialized competitors, and our position is continuing to slip. In the Connecticut Longitudinal Study, a research project conducted at Yale University that has followed children from kindergarten through high school, about 20 percent of elementary children are characterized as having serious reading difficulty, and many more find reading laborious and unrewarding, even though they can read within the average range on standardized tests.[2] However, only 5 to 6 percent of our children nationally are actually classified by schools as having learning disabilities and are eligible to receive "special" instruction. President Clinton has promoted his America Reads Challenge in his second term in office, encouraging all children to read on grade level by third grade with the help of student tutors. Parents, who care about their children's reading, spelling, and basic math skills more than any other goal of education, have resorted to buying home reading programs in increasing numbers because of frustration with school-based reading instruction.

The concerns about reading achievement are occurring at a time when our society is demanding higher reading levels than ever before. The U.S. Office of Technology has estimated that 25 percent of the adult workforce does not read well enough to meet the routine requirements of today's workplace. With computers and other technology replacing manual tasks, it is impossible to participate fully in our society without being able to read well. According to Dr. Marilyn Adams, whose award-winning book synthesized most extant reading research in 1990, reading instruction needs to work better now than it did even a few years ago. As Dr. Adams points out in *Beginning to Read:*

> It is no longer possible to guess, much less dictate, what knowledge and skills will be critical to students in their futures. Each of them must be prepared with the abilities to acquire, understand, use, and communicate information accurately, efficiently, and independently. Levels of literacy that were once held—even very recently held—to be satisfactory, will be marginal by the year 2000.[3]

What About the Personal Cost of Children Failing to Read Well?

Parents know about the reading crisis when, in addition to the hard facts that point to widespread reading difficulty in our nation's children, a child of their own does not read well. When a child is laboring to learn, a parent's immediate concern is the unhappiness and frustration that the child experiences daily. Parents and the rest of the family at home are deeply affected by a child's reading problem. I know because one of my two children had difficulty learning to read. My son's battle with print not only overwhelmed him with doubt and anxiety, but also consumed me. During the middle of our child's first-grade year I spent an inestimable number of hours trying to figure out what was bothering him and then searching for what to do to solve the problem. My quest became a mission fueled by curiosity, need, and subsequent outrage at what was happening to my son and to other children affected by reading instruction in this country. My quest ultimately generated help for my son—and this book.

The parent of a struggling reader embarks on a long journey fraught with confusion and self-doubt. Simply identifying the real problem that is making the child unhappy with school can be an elusive goal. What the parent sees is a child who is reluctant to go out the door, who is unenthusiastic or even fearful of school, or whose behavior during school days changes unexpectedly. Most six-year-olds cannot tell you that the reason they are increasingly uncomfortable at school is embarrassment that reading is a mystery for them when other children have figured it out. Once a parent has finally surmised that poor reading is the source of her child's problems, she is likely to ask numerous questions for which answers seem elusive.

In our case, we discovered that my son simply needed to be taught to read with an approach different from the one used in his class. He was among the large number of children who would never read well without explicit and systematic instruction in how our alphabet represents sounds. His reading took off within about three months after we hired a tutor who knew how to teach him.

He is a good reader today who can read the words and comprehend their meaning—and that's what reading is about.

We discovered as well that reading instruction in education has gone through pendulum swings from one method to the next, and that a method that is "in vogue" may not match the needs of many children. Unfortunately for my child, the reading approach that was popular when he was in first grade was not effective for him. During the year that it took us to diagnose what was wrong and determine what intervention strategy would be most effective, I initiated a search for understanding and solutions without the help of school personnel. And it wasn't an easy process. During that quest my feelings about our educational system evolved from confusion to frustration. What would have happened to my son if we had relied upon the school to teach him to read? His teacher didn't even think that his labored reading was a problem. She told us that it was simply a developmental lag. Would he have always been an underachiever, never working to his full potential? That possibility alarms me and spurs me to share with parents what I learned during my journey to understand reading instruction in our schools.

TYPICAL QUESTIONS PARENTS ASK

- Why is my otherwise competent child having so much trouble with a basic school skill? Is he really unusual?
- Should my child be tested for learning problems?
- What is a learning disability?
- What do we need to do so my child will be able to read?
- Why do educators argue about phonics and whole language methods for teaching reading?
- Is one method better than another, and what is my child really getting at school?
- What can I do to help my child at home?
- Will my child ever be successful at school again?

What Happens to Children Who Fail to Read Well?

Reading is *the* most important skill for success in school and society. Children who fail to learn to read will surely fail to reach their full potential. According to the International Dyslexia Association, people in the United States who are illiterate represent:

- 75 percent of the unemployed
- ⅓ of mothers receiving Aid to Families with Dependent Children
- 85 percent of the juveniles who appear in court
- 60 percent of prison inmates[4]

Students who have milder but chronic difficulties with reading, according to the Connecticut Longitudinal Study, are often affected in less dramatic but important ways: they socialize less, engage in fewer extracurricular activities in school, curtail their education before their career aspirations may be realized, and are less likely to develop into people with diverse involvements and interests. When we look at the evidence for declining reading levels in many parts of the country, we believe the word "crisis" is justified. As Elizabeth McPike, editor of the journal of the American Federation of Teachers, remarked, "This we can say with certainty: If a child in a modern society like ours does not learn to read, he doesn't make it in life."[5]

Causes of the Reading Crisis

What Caused the Reading Crisis?

The decline in reading scores and the increase in the number of children having difficulty reading go hand in hand with a change in how reading is being taught in our schools. A new method of teaching reading swept the country about 15 years ago, and took root about 10 years ago. Although classroom instruction may not be the only factor that accounts for reading achievement in students, adoption of this new method is associated with the decline in reading achievement among our children, as measured by reading test scores.

The controversial approach to teaching reading is commonly referred to as the "whole language" philosophy in which reading is taught through immersion in children's literature—without direct, systematic, cumulative teaching of phonics, spelling, grammar, or comprehension. The term "whole language" means to teach reading without breaking language down into its parts. Whole language methods presume that children will learn to read naturally, through exposure to literature, with minimal and incidental instruction in the component skills of reading, such as knowing the sounds in words and how to spell them. Whole language replaced teaching that emphasized direct instruction in word analysis and the skill of sounding words out—thus, a "meaning-emphasis" approach. In whole language teaching, a child is instructed to look at the pictures of a children's book and to use the context or meaning to guess at unknown words; the emphasis is on guessing at words from the overall story rather than deciphering each word by sounding it out. As discussed in a March 2, 1997, article in the *Chicago Tribune* entitled, "Reading Wars: Endless Squabbles Keep Kids from Getting the Help They Need," the number of children affected by the shift to whole language has been huge:

> That Johnny can't read is hardly news. But why one out of five schoolchildren is reading-impaired by the time he or she reaches 4th grade and what can be done to keep such kids from falling through the cracks are issues that pose unprecedented challenges for the education and scientific communities.
>
> "We know what to do. We have the information within our grasp. We just can't get the message across," said Reid Lyon, research director of the National Institute of Child Health and Human Development. "That's what makes this issue so frustrating."[6]

The very fact that a book such as this is needed reflects the continuing rift between mainstream reading instruction and reading research. Reputable experts who conduct reading research have gathered consistent evidence that explicit instruction in how to read the words is the first critical component of a balanced, comprehensive reading program.[7] Sound awareness, letter knowledge, and vocabulary are essential foundations, especially for children who do not already read fluently. Phonics is a necessary part of any reading program, along with sight word learning, vocabulary study, independent reading to increase speed, comprehension instruction, and motivational incentives. All this can and should take place in a class that surrounds children with good literature and leads them to write about it. Classrooms of primary children who are taught to sound words out, after they learn speech sounds and letters, do better on word reading, spelling, and passage comprehension than children who are not so taught.[8] Yet many teachers in classrooms across the country continue to teach reading without systematic code instruction in spite of the evidence that the approach helps fewer children and does not lead to better reading for the majority.

Many professors of education, curriculum advisors for school districts, and individual teachers continue the debate about reading approaches. Sometimes education professors become aligned with a publishing company, which reaps considerable monetary rewards from sales of books supporting one approach. Whole language subscribers cannot point to hard data to support their beliefs about reading, and are sometimes hostile to objective methods of determining what works best. The debate about reading methods is seldom civil or scholarly; researchers whose studies have not supported whole language have been the targets of character attacks, slanderous accusations, and heated criticism. Nevertheless, the data are on their side. The impact of this heated debate within universities is discussed in an article which appeared on the front page of the *Wall Street Journal* in October of 1996:

> So divisive is the issue in academia that some teacher-training colleges are unable to fill faculty posts for those who teach reading methods. The reason: Candidates are often considered to be either too "pro-phonics" or too "pro-whole language," depending on the bent of the selection committees.
>
> In this debate, "there are literally no survivors. It's completely beyond the pale," says Richard Elmore, a professor at Harvard University's graduate school of education.[9]

How Much Have Reading Scores Fallen?

According to Dr. Marilyn Adams, reading in the United States is declining in relation to what is required:

> But even as we come to recognize this situation (increased reading levels required), we are confronted with statistics that the ability of our students to read advanced materials is slowly but steadily declining; that among industrial nations, American students' reading achievement is average or even below; that compared to its industrial competitors, the United States is raising a disproportionate number of *very* poor readers; that already one out of five adult Americans is functionally illiterate and that these ranks are swelling by about 2.3 million each year.[10]

Because there are no standard tests given to schoolchildren throughout the country, it is difficult to make statements about national trends in reading achievement. States use different tests. What we can do is track scores within a given state and look at changes across time. A look at the story of the reading decline in two states suggests what may be occurring in other states across the country.

The California and Illinois Stories

The California Story

California officially adopted a whole language philosophy in its state policies and educational materials in 1987. At that time, the California legislature passed a bill requiring an "integrated" approach that discouraged teaching phonics, spelling, and other skills. Although it was intended that teachers would continue to teach basic reading skills as they concentrated on literature and meaning-emphasis with children, many teachers were censured for doing so, and teaching component skills became a lost art. The instructional materials adopted for use typically did not include direct teaching of sound awareness, phonics, word attack, spelling, grammar, or other language skills. Teachers in training were not schooled in how to teach reading, spelling, or writing skills but in discussion of literature and composition. These practices, in conjunction with an escalation in class size, contributed to a disastrous decline in reading proficiency in relation to other states. When California adopted whole language in 1987, its reading scores were in the top 20 percent of states. In 1993, approximately seven years later, California tied with Louisiana for last place in the country among the 40 states participating in the National Assessment of Educational Progress reading exam given to fourth-graders.

Analysis of the scores reveals that declines in reading achievement were experienced by all groups of children, not just those for whom English is a second language. Even more heartbreaking for parents is that children from homes that had provided enriched reading experiences to preschoolers were not reading well either. As a writer for the *Chicago Tribune* described in an article during May 1996 entitled, "In Blast From Past, California Schools Plan to Re-Embrace Phonics":

> "We're not just talking about low-income students or kids who can't speak English," said Maureen DiMarco, the governor's chief education adviser. "We found that 50 percent of the kids where both parents are college educated were also reading below (grade) level."
>
> California's love-hate relationship with cutting-edge concepts and new flirtation with the back-to-basics movement are a reflection of the trend-driven frenzy of public education in America.[11]

Dr. Bill Honig, who was State Superintendent of Public Instruction for California from 1983 to 1993, guided the curriculum adoption during the shift to whole language. He has written a book for educators, published in 1996, in which he readily admits and analyzes the ways in which his prior decisions were misinformed.[12] Reversing positions, he recognizes the problems with whole language instruction, invokes lessons from reading psychology to explain why California's policy was wrong, and argues for a balanced approach. He currently lectures to groups throughout the country, arguing that good instruction integrates components of both whole language and phonics, and cites the merits of direct skill instruction.

In 1996 the California legislature passed a series of interrelated laws known as the California Reading Initiative. These laws addressed every aspect of reading instruction including the way teachers are trained, the way they continue their training, the materials they use, the size of their classes, and the information that is disseminated by the state about reading instruction. The laws specify that "systematic, explicit phonics, spelling, and basic computational skills" be included in the curriculum, along with the study of literature. Reading teachers must pass a competency evaluation before they can be licensed. Reading courses in universities must teach a wide range of skills and knowledge, or programs may lose their accreditation. People who provide in-service training must be approved by the state board of education before public money can be spent to support their work. Classroom instructional materials have been approved and adopted, and although many of these need improvement, the most incomplete and ill-conceived were dropped from the adoption list in December of 1996.

The Illinois Story

Illinois's movement toward whole language followed a course more typical of other states. Whole language wasn't adopted as early, nor rigidly; however, the change was still quite sweeping. Because school districts adopted whole language as the standard and eliminated use of a basal reading series (reading textbooks used in classrooms), teachers were required to teach using "authentic literature," but without textbooks for phonics, spelling, grammar, or component comprehension skills. Some teachers (primarily experienced teachers) continued to integrate some phonics into their reading curriculum. Phonics books were not confiscated from classrooms, as they were in isolated incidents in California.

During the past decade, teachers colleges taught the new approach and dispensed with the old. Most teachers graduating from undergraduate and graduate education programs in Illinois over the past 10 years were taught the whole language approach, but given little or no instruction in how to teach the structure of syllables, words, or sentences, or how to teach students who failed to learn easily when exposed to good books.

The wake-up call for Illinois came with the results of the 1995 IGAP (Illinois Goals Assessment Program). Reading scores of Illinois schoolchildren had dropped significantly. Not only had these reading scores reached the lowest level since IGAP testing began in 1988, but scores declined at all tested grade levels. The front-page article in the *Chicago Sun-Times* in early September of 1997 continued to discuss the severity of the problem:

> Illinois reading scores tumbled across the board again this year with the worst decline coming in sixth grade, where scores dropped nearly 8 percent.
>
> In fact, compared with five years ago, sixth-, eighth-, and 10th-grade state reading scores look as if they've fallen off a cliff, with drops of as much as 17 percent, an analysis obtained by the *Sun-Times* showed. . . .
>
> "This is not a bleed. This is a hemorrhage," Spagnolo said. (State Superintendent of Schools) "We need to do something right away."[13]

The State Superintendent of Education assembled a team to determine whether the scores reflected a true decline in reading or reflected some bias in testing. The team reported back that there were no errors in testing and that the tests were not racially or ethnically biased. In fact, reading proficiency in the state had declined.

Consequently, a group of educators assembled for a reading summit. In a report documenting the discussions of this two-day summit, held in August 1996, attention was drawn to the fact that whole language was widely used and other instructional approaches to teaching reading were discouraged. Much of the report discusses the research findings showing that ideal reading instruction includes direct training in awareness of speech sounds, the alphabet, letter-sound correspondence, and other word attack skills, contrary to whole language philosophy.[14] The summit participants struggled with the issue of how to implement these "best practices" into classroom instruction and teacher preparation throughout the state. This is a challenging task because control over curriculum rests with the hundreds of individual school districts, typically governed by local school boards. Unlike California, Illinois has a decentralized form of educational administration in which local districts retain decision-making power. Compliance with "best practice" advisories is purely elective; there are no financial consequences for failing to adapt or improve, as there are now in California.

Research Support for Better Reading Practices

Does Research Really Support a Best Approach?

Within the past 30 years the research from several fields outside of education has revealed a great deal about how people learn to read, why reading is difficult for many children, and what can be done about the problem. Brain scientists using sophisticated scanning equipment and psychologists using computer eye-scanning devices have helped in piecing together this complex puzzle. The largest body of work addresses the relationship between spoken language and written language learning, and shows that reading is primarily a language activity, not a function of rote memory or a simple visual skill. Children who have trouble learning to read English usually have a basic problem recognizing printed words accurately and fluently because they do not have a well-developed sense of the speech sounds that the letters represent in our writing system. This critical weakness has to do with something called phonological or phoneme awareness.

Although researchers have not concluded that there is any one program or method that teaches all students equally well, they generally agree that certain components of reading instruction are necessary for optimum results. These components should be taught in combination, in a logical sequence, and in relation to what the children are ready to learn at their stage of reading development.

GOOD EARLY READING INSTRUCTION TEACHES:

- speech sound, or phonological awareness
- letter recognition

- sound-symbol connections (sound-letter correspondence)
- advanced word attack
- sight vocabulary
- fluent reading of text
- spelling
- understanding the language in books (words, sentences, paragraphs)
- written composition
- listening and speaking

Reading programs that omit any component are missing something important and putting children at risk for low achievement.

Most researchers agree that reading instruction needs to be balanced and comprehensive. Most even say that phonics is necessary. According to Dr. Keith E. Stanovich, a leading reading expert from Canada, in an article in the January 1994 issue of *The Reading Teacher,* a publication of the International Reading Association:

> That direct instruction in alphabetic coding facilitates early reading acquisition is one of the most well established conclusions in all of behavioral science.[15]

Unfortunately, this is not enough of a conclusion to defuse the Great Debate. The area of greatest disagreement among reading professionals has concerned how to teach phonics, at what point in the curriculum, and to whom. The arguments continue because phonics instruction is not the same from program to program.

ALL PHONICS INSTRUCTION IS NOT ALIKE

- Some phonics lessons are silent; others are vocal.
- Some are random; others are systematic.
- Some deal only with some letter-sound correspondences; others deal with most of them.
- Some teach phonics out of context; others teach phonics in context of reading material.

The methods vary, so that whole language teachers can claim that they teach phonics, when in fact they may be teaching a little bit of phonics, unsystematically, inaccurately, ineffectively, and with insufficient reinforcement and practice for the skills to be useful in sounding words out. Therefore, simple descriptions can be very misleading to parents trying to find out what is happening in their child's school.

Why Classroom Practice Has Been Slow to Change

Are Teachers Aware of Reading Research? If Not, Why Not?

Typically and unfortunately, most educators have not kept abreast of the research on learning to read. Teachers may not understand why certain practices are better than others; they do care, but the structure of our educational system doesn't encourage them to keep up with the research in their field. Research results usually appear in scholarly scientific journals that teachers rarely read. These articles typically don't contain the practical link of how to implement best practices in the classroom. In fact, researchers often don't interact with people in classrooms or the commercial publishing houses that produce reading materials.

Teachers aren't expected to know current research findings. They aren't rewarded in additional compensation, promotion opportunities, or even reputation for scholarship about reading psychology. There are even some forces working against their continuing education. School systems often devote very little of their budgets to teacher training. Administrators sometimes resist the disruption of teachers missing classroom days to attend training. In almost any other profession that is regulated by standards and licensing procedures, such as dental hygiene, speech/language pathology, surgery, plumbing, or even hair dressing, continuing education in the latest, tested methods in a field is a requirement of continued licensure. Teachers are almost never expected to learn a specific body of information because it is deemed by learned authorities to be essential. The continuing education for which teachers receive credit does not have to meet standards in most instances.

Why Else Would Educators Be Resistant to Change?

Some educators intentionally ignore the findings of research because they prefer to do what they have already learned. They simply don't want to change because they are invested in what they are doing, and change is difficult unless there are strong incentives and consistent support. Resources, reading materials, and programs on a large scale have already been committed to, and they are thus not inclined to change without pressure.

Another obstacle for change is that teachers themselves are often unfamiliar with how to explicitly teach sounds, letters, and spellings. Most new teachers are not taught phonics in school and work with materials that do not teach it well. One professor at the Harvard Graduate School of Education recently stated that she had had young master's degree students who did not know a vowel from a consonant. Of course such teachers will not understand why it is important to teach phonics to their children. A survey of experienced teachers' knowledge of sounds, spellings, and language structure showed that fewer than 20 percent knew the information well.[16] But why is their knowledge in our writing system often too meager to allow skillful instruction? Many states have such weak course requirements for teachers that it's no wonder the teachers don't know how to teach reading skills. In Illinois, for example, a student need only take one two-hour course in reading to be granted an early education certification. This is the certification many graduates who ultimately end up teaching first grade receive. Surveys of the content of typical reading courses in teachers colleges reveal that phonics—sounds and spellings—are often taught to teachers as a jumbled, illogical mess.[17] In reading instruction, we learn behavior patterns by modeling and experience. Teachers must be shown how to teach skills and must learn the content well themselves to be truly effective.

Our education system not only doesn't offer much training during college or on the job, but it also fosters an environment of independence and isolation. Teachers work independently in their classrooms with little supervision or systems to ensure that they know what is best. In the absence of research-based standards and accountability, teachers make decisions about instruction, relying on their own instincts and impressions about how children learn. Rarely do teachers have mentors, or strong relationships with master teachers. Sometimes teachers witness presentations given by people selling educational products whose company claims that the product is "research-based." Since many of these products have not been subjected to a true scientific test, it is understandable that teachers are skeptical of research claims. School boards rarely ask about the research before adopting materials for teaching. In the future, it will be important for educators to have access to the findings of reputable research and to determine which studies or scientific authorities can be trusted.

REASONS TEACHERS MAY BE RESISTANT TO CHANGE

- prefer to continue doing what they have already learned
- didn't learn in teacher training how to teach reading by directly instructing in sounds, letters, spelling, phonics, and language structure
- are skeptical about claims that an approach is "research-based"
- lack knowledge about what constitutes a scientifically rigorous research result
- have difficulty in comparing the effectiveness of alternative approaches

---

What Other Factors Preserve Whole Language Practices?

The problem of teachers resisting change runs deeper than teachers just not knowing how to teach phonics. It's undoubtedly more fun to be immediately immersed in children's literature, spending reading time with books and passing over structured systematic language activities. If no initial time is spent on letter-sound instruction, the year begins with reading stories. From the beginning, using big books, the teacher and students read together, or the students follow along with the text as the teacher reads aloud. Children will memorize words and "read" stories by themselves, because that is the basis of the approach. In a more phonics (or skills-based) classroom, at least the first half of first grade is spent on letter-sound correspondences, recognizing letter combinations such as *ch*, *sh*, and *ck*, and looking at word families, such as all words made up of a consonant followed by the letters *at* (such as *rat, cat, sat, mat*).

Another reason that some teachers are attracted to whole language is that they have more freedom over the curriculum. Without a structured sequence of skills to teach, they have virtually complete control over what is taught and how it is taught. Clearly teachers enjoy having more control over the curriculum, and whole language offers them an outlet for their creativity and a sense of ownership in their classrooms. Any business-minded layperson, however, who sees the amount of choice over reading curriculum in some classrooms would immediately ask, "Where's the quality control?" How can we be sure that reading is being taught using tested, proven principles in all classrooms in the same school or across a district or state or nation? We can't. Typical of most subjects in education there is no quality control in the way reading has been taught in most of our schools. Researchers who attempt to document the results of whole language teaching have difficulty arriving at a consistent description of what a whole language teacher does when he or she teaches. As experience has taught us, consistency from class to class or school to school is impossible without a curriculum guide and student materials. A principal of a typical elementary school supervises teachers in 25 classrooms, far more employees than any businessperson would think optimum. In addition, it has been a long time since teachers submitted weekly lesson plans to the principal for review.

Regardless of an individual teacher's willingness to concede that reading needs to include skills and literature, school systems are hampered by inertia and the fact that once they are invested in an approach, it is hard to change. Now that they have taught reading under whole language for a number of years, school systems must adopt new materials, retrain teachers, and change the way teachers and students are evaluated. The mobilization of resources takes time and money—two scarce commodities in public education. At this point only a few states in addition to California are considering launching comprehensive initiatives in reading.

Many teachers are afraid that the evidence in support of skills-based language instruction will result in a return to "skill and drill" teaching, when children did workbook exercises and did not spend enough time reading for comprehension. Teachers who are enjoying the literature in current reading programs and who see the advances children have made in expressive writing don't want to give up the more meaningful and enjoyable practices and return to "boring" stories of two decades ago. These teachers seem to be confusing the issue of *what* to teach with *how* to teach it. There is no need to de-emphasize literature just because decoding is taught. They have been prejudiced against teaching skills because they mistakenly assume that the instruction must be rote, boring, or meaningless for children.

Often educators observe that some students seem to learn better with a whole word approach and that others struggle with phonics. Many years of reading research does indicate that roughly a third of the children will learn to read no matter what approach is used, as long as they are taught in an organized way. These children enjoy the emphasis on literature and are basically able to teach themselves some of the skills they need. They have an easier time because they may be neurologically "wired" to easily process language and reading. The ease with which this one-third of the children learn to read has often been inaccurately used to defend the practice of not teaching skills at all. Of the remaining children, the average ones benefit from instruction in sounds and spellings, and the bottom quarter can't learn to read without it. This is why a balanced approach, including instruction in skills integrated with rich literature, is the only sensible course for a whole class. Over the past 10 years of leaving phonics, spelling, and other skills out, too many children were left behind; this approach has deprived them, and even those children who prosper within a whole language approach, of an important strategy for reading and spelling unfamiliar words.

Although the staunch whole language advocates insist that tests don't measure competency, many of them dispute the decline in reading achievement. They claim there is no reading problem in the United States, and, therefore, there must be nothing wrong with the prevailing modes of instruction. In California, educators would insist that large class sizes, the influx of Spanish and other language–speaking groups, and the influence of television were responsible for the decline in reading. Yet they were ignoring the facts that New York and Texas, which are also "melting pot" states, did much better than California on the National Assessment of Educational Progress and that children of white, middle-class, educated parents were also at the bottom of the nation in their respective comparison groups.

REASONS TEACHERS LIKE WHOLE LANGUAGE

- greater freedom to determine reading curriculum
- ability to be creative and feel ownership of curriculum
- more fun because children start with literature instead of phonics lessons
- concern about returning to "skill and drill" teaching of the past
- observation that some students learn well with a whole word approach

---

In summary, educators have not been expected to base instructional decisions on objective studies and are not held accountable for the results of their practices. Whole language was adopted without a critical evaluation of its effectiveness in comparison to other more skills-oriented approaches. With the benefit of hindsight, educators will perhaps be more ready to pilot, study, and select new approaches based on their effectiveness in helping certain kinds of children. We certainly expect this process in medicine. Why not in education?

What About the Poorest Readers—Those with Dyslexia and Learning Disabilities? Are They Getting Sufficient Help?

Although many school districts are conscientious about identifying children who are experiencing difficulty learning to read and then delivering timely and appropriate services, there is unfortunately a very disturbing trend toward nonidentification. Many schools have a policy of waiting until a child is one full year behind grade level before initiating testing. Educational tests, however, are generally the first step in understanding why a child is experiencing a difficulty. Some schools are reluctant to begin testing because they are required to deliver services, some of which are expensive, once a specific problem has been identified.

While it is certainly true that administering an expensive battery of tests to any child who falls a little behind would not be a prudent use of taxpayers' money, it is inexcusable to delay testing a child who is really struggling, a practice that has become all too prevalent. Delaying testing of students may appear on the surface to be an efficient way for cash-strapped schools to sort out severe problems, simply by waiting. However research demonstrates that prevention and remediation of some reading problems, if identified early, may actually cost taxpayers less than offering services later. Parents are all too often told in conferences that their child merely has a developmental lag and are assured that he will catch up. While some children do experience developmental lags that improve without treatment, in the Connecticut Longitudinal Study of reading done at Yale University, only one child in five closed the gap after falling behind by third grade. Early screening programs done with a whole class and individual assessments for those falling behind are essential from the middle of kindergarten onward. Diagnostic testing is important for those who do not respond well to classroom instruction, even if the instruction is well designed. Unfortunately many parents are unaware of their rights to have their child tested by the school.

Research from the National Institute of Child Health and Human Development (NICHD) documents that early identification is critical.[18] Bonnie Miller Rubin quotes Dr. Reid Lyon from the NICHD in a March 2, 1997, article in the *Chicago Tribune* entitled, "Reading Wars":

> It is particularly distressing that government research shows that children can be identified as poor readers when they're as young as 4 or 5, based merely on how they hear, remember and repeat the subtle sounds found in everyday speech. Yet schools often don't jump on the problem until children are 8 or 9.
>
> If a youngster does not receive special help until age 9, "it takes four times as long to move the same skill the same distance," Lyon said.
>
> "That means what could be addressed in 30 minutes a day in kindergarten now can take two hours a day by the 4th grade. The 8th-grade teacher will have it even tougher with more ground to cover to even catch up—not to mention all the failure that the student has already experienced and the toll that takes on self-esteem."[19]

Many research studies, both within the NICHD and outside of it, have sought to determine if it is possible to test kindergartners for the precursor skills of reading and reliably identify those children who will subsequently experience difficulty learning to read. At this point results are very promising; instruction in kindergarten that is based on the findings of kindergarten screening tests has reduced reading failure substantially in first- and second-graders.[20] The tests, which focus on the ability of the child to detect the individual speech sounds in words, to recognize and name letters, and to understand how a book represents language, will help in the critical task of early identification of children at risk for reading failure.

Early identification of the children who are struggling is only one side of the coin. After determining which children need help, the other critical component is delivering the appropriate type of help. Too often, school districts are delivering the wrong kind of help at too low a level of intensity. Take, for example, the person in a school located in a northern suburb of Chicago whose title is "Reading Assistant" and whose job it is to provide reading help to students individually and in small groups who have been identified by their classroom teacher as needing this pull-out service once or twice a week. This reading assistant was previously a regular classroom teacher. She has not been trained in systematic and intensive phonics approaches and does not have a special education background. The district doesn't view reading to be a serious problem and, in these times of budget cutbacks, her salary is far less than if they hired a trained reading specialist. This individual is dedicated and tries hard, but hasn't been equipped with the best tools and techniques to do her job. Parents assume that she is well trained. Some children will demonstrate a level of improvement through intensive help of this sort. But the improvement is far less than if that child had been given an informed approach aimed at the right level of instructional readiness. In other cases, providing more hours of an approach not all that dissimilar from what the child gets in his classroom will never remediate the child's distinct weakness. Therefore he will continue to be held back from making that explosive reading breakthrough we know to be possible when the intervention is targeted and timely.

Why Can't Someone Do Something to Resolve This Educational Debate?

For parents who want their child educated, this is a pressing and puzzling question. Parents are confused about why too little is being done. They are hard-pressed to understand why any school district, anywhere in this country, would fail to use the most effective approach to teaching reading, as documented by the research evidence.

In seeking to explain why there is such a gap between research and practice, parents must understand that policy decisions about education are made by local school boards in communities across our country. Even if a state board of education wanted to prescribe a curriculum approach to teaching reading, it would lack the necessary authority to do so. While a board of education can advocate and require accountability for performance, it cannot control the specific means that a district chooses to implement its recommendations and policies. It can take away a school's license or funding on grounds such as safety noncompliance or failure to meet reasonable standards of performance, but it generally has no authority over the specific curriculum used.

Many states have considered and passed legislation dealing with the issue of reading instruction. In the past few years several states have passed legislation to ensure that phonics is included in a comprehensive, balanced reading program. One very early state was Ohio, which adopted legislation in 1989 to require phonics instruction in all schools and training in teaching phonics for the students at Ohio's teachers colleges. Legislation to restore the entire spectrum of reading instruction is in varying stages of implementation in New York, North Carolina, South Carolina, Wisconsin, and Texas. In most of this legislation, the wording stipulates that the code component must be "explicit and systematic" phonics.

In Wisconsin, legislation was passed which requires course work in phonics in order to acquire certification to teach reading. No teaching license will be issued to anyone who will teach language arts in any prekindergarten through sixth-grade classroom if the applicant has not successfully completed instruction in how to teach the code within a complete reading program. California has specified a whole range of competencies for teachers of reading which will be tested by a Reading Instruction Competency Evaluation given to teacher candidates.

Reading has become a political issue at the national level. Consider President Clinton's America Reads Challenge. In his acceptance speech at the Democratic National Convention in August

1996, President Clinton highlighted our nation's reading problem. He requested funding to assure that all children will be reading at grade level by the third grade. However, his proposal was to use one million work-study students to help children learn to read. Doesn't it seem strange to use one million untrained students to do what teachers should be doing? Clinton might have called for a change in how reading is taught in our schools, but in doing so, he might have lost some valuable political support from teachers' unions. At least the America Reads Challenge administrators distributed a summary of the NICHD research findings on reading with all their other literature on reading.

What Will It Take to Solve the Problem of How to Teach Reading?

For change to occur, for instruction to become research-based, many different groups of people must become educated and insistent on the goal of reading success. Parents, administrators, board members, teachers, professors, and publishers need to act in concert to achieve results. If all educators agreed that we need to put sound awareness, phonics, spelling, word analysis, grammar, and comprehension skills back into the curriculum, along with the literature emphasis of whole language, surely they could make it happen! Imagine how easily a change could be approved by a school board if the teachers and administrators unanimously supported the adoption of a proven curriculum for teaching beginning reading.

Given the polarization within the educational community, however, children's needs may still take a back seat to adult professional egos. Too many people have staked their reputations or resources on their current ideas and practices to change overnight, and there are still too few ways for the public to find out about reading research. While some educators are resisting change in their entrenched belief systems, the research community is developing an even better understanding of how people learn to read. Reading experts are recommending comprehensive, balanced, informed instruction in which all the parts of reading are taught well. This new approach is much more than an unsatisfactory compromise between two opposing schools of thought. The more sophisticated approach emphasizes the importance of specific skills for specific children at specific times, in the context of a literature-rich program. No pieces are left out.

Parents can be instrumental in bringing about a more rapid change to reading practices that make scientific and practical sense. It is our children who are hurt by the philosophical polarizations and the gap between research and practice. It is our children whose well-being is threatened when we do not use the best of what we know from evidence.

If a change is to be accomplished through legislation, then parents need to be informed so that they can approach their legislative representatives. As in California, the wording of any state legislation must be specific about what is intended, and accountability for compliance with the law must be supported.[21] Initiatives are needed to revamp teacher preparation programs, teacher in-service training, instructional materials adoptions, academic standards and frameworks, and public education about reading. States will need to launch major initiatives to train teachers already on the job.

What Parents Can Do

Any concerned parent wishing to approach a school board or legislator can be assured of the following:

- There is scientifically based, objective evidence that systematic, structured teaching of both skills and comprehension must be included in effective reading programs.
- Educators are not yet fully aware of this evidence or willing to act on it.
- Some reading programs have track records that are significantly better than others.
- Educators are not yet accountable for using programs and methods that are likely to minimize failure and help most children learn to read.
- Consequently, our children's reading and spelling is suffering, and too many children will struggle unnecessarily.

As parents, we tend to feel as if there is little we can do in time to help our own child. It was *one parent,* however, who initiated the change in California. A simple place to begin is by asking questions of school authorities. Some other actions we can take include the following:

WHAT YOU CAN DO

- Become familiar with the scientific evidence about reading.
- Monitor your child's reading progress throughout the elementary years.
- Take immediate action if your child is experiencing difficulty learning to read.
- Assume the role of your child's reading coach.

All of these topics are covered in this book. The first five chapters give background about reading methods, reading development, and your role. The chapters in the middle section discuss what a child should be able to do during preschool and kindergarten, first grade, second grade, and third grade. Activities, games, and books are described. The final chapter gives information about reading difficulties and learning disabilities. If your child is experiencing difficulty learning to read during first grade, you need to take action. Concrete advice on what to do and when to do it is included in the chapter on reading difficulties. Throughout the whole book we discuss what it means to be your child's reading coach.

Chapter Two

Who Teaches My Child to Read?

> . . . the likelihood that a child will succeed in the first grade depends most of all on how much she or he has already learned about reading before getting there . . .
>
> *Dr. Marilyn Adams, from* Beginning to Read[1]

In this quote Dr. Adams implies that parents play a major role in helping their child learn to read. Given that Dr. Marilyn Adams is one of the nation's leading reading experts, she's worth listening to. Dr. Adams achieved this recognition because, while working on a project for the U.S. Department of Education during the late 1980s, she thoroughly reviewed reading research to learn what makes children become good readers. Therefore when this expert says that your child's reading development begins with what you and your child do at home before your child gets to first grade, parents should take note. Yet Dr. Adams's statement brings several questions to mind:

- What is a parent's role in teaching a child to read?
- What exactly is a parent supposed to *do* to better prepare a child for reading instruction?

The School's Role

Doesn't My Child Learn to Read at School?

It's impossible to think about the parent's role without simultaneously defining the school's role in teaching reading. Many parents assume that first-grade teachers are well trained in methods of teaching reading and equipped with materials and practices to instruct in a systematic and sequential manner. To the extent that parents believe that teaching reading requires skills and training, they will be less inclined to start the process at home. Parents naturally try not to do things at home that would conflict with teaching methods at school.

During the time my oldest child was learning to read I was forced to examine my assumptions about my role and the school's role in teaching my child to read. Before he entered school I believed that it was the school's responsibility to teach my child to read and that my role was limited. My view has changed a great deal after my experiences with my two children—one who struggled in learning to read, and one who read easily. My insights offer perspective to parents about a more proactive role of the parent in this process. My story may help you reflect on your assumptions about who's going to teach your child to read.

A Parent's Story of Her Child's Struggle to Learn to Read

When my first child finished preschool and started elementary school, I remember looking forward to him learning to read. In my motherly fantasies, I would visualize him curled up on a corner of the couch so entranced in a book that he was oblivious to the activity surrounding him. He was clearly interested in reading because he would sit for more than an hour listening to me read him a story and beg for more when I stopped. His ability to sit still and listen always amazed me because he was the most active toddler in our play group of six boys. I was just sure that he would love to read because I do, and because I had done what people always told me to do:

- teach the alphabet, and
- read, read, read to your child.

I felt I had done my part in preparing this child for reading instruction. As for direct instruction in how to read—that was the school's job. Now it was the school's turn to take my highly prepared child and make him a great reader.

In October of first grade, I attended curriculum night at school and heard all about what he would be studying this year. This was an excellent school in an affluent suburb of Chicago, which attracted professional couples, many of whom had graduate degrees from the top universities in the nation. We chose this suburb based on its reputation for excellent schools. My son's teacher took a loving approach with the children, and I was confident that she would teach him to read. I assumed that because she was a first-grade teacher, she must have expertise and experience in teaching children how to read. Therefore we would wait for her to systematically instruct him in how to read while my husband and I continued to read to him daily.

Throughout the first few months of first grade everything seemed to be just fine. My son looked forward to school each morning. After school when he bounced out of the classroom where I waited to pick him up, he could hardly wait to tell me about what he did that day. He dragged me by the hand back into the classroom to show me his spider web made of yarn and construction paper, which was suspended above his desk from a wire attached to the ceiling. As we walked home together he would tell me in great detail about what he had built in the block corner that day, or about the story the teacher had read to the class. He might tell me about whom he ate lunch with, and which game their class played in gym, including details about who was on his team and who had made the last point. The details about his day were rich, lively, engaged, and full of a range of emotions.

During January things began to change. As he walked out of

the classroom each afternoon, his manner didn't seem as assured and upbeat. On the way home when I asked my usual question, "How was school today?" he would say very little. The few things he did tell me about his day he described in a more detached tone and manner. At home in the evening he seemed more easily frustrated than usual. He would erupt over the slightest imbalance in his Legos building, an activity that previously had provided long, quiet stretches of complete engagement and joy. The clues about his feelings were in his downbeat mood and mannerisms, and in the contrast with how he had talked about his school day in the fall.

It was clear something was bothering him, but I couldn't tell what it was. No matter what question I asked it didn't seem as if I was putting my finger on what was happening to my son. Even in those quiet moments of sharing, he wasn't saying what was bothering him. Ever since he was about two years old, we had enjoyed a private sharing time at night, just after a story and right before tucking him into bed. The routine was for me to ask him what he liked best that day, and whether there was anything that happened that he didn't like. He did tell me things that had not gone well about his day. But they were the same types of things that he had always talked about—the kid who pushed him on the playground, what he didn't like about his lunch, or what someone had said that hurt his feelings. There was no new information that would explain his diminishing enthusiasm for school or the obvious irritability in his behavior.

I tried to look for a pattern in what he said he didn't like about school. Was it a problem with one of the other children in his class? I thought about whether he had mentioned repeated altercations with any one child. Could it be his teacher? I knew he liked the teacher, but could it be that she wasn't receptive to his ideas in class? Because he wasn't able to tell me what was wrong, I needed to get into that classroom to make my own observations. At the end of January I volunteered to help on a multidisciplinary project about Japan. Each mom would spend a couple of hours in the classroom over a week working with her own child plus several other children to study one aspect of the country. My group was studying holidays. The plan was that each child would read one page of a handout in round-robin style, and then we would make models of objects that were symbolic of key holidays.

On the designated day I arrived in the classroom and sat in a circle on the floor with my group of students. After passing out a copy of the handout to everyone, I asked the child sitting to my right to read first. This girl read aloud her page with great ease and accuracy, making no mistakes. I wasn't surprised she was an excellent reader because I knew she came from a family of readers. The second child, also a girl, read. I was surprised at how well she also read, missing very few words. The third and fourth children were both boys. Although their reading wasn't as fluent as either of the girls, each did a good job overall. Each boy accepted help with a couple of words. At this point I realized that these children all read quite a bit better than my child did. Then my son, who sat next to me on my left, had his turn to read. His reading was slower and more choppy, and he required me to tell him more new words than the other children had. He read several easy words incorrectly (such as reading *was* for *saw*) and just couldn't begin to figure out several unknown words.

When I looked at my son as he read aloud he looked sheepish and embarrassed. It was instantly clear to me what was wrong. My son's reading was at a level well behind the four other children in our group. He knew it, and it was clearly bothering him. My son has always been a very competitive child. He believed he ought to read as well as the other children, and he was frustrated that he wasn't able to.

That evening I asked him a few questions about our Japan project, which eventually led to a discussion about how he felt while reading to his classmates. He said he was embarrassed that he couldn't read as well as the other children. As we sat on his bed that evening, he looked at me and said, "Why am I the first one in the class to finish the math worksheets, but I'm in the lowest reading group?" Until that moment I didn't know that he was in the lowest reading group. It was clear that he was upset that he was in the lowest reading group. His teacher had never mentioned during the fall parent-teacher conference, or any of several more recent casual conversations with her, that he was having any difficulty learning to read.

Over the following week I began observing my son's reading much more closely. This effort resulted in some interesting observations about how he was reading.

MY OBSERVATIONS ABOUT MY SON'S READING

- Although he would listen to me read aloud forever, he resisted reading to me.
- Reading seemed to be a very laborious task for him.
- He complained that reading was very hard.
- He seemed to rely upon his ability to memorize words he had seen before.
- When he reached an unknown word, his first approach was to look at the pictures or the rest of the sentence.
- He couldn't sound out an unknown word.

These observations prompted me into action. I spoke with the teacher to express my concern that my son was frustrated with his reading. I told her I was prepared to help him at home and asked for ideas about what I could do. Maybe what he needed was some extra time and attention one-on-one, which I was fully prepared to provide. His teacher said that his reading was developing a little slowly and not to worry about it because all children read at their own pace. She said that spending some extra time working with him on reading at home was a great idea. The only concrete suggestion she made was to try to find some controlled vocabulary books.

It was at about this time that an interesting experience occurred. During one of my many trips to the library in search of beginning reader books, I saw another mother whom I knew. She asked how my children were, as mothers do, so I asked her for advice on what to do if your child doesn't seem to be reading as well as his peers. She gave me some ideas, although mostly just support, and then she left the library. As I sat perusing the children's books, an Eastern European woman who had been sitting nearby leaned over and said, "Excuse me, but I couldn't help hearing your conversation." She then began practically lecturing me in very emphatic language that it was *my* responsibility to teach my child to read. With her heavy Russian-sounding accent she said to me, "You must *do* something. *You* must teach him to read. You cannot wait for the schools to do something if he is falling behind. He will start to feel badly about himself if he can't read." She relayed her story about how she taught her children to read. She said, "You just listen to them read, and help them learn to sound out the words." This Russian woman then told me how important reading is to a child's self-esteem at this age. In about five minutes of conversation with a woman whose name I do not even know, my assumption that my child's teacher would be the person who would teach him to read was forever shattered.

I eventually discovered that my son needed more phonics than he was learning from his first-grade teacher, who taught reading principally through the whole language approach. Furthermore, his teacher didn't notice that he was reading at a level far below his capabilities. I hired a reading tutor to work with my son—one who principally uses a systematic phonics approach to teaching reading. After three months of two hourly sessions per week with the tutor, my son was moved up to a reading group in about the middle of the class. The tutor taught him how to sound out unknown words and to look for letter patterns; over time he gained speed and fluency and became a good reader. His self-esteem came back, and he once again enjoyed going to school. Fortunately for my son, his difficulty was identified early, and he was provided with the kind of help he needed.

Parents sometimes blindly trust that their child's first-grade teacher will be an expert in teaching reading. Their assumption is that the teacher is trained and works for a school district where there are curriculum guidelines. However, none of those factors helped assure that my son learned to read from what his first-grade teacher taught in class. It's not surprising that more and more parents are questioning why their children can't read well enough, or don't spell well. Parents are asking more questions about how math and reading are taught.

This change in perspective can be compared to another major societal change—the changes in health care. Twenty years ago people blindly trusted decisions about their medical care to their doctors. Now we get second opinions, do our own research prior to deciding on a course of care, and more aggressively ask about a doctor's credentials and experience with a particular medical condition. In the case of health care, other factors are driving the change toward individuals assuming more responsibility for decision making. Insurance companies are encouraging this shift toward clients questioning and seeking second opinions because of their vested interest in cutting costs.

As with health care, the public's view of educational responsibility is changing. Parents are becoming more informed about, and involved in, their children's education. A generation ago parents assumed that by residing in a good school district, they were assured their child would get a good education. They believed that their responsibilities ended after making sure their child got to school well rested and with homework completed. Parents were hesitant to intervene at school on behalf of their child. According to administrators, parents today are more involved in trying to influence what happens at school. Parents are more involved in:

- requesting that their child be placed with a specific teacher
- complaining about bad teachers
- helping improve their child's poor spelling or reading skills
- determining how much time their child spends studying core curriculum

Another indicator of the shifting roles of schools and parents is the huge increase in the number of parents homeschooling their children. Today's parents understand the importance of being more active and involved in what is happening at school.

Our Proposal for the Parent's Role

What Is My Role in Teaching My Child to Read?

We believe that **teaching a child to read is a shared responsibility between school and parents.** What parents do at home to encourage and support their child's reading development is very important. The parent's role is not just to read aloud and teach the child the alphabet—it's much more.

PROPOSED ROLE OF THE PARENT

1. **Coach**—Nurture your child's interest in reading by
   - providing positive introductions to reading,
   - choosing appropriate books, and
   - encouraging the development of reading skills.
2. **Monitor**—Assess your child's reading development against benchmarks.
3. **Advocate**—Become involved if reading development doesn't seem to be "on track."

Each of these roles is described on the following pages.

How to Be Your Child's Reading Coach

Parents can play a critical role in teaching their child to read. Dr. Marilyn Adams clearly states that what parents do at home prepares their child for reading instruction at school:

> Research reviewed later in the book confirms that letter recognition facility and phonemic awareness are causally related to reading acquisition and that each is prerequisite for the young reader. Even so, a catch-22 emerges. Closer analysis indicates that children who have learned their letters and acquired a solid level of phonemic awareness

> before entering school have also begun to learn to read before entering school. By implication, we are left with the conclusion that the likelihood that a child will succeed in first grade depends, most of all, on how much she or he has already learned about reading before getting there.[2]

Notice that Dr. Adams talks about two crucial skills that preschoolers need before the alphabetic writing system can be deciphered: recognizing the alphabet letters and something called "phonemic awareness." This term means that the child must be aware of the separate speech sounds in a word, not just be able to recognize letters. Because of the importance of this skill as a precursor to reading, it will be discussed, along with suggested activities, in the preschool and kindergarten chapter later in this book.

The International Reading Association distributes a brochure to parents entitled "Your Home Is Your Child's First School." In this brochure the association communicates to parents the message from the work of Dr. Adams and other reading experts.

> Your child's ability to begin reading instruction once he or she enters school will depend to a great extent on what you have done before school starts. Readiness for reading . . . begins for your child in your home, and you are the most important stimulus in your child's progress towards preparation for reading instruction in school.[3]

Let's examine some of the ways parents prepare their child for reading instruction. The most obvious activity is reading aloud to your child. Many parents don't realize the important things a child gains from listening to stories. While listening to stories your child learns not only that reading is enjoyable, but also that a book is read from left to right, from front to back, that the letters on the page correspond with the words in our speaking vocabularies, and general familiarity with the language in books. The child also gains crucial background knowledge about the world. Because it is so important, the entire next chapter in this book is dedicated to reading aloud.

Parents know that their child needs to master the alphabet

before they start to read. Many parents are actively involved in teaching their child the letters through singing the alphabet song, looking at alphabet books together, and pointing out letters on signs and in print. Although parents often do a great job at making sure their children know the alphabet, most parents are unaware of how important a related skill is—knowing the sounds each letter makes and being able to hear distinct sounds in words.

Dr. Marilyn Adams suggests comparing the number of hours parents spend reading at home to their child versus the amount of time a first-grade teacher spends on the instruction of reading.[4] Assume you read to your child 15 minutes each night at bedtime. If you start this practice when your child is six months old, you will have spent more than 500 hours reading to your child by the time your child is six years old. It's difficult to determine how much time is spent specifically on reading instruction in classrooms with integrated projects. However, if we assume your child's first-grade teacher spends an hour on reading each school day, then 180 hours (5 hours/week x 36 weeks in school) will be spent on reading instruction. Your bedtime story time would already total nearly three times the time spent in first-grade classroom instruction time. Parents have a tremendous opportunity to assist in the development of reading skills during this read-aloud time. If you read to your child at other times of the day as well, the time you spend on reading versus the teacher is even greater. And this reading aloud time does not include the time spent working with magnetic letters, watching *Sesame Street*, singing the alphabet song, talking about the letters in a stop sign, and all the other reading readiness activities you do at home. During the majority of the instruction time at school, the teacher works with 20 to 30 children, when it is difficult for the teacher to individually coach your child and address her individual needs.

When your child is learning to read, you will probably spend more hours one-on-one listening to your child read than her teacher will. Therefore it is critical that you be informed about how to help your child. Some of the typical questions parents ask as their child learns to read are:

- Should I supply an unknown word, or ask the child to sound it out?
- If my child wants to skip an unknown word or look at the pictures for clues, should I discourage her?
- How do I know what books are at my child's reading level?
- My child resists reading. What can I do to encourage her to read?

All of these questions, and more, are answered in Chapter 7.

Even if you are convinced that parents play an important role in their child's reading development, why describe that role as a coach? A coach is a role we frequently associate with sports. Good coaches are people who inspire and guide a child's development in learning a new skill. A coach is responsible for planning a set of activities that enable the learner to practice a skill and to concentrate on skills that are deficient. A coach knows what his students need to work on and how to help them improve their skills.

In coaching your child to literacy, your role will change over time. While your child is a preschooler, you can help her learn to name the letters and know the sounds each letter makes. As you are reading a story to your four-year-old child, make sure she knows you are reading words and that the words are read left to right. When your child reaches first grade, help her learn how to sound out unknown words. You can help her recognize that a compound word is composed of two words she already knows. Throughout her school years, you can become a major influence in her reading development through establishing good reading habits in your house and supplying your child with interesting materials to read.

YOUR ROLE AS YOUR CHILD'S READING COACH

- Read aloud to your child.
- Supply engaging books.
- Create a reading environment in your home.

- Listen to your child read.
- Help your child develop specific reading skills.

How to Monitor Your Child's Reading Progress

One of the critical roles for parents is to monitor their child's progress. One parent beautifully describes the importance of monitoring what is happening in school. She watched her first-grade daughter lose self-confidence as the year progressed. Her daughter, whom we shall call Kelly, had a miserable year at school with a teacher who didn't understand her and made disparaging comments about her to her mother. Kelly's mother described how Kelly's demeanor deteriorated. She experienced her as a different child in and out of school. While watching her daughter walk down the hallway at school, she saw her child walking with her head down, body slumped over, and looking at the floor. Kelly's mother observed that she seemed anxious, smiled infrequently, and demonstrated no excitement about going to school. This was such a contrast to the child who lightheartedly giggled and laughed in her room with a friend who was sleeping over. Kelly became apprehensive about her academic skills and was reluctant to read at home. She became almost angry if her parents tried to encourage her by sitting with her as she did her homework.

By February her distraught parents decided to have her tested to determine if she had a learning disability; they were especially concerned about whether she had an attention deficit disorder (ADD) because her teacher described her as "spacey," or daydreaming, a lot at school. The testing revealed that Kelly was a little behind in some academic areas but that she had no specific learning disabilities. The parents hired a private tutor in March, and by early June, Kelly had completely caught up.

This mother said the major warning sign of an emerging school problem was Kelly's lack of attention to, and follow-through, on schoolwork. Kelly's mother advises other parents that the most important thing is to be in tune with your child's demeanor. You need to know how your child is feeling about herself at school. Go to school and watch your child. Ask the teacher to describe how your child acts when she's at school.

As a parent, you know what kind of preparation your child received before starting first grade. You know how much your child was read to, how frequently she heard about letter sounds, how much she was exposed to the naming of letters, and how much she watched *Sesame Street.* Your child's first-grade teacher knows none of this information. The teacher may therefore assume a child who is struggling had less prereading preparation. In fact, with 20–30 children in the classroom, your child's teacher may be spending a limited amount of time thinking about your child.

I will never forget when my son's first-grade teacher mentioned at our spring parent-teacher conference that his "word attack skills are weak." After asking what that meant and whether this was a concern, the teacher assured us that we should not worry because it was probably a "developmental lag." This didn't make sense to me because I knew his prereading preparation was as strong as any child's, and that he was one of the oldest in his class. When I pointed this out and asked how she could attribute his delay to a developmental lag, his teacher looked as if she hadn't even checked his file to realize that he was one of the oldest in the class.

How do you know whether your child's reading development is progressing on schedule? Included in Chapter 7 of this book are benchmarks of reading achievement. These benchmarks are provided in this book for parents so *you* can monitor your child's progress. Just as you can check any baby book for information about when your infant should be crawling or walking, you need to be able to check your child's reading development against some objective developmental benchmarks.

Another key to being effective at monitoring your child's reading progress is to understand how reading is being taught in her classroom. This knowledge will help you evaluate how that technique is working for your child. Although I had heard the terms "whole language" and "phonics" when my child entered first grade, little did I know that my understanding of each of these approaches would be a critical element in my child learning to read well. It is imperative that you as parents ask pointed questions about teaching methodology, and be able to evaluate whether your child is getting what she needs in terms of skills instruction. My son's difficulty in learning to read was directly related to the teaching method used in his classroom; he is one of the 20–30 percent of the children who really don't learn to read well without phonics. The information included in Chapter 4 will provide you a broad overview of alternative approaches to teaching reading and specific questions you can use to evaluate the method used in your child's classroom.

According to experts who conduct diagnostic testing, it is the parent who often suspects a possible reading problem well before the school does. Parents sometimes notice that their child's development is different from her peers as early as the toddler or preschool years. The parent has been with the child throughout her development, and therefore has more information than any teacher. To be an effective reading monitor, parents need the information about stages of reading development provided in the chapters in the second half of this book.

Why You Need to Advocate When Your Child Falls Behind

No one cares as deeply about your child as you do, and no one else can be as effective an advocate. Parents can nudge the school to notice a problem and provide individualized help and attention earlier than they otherwise would have. The school has to balance the interests of all the children and ration a budget for diagnostic testing or special services. Your only concern is that your child gets what she needs to become a good reader. You must become your child's advocate. Parents whose children have difficulty reading often complain that the school waited too long to test the child. Often the school's reading specialist isn't trained in the teaching approach that is best for a child. Parents who know their rights have corrected these situations.

Being an advocate for your child involves a wide range of roles, from simply asking the teacher questions to launching a legal battle to assure that special services are provided to your child. The process of advocating on behalf of your child almost always involves collecting information from sources other than the school. In order to know when to test and what type of tutoring your child may need, parents need to gather information from a variety of sources. See Chapter 10 for more information about this.

Early identification of reading difficulties is critical, as shown by research funded by the National Institute of Child Health and Human Development. Children with reading difficulties who are identified after the age of nine will have a much more difficult time learning to read. However, with early identification and proper intervention, these children can read with far less difficulty.

Trust your instincts. If your child seems to be struggling in learning to read, ask questions until you are satisfied with the answers. Getting the right kind of help for your child early can make an enormous difference in her ability to succeed in school.

What Can I Do to Help My Child Be a Good Reader?

The objective of this book is to show parents how to prepare their child for reading instruction. This book is not about drilling your child at home so she will be the earliest child in your play group to read. Unlike some books, this book does not supply step-by-step instructions for how to teach your child to read. Our philosophy is that parents and teachers each have a distinct role in the teaching of reading. We don't view the parent's activities as replacing effective reading instruction in school. Instead, we see the parent's role as preparing the child for reading instruction, monitoring her progress, and becoming her advocate, if needed.

Many children do teach themselves to read before they enter school. Some children read early because they have been exposed to prereading skills, and they have an easy time making the link between sounds and letters. Children who learn to read early are the exception, however, and are not the focus of this book.

Think about a child you know who excels at playing a sport or a musical instrument. In order for that child to have reached that level of proficiency, most likely at least one of her parents took an interest in that activity. The parent drove that child to lessons or practices, purchased the needed equipment, attended games or recitals, talked to coaches or teachers, and generally supported the child's interest. Supporting your child in developing an interest in reading is not all that different. If you want your child to read well, you need to invest some time and effort in obtaining appropriate books, including time for reading in your child's schedule, and reading to your child.

THINGS YOU CAN DO TO CREATE A READING ENVIRONMENT AT HOME

- Fill your house with books.
- Establish good reading habits.
- Offer incentives for reading.
- Set an example through your reading.
- Help your child choose books.

Fill Your House with Books

If you want your child to be a reader, have lots of children's books in different rooms in the house. Placing books in different rooms is important because sometimes you can squeeze in a story during a lag time. While waiting for the camp bus or car pool to pick up your child, read a chapter each day. Keep books in a handy spot for grabbing as you're walking out the door. If your younger child rides along to pick up an older sibling from practice, bring along a book and read during those unavoidable minutes of waiting time.

Place books that are enjoyed by all of your children in the family room. Include an anthology of stories such as William Bennett's *Children's Book of Virtues, Aesop's Fables,* or *Grimm's Fairy Tales.* These stories can be enjoyed by children of many ages and promote discussions about values.

Place some books in each child's bedroom so they are handy for bedtime stories. As your children get older, switch the books in each child's room so that the stories are age-appropriate and there are some new stories to enjoy. You may even find your child reading while she's in her room waiting for her time-out to be over.

Buy some of the classic children's stories that you will enjoy reading over and over with each child. A list of books recommended by age category is provided in Appendix 3. There are many good sources of information about children's literature, including the following:

- *The New York Times Parent's Guide to the Best Books for Children,* by Eden Ross Lipson (Times Books)
- *American Library Association Best of the Best for Children,* by Denise Perry Donavin (Random House)
- *The Read-Aloud Handbook,* by Jim Trelease (Penguin Books)
- Newberry awards for stories, and Caldecott awards for illustrations

Position a trip to the bookstore as a treat for your child. Instead of always getting ice cream for a treat, consider a trip to the bookstore. If you do this from an early age, your child will get the strong signal that books are special. If your child seems reluctant, you may be surprised. Once you're at the bookstore she may want to purchase more books than you are prepared to buy. Try telling her that she can get one or two books today, and once she's finished these, she'll be able to come back and pick out more. When your child is a preschooler start a routine of going to the library weekly. Get your child her own library card as soon as she can write her name.

Establish Good Reading Habits

Good reading habits depend upon first making time for reading. If your child's schedule is so full of sports and enrichment activities, there may not be enough time for your child to have "down time" to read. Limit TV time to one 30-minute children's program per day once your child reaches school age. Start the bedtime preparations early once in a while in order to allow a little extra time for reading. Have a reading hour after dinner when everyone in the family reads during that time—including parents. Offer to read a story to your child when she has had a bad day or can't think of what to do because no one can play. Read aloud a special book to your children; choose a book that you really enjoy, such as *Charlotte's Web* by E. B. White. If Mom is the parent who is more interested in reading to the child, then ask Dad to select a topic to explore with his child. Most public libraries have excellent nonfiction children's books on topics such as animals, sports, countries, space exploration, history, and science.

It is critical to establish a reading routine prior to your child learning how to read. Initially you will be reading aloud to your child. But as your child learns to read, some of this time she will now read to you. If your child does have trouble learning to read, you will already have established a habit of setting aside time to read together. Parents of children who are having difficulty learning to read describe how their child often resists reading to them. Whether it is because reading is so laborious, or because the child doesn't like to reveal how poorly she reads, she may resist reading at home. That way the parent can say to the child "we always read at bedtime," and it doesn't appear that there is a sudden focus on reading because there's a problem. A child with reading difficulties needs to be listening to stories read aloud to keep up with the vocabulary development that her peers are gaining through their own reading.

Offer Incentives for Reading

If your child is reluctant to read, try some positive incentives to get started. Most first- and second-grade teachers encourage children to read more by sending home weekly sheets for the child to list what books she reads for 15 minutes at home each evening. Many teachers offer incentives to encourage reading, such as a visit to the toy box or recognition on a blackboard. Continue this same system at home throughout the summer, or into the next school year if your child's teacher hasn't initiated a system. Allow your child to select educational activity kits, or a toy or video, to be earned through logging daily reading time or pages read. Nagging your child to read probably won't work. Try offering incentives instead.

Set an Example Through Your Reading

Your attitude toward reading can have an effect on whether your child will be a reader. Your child will sense your level of interest in her reading based on whether you spend time reading to her or listening to her read. However, it is also important for her to see you choosing to read as a priority activity in your life. Our actions speak louder than our words. Therefore, choosing to watch TV each night after dinner rather than reading sends a strong message to our children about which activities we value.

I personally struggle with how to read during times when my children might see me. I read every night before going to sleep, but my children never see me read at that hour. Last summer during our family vacation I began reading a novel selected specially for this trip. As my husband played with the children in the pool, I sat in a lounge chair captivated by my novel. When they left the pool to get ready to go out to dinner, I stayed put so I could finish a thrilling scene in my novel. The family then had to wait for me to get ready to leave because I had trailed behind them in returning to our room from the pool. My children suddenly wanted to know about the story in my book. They clearly got the message that I was entertained by reading.

Try to create moments of shared reading time. Ask your child to bring her selected book and cuddle up next to you while you both read silently in front of the fireplace.

Beware of the signals either parent may be sending by not reading to the children. In Paul Kropp's book, *Raising a Reader,* he describes a mother, a school librarian, who approached him for help in figuring out why her son doesn't like to read. In response to his question about whether the boy's father read to her son, he relates:

> The woman gave me a surprised look. "My husband? My husband doesn't have time to read—he's a man."

Despite years of teacher training, the woman just couldn't see how the hidden family attitude—reading is something only women do—was crippling her son's reading progress.[5]

Help Your Child Choose Books

You will determine your child's early exposure to children's literature, from her first board books through her early readers. The books you select depend upon what you know about choosing quality books at an appropriate reading or listening level. When your child is an infant and toddler, she needs to hear lots of rhymes and hold board books with print she can study. While she is a preschooler she needs to hear lots of rich children's stories.

Even after your child learns to read, you play an important role in supplying her books. Once you discover a series your child likes, make another book appear just as she is finishing the last one. Sometimes a trip to the zoo or a museum, or a curriculum unit in school, will prompt an interest in a topic. Then provide nonfiction books from the library on that topic. Whether it's chipmunks, space, Mexico, or foreign currencies, be a magician and have the books appear in her room.

Well after your child is a good reader, you need to be aware of what your child is reading. In addition to monitoring the quality of what your child reads, you need to watch for periods where your child seems to lose interest in reading. Some experts believe that even good readers go through slumps where they lose interest in reading for a period of time. Rise to the challenge and try to discover what type of materials it will take to get your child hooked on reading again.

Is This Worth the Effort?

Yes. We believe that parents have an important role in helping a child learn to read. Every effort you make to be involved and play an active role will pay off later. As Dr. Marilyn Adams says in an emotional plea in her otherwise very scholarly summary of reading research in her book, *Beginning to Read:*

> But even before children enter grade school, we must become universally committed to developing their appreciation of and familiarity with text. We hug them, we give them treats and good things to eat; we try to teach them to be clean and polite, good natured, thoughtful, and fair. We do these things because it is the best way we know to set them off on happy, healthy lives. We must do as much with reading. In our society, their lives depend on it.[6]

The parent's role we advocate throughout this book is to:

- **Coach** in the development of reading skills.
- **Monitor** reading progress.
- **Advocate** if progress doesn't seem to be on track.

CHAPTER THREE

Why Reading to Children Is Important

> The single most important activity for building the knowledge required for eventual success in reading is reading aloud to children. This is especially so during the preschool years.[1]
>
> *from* Becoming a Nation of Readers

This conclusion, from an influential report entitled, *Becoming a Nation of Readers: The Report of the Commission on Reading,* resulted from a study sponsored by the National Institute of Education. The purpose of this review was to summarize the findings from research about reading and to make recommendations for instruction. This report, which was published in 1984, is still recognized as a landmark summary of research in reading and is frequently quoted in educators' books.

The fact that the Commission on Reading proclaimed the importance of reading to children may not surprise many parents; most parents have been told in many ways to read to their children. As a first-time parent, however, I became aware that although I had been repeatedly advised to read to my child, no one had ever explained *why* it was important.

When my first child was born, I was working full-time and feeling very overextended. I read many popular parenting books and worried about what my child ate, how to childproof the house, how to evaluate child-care options, and so forth. After a few months of feeling overwhelmed with how much there was to learn and do as a new parent, I decided to choose a couple of things that were important to me and do those really well. I chose two areas to concentrate on in my parenting, knowing I could not be an expert on every aspect of child rearing. Driven by interest, I made a commitment to do a particularly diligent job with building self-esteem and getting my child ready to read. My goal was to raise a child who loved to read and who had strong self-esteem. Little did I know at the time how connected these two goals are.

My choice of parenting goals may be of interest because one is a gift my parents gave to me and the other is a gift I discovered myself. My parents were amazingly intuitive about how to parent in order to raise a child with strong self-esteem. However, my parents didn't read to me as a child, and our home contained very few books. If they had been advised that reading aloud was critical for success in school, I have no doubt that my parents would have read to me and my siblings in spite of the fact that neither parent read for pleasure. In the 1950s, the importance of reading aloud to children wasn't widely known or communicated to parents. Because reading was not emphasized or modeled at home, I did not discover reading for pleasure until my late teen years. I missed the pleasure of many classic children's stories in my own childhood; therefore, the prospect of sharing them with my own children was doubly inviting. I'd get what I'd missed; they'd get acquainted with the wonderful world of books.

Having decided that I wanted my children to be readers, I began paying close attention to anything written about how children learn to read. In my journey through all the parenting books, I was on the lookout for anything about reading. The recommendation that parents should read to their children came through loud and clear, so I began to purchase children's books and read aloud to my children. However, being an overly analytical person, I began to wonder about *why* I should read to my child and *what proof* there is that it really makes a difference. Although regularly reading aloud to our children was a habit my husband and I embraced, I was nagged with these questions and struck by the fact that I had never seen an explanation of how this activity benefits children's subsequent reading ability.

It was during my first course in a master's program in education called "Survey of Reading Methods and Materials" that the answers emerged. One summer as I sat on my deck reading the textbook for this course, it all began to make sense. The information about what reading aloud to a child accomplishes was there in the textbooks for educators. But why wasn't this information in parenting books? That was probably the moment of conception for this book.

Six Reasons Why Reading Aloud Helps

How Does Reading Stories Aloud Benefit My Child?

There are some well-researched benefits to a child whose parents read aloud to him.

BENEFITS FROM READING ALOUD

The child

- develops background knowledge about a variety of topics
- builds his vocabulary
- becomes familiar with rich language patterns
- develops familiarity with story structure
- acquires familiarity with the reading process
- identifies reading as a pleasurable activity

Each of these benefits is explored in this chapter, along with evidence that reading aloud to our children will encourage them to be readers.

Benefit: Builds Background Knowledge

Probably the most critical benefit of all those hours of reading stories to our children is that the child gains knowledge of things, people, and places that he is less likely to acquire from any other source. Every story a parent reads to a child gives information about an environment and images of things that happen in that environment. It is almost as if we are creating a huge inventory of mental images of life's experiences and doing so much more rapidly than the child could experience firsthand, even in families that emphasize travel and conversation. Later, when the child reads a sentence or passage about a topic he is at least somewhat familiar with, it is so much easier for him to determine unknown words and comprehend what he is reading. Having background, or prior knowledge, about the topic when reading a new book is a critical component of later comprehension after the child has learned to read the words.

After reading about background knowledge in my education textbook, I began examining children's stories to see what kind of information is contained in them. Let's take a popular children's story and assess it from the perspective of what it provides the child. My oldest child loved *Curious George* stories written by H. A. Rey. Because I have fond memories of how much we enjoyed reading these stories, I've chosen one for an analysis of the background information provided in it.

Overview of the Story—*Curious George Gets a Medal*

In this classic children's book, a monkey named George is the center of the story. He is very curious and causes some difficulty each time he pursues his curiosity by exploring something. In this 47-page illustrated book, George, who is home alone, receives a letter. While trying to write a response, he spills ink which he is trying to pour from a bottle into a fountain pen. The mess becomes much worse as he tries to clean up the ink with soap flakes and water from a garden hose. Having partially filled a room with lather and water, he runs to a nearby farm where he remembers seeing a portable pump.

The events at the farm continue with difficulties. Because the pump is too heavy for him, he decides that he can get a farm animal to pull the pump back to his house. However, his first effort to get a pig to pull the pump results in all the pigs rushing out of the fence once he lifts the latch. He finally realizes that a cow is a better choice and begins the journey home on the cow's back with the pump pulled behind them. However, the farmers see them and a chase begins. George hides in some laundry on a clothesline and then jumps in the back of a passing pickup truck.

The truck happens to be on its way to the Museum of Science to deliver a large box. George, who does not know what a museum is, goes inside to satisfy his curiosity. He explores the rooms with stuffed prehistoric animals and eventually spots some nuts on a tree in the dinosaur exhibit. Since he is hungry he climbs onto the dinosaur's head and accidentally pulls the artificial tree over, knocking down the dinosaur. The guards catch him and lock him in a cage. His friend, "the man with the yellow hat" (who had brought him from Africa in the first book) arrives just in time to save him from being taken to the zoo.

George's friend is carrying the letter that had been delivered by the mailman at the beginning of the story. The letter was written by "Professor Wiseman," the director of the museum, to invite George to ride in a spaceship which has been built as an experiment. In order to be forgiven for the mess he made at the dinosaur exhibit, George agrees. George blasts off in a tiny spaceship and must bail out by pulling a lever when a light is illuminated inside the ship by remote control from Earth. He parachutes out just in the nick of time and receives a medal for being the First Space Monkey.

Background Information from the Story

There is an amazing amount of background information in this story. Our lovable, curious monkey demonstrates practical things, such as how fountain pens are filled with ink and what happens when soap flakes are sprayed with water from a garden hose. While George goes to the farm, he observes the pigs squealing and grunting and running away as fast as they can. He also contrasts the pigs' behavior to that of the cows, who were gentle and strong and far better candidates to pull the pump for him. All these observations provide background information for the child about the behavior of different farm animals.

George, who had never been to a museum before, makes observations about this unfamiliar environment. George observes that the large animals he sees do not move. The author writes:

> They were not alive. They were stuffed animals, put into the Museum so that everybody could get a look at them.[2]

The book provides illustrations of the several rooms of stuffed animals, including the dinosaur exhibits. For a very young child, this may be his first exposure to a museum of this sort.

As the story continues through the spaceship scenes, there is some additional background provided. George is dressed in a space suit with a helmet, air tank, gloves, and shoes. A satellite dish and monitor screen are shown in the illustrations to explain how the people on earth communicate with the monkey in the spaceship. The blastoff scene is complete with a countdown before the rocket engine is ignited and the ship blasts off. The description of the ship continues:

> He pressed the button and the ship rose into the air, slowly first, and then faster and faster and higher and higher, until they could no longer see it in the sky. But on the screen they saw George clearly all the time.[3]

A young child hearing this story retains an impression of the blasting off of a spaceship and continued communications with Earth.

This classic children's story was written in 1957 and offers the opportunity for a parent to explain that there were no manned space flights then, yet we have achieved enormous progress in space flight during the last 40 years. Other scenes that date the book include the use of a fountain pen with a blotter and the laundry hanging on the outdoor clothesline. These nuances provide an experience from which to launch a discussion about the differences in technology and life in the 1950s versus today.

Benefit: Builds Vocabulary

A child with a large listening and speaking vocabulary has an enormous advantage in learning to read. Reading comprehension depends more than any other single skill on knowing the meanings of the individual words in the passage. When a child is trying to read an unfamiliar word after he has learned some phonics and word attack skills, he should begin to sound out the word. The process of relating the print to a spoken word is faster and more accurate when that word is already in the child's speaking vocabulary. For example, if a child encounters the word *museum* for the first time in print, he is likely to say the word correctly if he recognizes that it is a word he has heard and can interpret. And not only can the child figure out the new word faster, but because word recognition has required less time and effort, he has more attention to devote to comprehending the passage.

Imagine that a child who is an early reader doesn't know the word *rocket* and is reading the following sentence:

> When we flash you a signal you will have to open the door and bail out with the help of emergency rockets.[4]

As he sounds out *rock-ets* he will more quickly recognize that he has read this unknown word correctly if this word is already part of his speaking vocabulary, and he knows what it means. The context will help him know that he has deciphered the word correctly, and he will have a sense that the word fits the meaning of the sentence. Having a big mental dictionary of words facilitates reading comprehension and reading fluency, and young children acquire a big mental dictionary from having books read to them.

Continuing with our *Curious George* example, let's examine the vocabulary words that appear in this children's story. During the beginning scenes at the house involving the letter writing and attempted cleanup of the spilled ink, lots of rich vocabulary is used. Then while George is on the farm, completely different words are included. The story continues with more rich experiences and vocabulary as George is asked to go up in a spaceship and bail out using a parachute to land safely.

On the next page is a list of 28 sample words from this book. Although some of these words may be spoken in our daily interaction with our children, many are words we would not use regularly, and so the child's vocabulary expands. It has been proven that children do not typically learn such words from television, from

Sample Vocabulary Words in *Curious George Gets a Medal*

Scenes at the House	*Scenes at the Farm*	*Scenes at the Spaceship*
• curious	• shed	• professor
• fountain pen	• loop	• flash
• funnel	• hurled	• signal
• blotter	• latch	• bail out
• garden hose	• grunting	• emergency rockets
• tap	• squealing	• permit
• lather	• grazing	• space suit
• escape	• rattling	• launching site
• portable pump		• lever
		• groping
		• parachute

each other, or simply from talking with adults. Reading books is the key to knowing words.

Benefit: Develops Familiarity with Rich Language Patterns

Not only is exposure to the background information and specific words in books important for children, but so is exposure to sentence patterns and special uses of language that are found only in books. The more exposure to complex and well-structured sentences, the more likely it is that the child will use such sentence patterns himself. Thus, the exposure helps not only comprehension but also speaking and writing ability as the child matures.

In the preschool years, children do not learn about sentence structure from being formally taught. They learn from listening to the patterns spoken around them and modeling their own language patterns after those of other speakers. The brain is hardwired to learn the rules and organization of a language system; all that is required is sufficient input for the brain to sort out the way words can be ordered to make sentences. As a child listens to sentence after sentence, he develops a familiarity with a range of possible sentence patterns and how ideas are communicated. The patterns become part of his internal rule system for putting words together. For example, he learns that questions can be made in different ways:

What did George do when he could not carry the pump?
Did George carry the pump?
(With a rising voice): George didn't carry the pump?

He learns as well that some words have to go in a certain order to fill "slots" in a sentence, and others are not bound by such rules. For example, he learns where to put an adjective that modifies a noun: before the noun, unless it is part of the verb phrase. In English we say *the curious monkey,* not *the monkey curious,* although we can say *the monkey was curious.* This part of language "learning," again, is not conscious or deliberately practiced in the preschool years; it will take place with exposure to language.

What is different about the language in books and the language of speech? Plenty. The language of books is much more complex. Sentences are complete in book language but tend to be incomplete and run-on in less formal conversations between people who are talking to each other face-to-face. Sentences tend to be longer and more complex in books—that is, they have clauses built into them, or they are joined by conjunctions that are carefully chosen to express an idea. They tend to be loaded with more modifiers—adjectives and adverbs—and to use correct grammar more than we do in casual speech. Printed language uses phrases and expressions in special ways that are peculiar to writing but uncommon in speech, such as the greetings and closings in letters. Finally, the way that sentences are ordered and strung together in writing is usually much more organized and less repetitious than the way we speak.

An example of well-written sentences from our *Curious George* book is the letter from the Professor to George, which is printed in the book, as follows:

> Dear George,
>
> A small space ship has been built by our experimental station. It is too small for a man, but could carry a little monkey. Would you be willing to go up in it?
>
> I have never met you, but I hear that you are a bright little monkey who can do all sorts of things and that is just what we need.
>
> We want you to do something nobody has ever done before: bail out of a spaceship in flight.
>
> When we flash you a signal you will have to open the door and bail out with the help of emergency rockets.
>
> We hope that you are willing and that your friend will permit you to go.
>
> Gratefully yours,
> Professor Wiseman
> Director of the Science Museum[5]

This passage also demonstrates some fundamentals of good letter composition. The first paragraph introduces the topic and tells why the Professor is writing to the monkey. The remainder of the letter clearly explains why a man can't go in the spaceship and why George has been invited to do this job. In addition the Professor describes what George would be asked to do. The last paragraph politely expresses the Professor's recognition that George will need his friend's permission to go.

Another example of the descriptive language appropriate for preschoolers is from the scene where they are waiting for George to react to the illuminated light and pull the lever to parachute from the spaceship. The author's writing is demonstrated in the following passage:

> They waited anxiously . . . At last George began to move. Slowly, as if in a daze, he was groping for the lever. Would he reach it in time? There—he had grabbed it!
>
> The door opened—hurrah—George was on his way!
>
> Out of the blue an open parachute came floating down to earth. The truck raced over to the spot where George would land.
>
> What a welcome for George!
>
> Professor Wiseman hung a big golden medal around his neck. "Because," he said, "you are the first living being to come back to earth from a space flight." And on the medal it said: TO GEORGE, THE FIRST SPACE MONKEY.

> Then a newspaperman took his picture and everybody shouted and cheered, even the farmer and his son, and the kind woman from next door (who had worked for hours to get the water out of the room).[6]

In summary, children who have been read to have learned that there is a different language, or a different way of expressing ideas, in books from the way we speak. They begin to develop an "ear" for written English versus spoken English. As described by Canadian educator M. Spencer:

> Being read to offers them [children] longer stretches of written language than at any other time, and moreover, this is language put together by someone that isn't there to be seen. The reader, adult or child, lends the text a different voice, so that "I'll huff and I'll puff and I'll blow your house down" becomes a language event of a particular kind.[7]

Benefit: Develops Familiarity with Story Structure

Children absorb a great deal about story structure from hearing many stories during their preschool years. This knowledge is helpful once the child begins to read and write his own stories. It helps with reading because, knowing what to expect, children form a mental outline of the events and remember the details much more easily. It helps with writing because, knowing what the pieces are and where a story should go, the child has a mold to put his words into. Preschoolers who have been read hundreds of stories begin to understand that stories have common characteristics.

COMMON CHARACTERISTICS OF STORIES

- The story has a title.
- There are characters, including a main character.
- The story takes place in a setting (time, place).
- The characters usually have a problem to solve.
- The action hinges on how the problem is solved.
- There is a resolution (climax) in the story, before it ends.
- Language is used to create the effect of surprise, sadness, climax, or humor.

Benefit: Acquires Familiarity with the Reading Process

Children learn about what reading is from observing others read to them. For the young child, early experiences of having someone read to them gives them an experience and impression about *how people read.* Children gain an impression about what a person does when he or she reads. Since we cannot see inside the mind, which is where the process is occurring, a child must guess about what the adult is doing. The child begins to form hypotheses about the print on the page corresponding to words that are the same as those the child hears in speaking and listening. This correlation between print and spoken words is an important step in learning about reading.

A study that was completed by educator E. H. Hiebert examined what preschool children believe an adult is reading on the page. Children were shown a book with pictures and print and asked to point to what a reader should read. In this study it was found that three-year-old children believed that it was the pictures that were being read.[8]

There is a set of other things a pre-reading child must learn that educators refer to as "print awareness" or "learning about print." These concepts are learned from being read to by an adult who shows the child the book and interacts with the child as the story is being read aloud. These concepts include the following:

CONCEPTS A CHILD MUST LEARN ABOUT PRINT

- how the book is turned when it is "right side up"
- that the print is read, not the pictures
- where the beginning of the book is
- the order of reading the print on a page
  –top to bottom
  –left to right
- what to do at the end of a line
- what to do at the end of a page

Benefit: Identifies Reading As a Pleasurable Activity

I can vividly remember the first time that I realized that reading was a great pleasure. It was during spring break of my senior year in high school, which my best friend and I spent in Florida visiting my grandparents. My friend, whose name was Madeline, tossed me her copy of Ayn Rand's *Atlas Shrugged* after she finished it. I devoured it during that week, reading late into the night several nights. Although this first "aha" experience came late for me, reading for pleasure has been a part of my life ever since. As a parent, it is my goal for my children to experience the joy of reading early in life and hopefully begin a lifelong love of reading.

Probably the most important thing about reading aloud to a child is to allow the child to experience reading as an enjoyable activity. If the child associates reading with pleasure, the child will have a greater desire to learn to read. As Jim Trelease wrote in the first chapter of his book, *The Read-Aloud Handbook:*

> Every time we read to a child, we're sending a "pleasure" message to the child's brain. You could even call it a commercial, conditioning the child to associate books and print with pleasure.[9]

There are many things parents can do to make reading pleasurable. Choose a location in the home that your children especially enjoy. My children love to read on the front porch swing during the summer; they have reminded me that we read *Charlotte's Web* one summer while waiting for the camp bus to pick them up each day. Especially in the winter my children love to cuddle up next to me while listening to a story. At an educators' conference that I attended, a European speaker showed slides of historical paintings depicting scenes about reading. His point in showing over a hundred slides of paintings was that the overwhelming majority of the paintings showed the child sitting on the adult's lap while reading a story. The proximity of closeness between parent and child while reading has been captured in art over many centuries.

Choose a time when you can read for an uninterrupted period. My children are very vocal about how much they dislike it when I answer a phone call and leave them "hanging" in the middle of a key passage of a story we are reading. Get involved and be dramatic: make the story more fun for you and your children by accentuating the animation of your voice for key lines.

It's important that parents allow their children to see them enjoying reading. When I was growing up the only thing I remember seeing my parents read was the daily newspaper. In fact I can vividly recall that my father always read the paper in his easy chair each evening after family dinner. Modeling that reading is pleasurable sends strong messages to our children.

Proof That Reading to Your Child Makes a Difference

The most definitive evidence is the quote that appears at the beginning of this chapter. It's worth repeating:

> The single most important activity for building the knowledge required for eventual success in reading is reading aloud to children. This is especially so during the preschool years.[10]

This quote, which is a key conclusion from the Commission on Reading, is the result of their analysis of an extensive body of reading research. The Commission believes that reading to children is so important that it is the first of the Commission's 17 recommendations from their study. At the end of the report, *Becoming a Nation of Readers,* the 17 recommendations are highlighted. These recommendations were given to the National Institute of Education and broadly publicized. The introduction to these recommendations and the first recommendation follows:

> The more elements of good parenting, good teaching, and good schooling that children experience, the greater the likelihood that they will achieve their potential as readers. The following recommendations encapsulate the information presented in this report about the conditions likely to produce citizens who read with high levels of skill and do so frequently with evident satisfaction.

Parents should read to preschool children and informally teach them about reading and writing. Reading to children, discussing stories and experiences with them, and—with a light touch—helping them learn letters and words are practices that are consistently associated with eventual success in reading.[11]

Practical Tips About How to Make Reading Aloud Enjoyable

When Do I Start Reading to My Child?

Although Jim Trelease, in his book, *The Read-Aloud Handbook,* advises that reading to a child should start as soon as the baby is born, my personal experience was different. Although I occasionally read to my infants when they were less than six months old, I found it awkward to cradle my infant and try to turn the pages of a picture book. Read to your infant if it provides stimulation for you during the sometimes tedious hours you spend holding and rocking your baby. However, don't feel compelled to read at this stage if you find it more rewarding to look into the child's eyes and talk to him instead. There's plenty of time to read later.

6–9 Months

Beginning to read to a child around 6–9 months of age is ideal. The child is sitting up and can hold small board books at this stage. It is great to allow a child to begin exploring books by himself during quiet moments in the crib or on the floor. Wonderful vinyl books are available, which are more durable when the child is slobbering during the teething stage. Place the more fragile board books with pop-out sections on the bookshelf to be saved for reading together. Keep several small books among your child's toys that are the right size and shape for him to turn the pages and carry without help from you. Rotate the books so that he doesn't grow bored with them.

12–18 Months

By the age of 12–18 months your goal is to have your child bring books to you, signaling he wants you to read him a story. It's a thrill to see your child with book in hand and arms lifted telling you that he wants to come up on your lap to hear the story he has chosen. This event signals that he enjoys listening to a story.

It is important to make reading times enjoyable ones; therefore, like so many other things in parenting, choosing the appropriate time and occasionally waiting for the child to be ready can be critical. When my active toddler son squirmed to get off my lap, I decided not to force it. Although I was anxious to begin reading to him, I decided to wait to avoid risking that his experience of reading would be negative. If your child wants to turn the pages faster than the words can be read, abandon reading the story as written and make up a story that corresponds with the pictures. Even with the very simple small board books of about a dozen pages with few words, discuss the pictures and talk about all the things your child sees on each page. Your dialogue about each page should take longer than the actual time to read the words on the page.

2 Years of Age

Establish a routine by the time your child is two years old that you always read a story at bedtime. This routine is important because even if you spend no other time reading during the day, at least this 15 minutes per day occurs religiously. While our child still slept in a crib, our favorite spot for bedtime reading was in a rocking chair in his room with the door closed to avoid interruption. In our family the routine of a bedtime story has continued to this day, and our children are 11 and 8 years old. Our pattern is that on nights when both parents are home at bedtime, one parent reads to one child. The pair then is swapped on the following night so that Dad reads to daughter one night and to son the next night, and Mom does vice versa. Bedtime stories will hopefully continue in our house until as long beyond age 10 as possible. After that age, the child may prefer to read to himself before bed.

6–8 Years of Age

Once the child is able to read himself, change the routine by having the child read for 15 minutes, followed by the parent reading to the child for 15 minutes. A child needs to practice to learn to be a good reader. If your child is a reluctant reader, have him read from a book on his reading level before you read to him from a book that is somewhat above his own reading level. When children are first learning to decode the words, there will be a gap between what they are able to read themselves and what they enjoy hearing read aloud. Encourage your child to practice reading books he can read comfortably. Then, it is important for the parent to continue reading to the child from books above the child's reading level in order to expand his background knowledge and enjoyment of literature.

What If My Child Resists Being Read To?

The intimacy of shared reading is not always easy to capture. When my son was a toddler it was difficult to feel close during our regular reading time. He was a very active child who frequently squirmed to get down from my lap because he had a greater interest in gross motor activities than in sitting. If your child isn't interested in hearing a story, abandon the effort and try again at another time. Do not push the issue and he will eventually come back to reading. Choose when to offer to read him a story and select very short stories initially, thereby matching the child's attention span. Select books on topics about which your child is keenly interested. Ease your child into longer and longer stretches of reading time.

When Do I Stop Reading Aloud?

Many parents believe that once their child begins to read himself, the days of reading storybooks aloud are over. However, there are some very important reasons for continuing to read to your child as he begins to learn to read. Especially in first and second grade while the child is learning to read, his listening level far exceeds his reading level; that is, he can understand passages read to him that far exceed what he is capable of reading himself. Continue to expose your child to good literature that mentally challenges him and enables his vocabulary and knowledge to continue growing. Do this as long as it is fun. Once children prefer to read silently, everyone can share a "Drop Everything And Read" (DEAR) time in the evening.

What Do I Do If My Child Wants to Look Ahead at the Pictures Before We Read?

As frustrating as looking ahead may be to the parent, most educators would encourage you to allow looking ahead at the pictures. This exercise helps the child to activate background knowledge about the setting and topic of the story. In first-grade reading instruction teachers usually take time to introduce a story before they begin reading it. Children are taught to think about the title of the book and anticipate what the story might be about. Typically a discussion is initiated about the topic of the book. If the story is about going to the zoo, the teacher leads a discussion about what you are likely to see at the zoo. Children will name the animals found at a zoo, as well as discussing the activities one might see, such as zookeepers feeding the animals. The purpose of this discussion is to activate prior knowledge for the children who have visited the zoo and to provide information to any child who has no prior information about this experience.

What Comes After Picture Books?

Before your child reaches age seven you will begin reading aloud chapter books that don't have pictures. *Charlotte's Web,* a story written by E. B. White about the friendship between a spider and a pig, is a wonderful example of a chapter book appropriate for this age. The vocabulary is challenging and interesting and the story is captivating for the child. There is plenty of background knowledge presented while the child is thoroughly entertained. Other books we enjoyed included *Mr. Popper's Penguins, The Indian in the Cupboard,* and *The American Girl Collection* books.

After your child can read himself, continue to look for opportunities to read aloud to your child. This can be done through round-robin reading of a classic book in front of the fireplace or through alternate oral reading—first the parent, then the child, switching every page or two—to foster better comprehension. It will also enable the family to have active discussions about the characters and the author's intended meaning. Your own love of literature will continue to be communicated through shared reading activities. Remember and find the books you loved as a child. Enjoy them again as you share them with your child.

What's So Special About a Bedtime Story?

An especially important time to continue reading to the child is at bedtime. Reading a story separates the activities of the day from the time when the child quiets himself to prepare to fall asleep. As the child gets older the selection of books may vary. Some children are much more interested in reading for information than they are in reading fiction. My 11-year-old son often chooses a nonfiction book about Native Americans, or animals in Australia, or what it was like to grow up in Abe Lincoln's day.

Regardless of the choice of book to read at bedtime, another very important thing occurs at this time of the day. I'm always amazed that, in spite of the fact that I am there when he arrives home from school and reports to me about his day, he brings up something about his day at bedtime that wasn't discussed earlier. This may be a residual habit from a tradition we started when he was around three years old. While tucking him in bed, usually before the story, I would ask him two questions:

- What was the best thing about your day?
- Is there anything that you didn't like that happened today?

It was helpful to learn about something that was really bothering my child, sometimes something that I did that he didn't like. What a great way to hear about it and be able to talk it through together right at the end of the day before he went to sleep!

Why Conversations Develop Skills for Later

Are There Activities Other than Reading Aloud That Can Help My Child Master Language?

There are other important things besides reading aloud that you can do at home. We are going to discuss three activities that involve talking and reading in combination. All of these activities help your child develop the critical language skills needed to be a good reader.

ACTIVITIES IN ADDITION TO READING ALOUD THAT DEVELOP LANGUAGE SKILLS

- Engage in extended conversations.
- Pursue interactive conversations about the content while reading stories.
- Discuss unknown vocabulary words.

Conversations at Home

Because we know that background knowledge, vocabulary, and familiarity with the language of stories are critical to success in reading, we should look once more at how children acquire that knowledge. Is it through television? Being around adults? Going to different places? We have already argued that children learn a great deal about written language from being read to. However, in addition to reading aloud, the kind of conversation we have at home with our children does have an impact on reading achievement.

In a section of *Becoming a Nation of Readers* entitled, "Talking and Learning about the World," the report reveals an interesting piece of research about skills children learn from conversations at home. Excerpts follow:

> Reading depends upon wide knowledge. The more knowledge children are able to acquire at home, the greater their chance for success in reading. . . . Children who have gone on trips, walked in parks, and gone to zoos and museums will have more background knowledge relevant to school reading than children who have not had these experiences.
>
> Wide experience alone is not enough, however. The way in which parents *talk* to their children about an experience influences what knowledge the children will gain from the experience and their later ability to draw on the knowledge when reading. It is talk about experience that extends the child's stock of concepts and associated vocabulary.
>
> The content of statements and questions and the manner in which they are phrased influence what children will learn from experience. Questions can be phrased in ways that require children merely to put some part of an experience into words or they can be phrased in a thought-provoking manner. For example, one parent may ask a child, "what do you see under the windshield wiper?", while another may ask, "Why do you think there's a slip of paper under the windshield wiper?" Thought-provoking questions stimulate the intellectual growth needed for success in reading.
>
> . . . Children who have extended conversations at home that make them reflect upon experience learn to construct meaning from events. They have a subsequent advantage in learning to read. A long-term study that followed children from age one to seven found that the content and style of the language parents used with their children predicted the children's school achievement in reading.[12]

In summary, it is the way in which we discuss events with our children that can make a difference. Reading well requires thinking, asking questions, integrating information, and drawing inferences. All of these are skills that parents can help their child learn through thought-provoking conversations at home. In our hurried lifestyle, conversation is often neglected. Make it as much of a priority as fixing dinner and tucking in your child.

WHEN TALKING WITH YOUR CHILD

- Ask open-ended, thought-provoking questions and listen to the answers.
- Challenge the child to draw meaning from events.
- Ask the child to give complete descriptions of things that happened and draw out what the important things were.

Interactive Story Reading

Have you ever felt frustrated when your child wants to stop you to ask questions while you are reading a story to him? When my children were preschoolers, I found it frustrating to be constantly interrupted by all their comments about the pictures and questions about the story. I decided that limiting the interruptions was a good thing, because when the child starts school his teacher wouldn't want to be stopped by incessant questions from 25 children. It also seemed that staying "on task" was an admirable skill to be learned.

However, this dialogue during the story reading is actually very positive and is something to be encouraged and developed. As described in *Becoming a Nation of Readers,* active discussion during reading is important:

> The benefits are greatest when the child is an active participant, engaging in discussions about stories, learning to identify letters and words, and talking about the meanings of words. One researcher who observed parents reading books to their children discovered differences in the quality and quantity of informal instruction that the parents provided.[13]

The importance of engaging the child as an active listener, rather than the parent reading the story from beginning to end without pause, has been researched by other educators. The most interesting of these was a study completed by G. Whitehurst and his colleagues in 1988, which demonstrated the impact of active engagement. In their study they provided training to the parents of 15 middle-class preschool children from two to three years old. The parents received a one-hour training session in interactive story reading in which they were shown how to engage in this technique. They were instructed to:

- pause periodically and ask open-ended questions
- expand on the child's answers
- suggest alternative possibilities
- pose progressively more challenging questions

An example of an open-ended question is "What is Curious George doing?" or "Why do you think he is doing that?" The key is to ask questions that cannot be answered with a yes/no response. A control group was identified with children of approximately the same age and language development. The parents of both groups tape-recorded their reading sessions for one month.

The tapes confirmed that both groups read equally often (about eight times per week) and that the trained parents followed the instructions for interactive story reading. The children in both groups were tested before and after the experimental month. The results showed that at the end of one month of interactive story reading the children in this group versus the control group:

- improved 8.5 months in verbal expression, and
- were 6 months ahead on a vocabulary test.[14]

The verbal expression measure assessed the child's capability in expressing ideas verbally. These are staggering results for children who have an average age of 30 months! Think what effect using an interactive story-reading approach might have over several years, versus the one month of this study.

Discussions About Unknown Words: Expanding Your Child's Vocabulary

The approach most children and adults use to figure out the meaning of an unfamiliar word is usually to learn as much as possible about the word from its context. In the following sentence, think what clues the context provides for the meaning of *cavalier:*

> *The boys were confident, even cavalier,*
> *about their prospects of winning tonight's big game.*

Knowledge of the word *confident* helps provide clues for the meaning of *cavalier.* Studies show that the first step in vocabulary development is to help the student be aware of unknown words. Then providing direct teaching of the word meaning is helpful, along with teaching strategies for how the child can learn word meanings on his own. Parents are advised to explain to the child that the clue provided by the word *confident* helps in inferring the meaning of the unknown word. The parent can extend the activity to include guessing the meaning, followed by looking it up in the dictionary. A good children's dictionary is a worthwhile investment, because it contains a larger typeface, pictures, and a carefully chosen vocabulary so that the size of the dictionary is not too overwhelming.

Research shows that vocabulary development continues through the early elementary years. Between grades three and seven, a child's vocabulary generally doubles.[15] Children come to school typically knowing at least 5,000 words; in the first three grades they learn at least 1,000 new words per year and, by grade four, are learning from 1,000 to 3,000 new words per year on average. Again, most of this new learning comes from reading.

There is some additional research about the differences among young children's, older children's, and adults' ways of defining the meaning of words. An older child or adult tends to define words by categories and then by differentiating characteristics of a word within a category. A younger child learns a piece of a word's meaning and adds to it as he is exposed to the word many times. How each group might define these words is shown on the next page. It is widely speculated that these differences in definition reflect the developmental stage of conceptual processing. It is believed that as children accumulate a greater background knowledge about where things come from and how things are made, they are able to define things into categories and understand that words are related to each other in meaning. Parents can help the

Word Definitions by Age Groups		
Word	*Older Child or Adult*	*Young Child*
straw	dried grass	It's yellow.
orange	citrus fruit	You eat it.

child learn how to categorize and notice differentiating characteristics through explanations offered while talking with children.

Reading aloud to a child is a critical activity in helping a child gain the knowledge and language skill that will enable good comprehension later on. Reading aloud increases background knowledge, builds vocabulary, and familiarizes children with the language in books. The Commission on Reading has advised that not only does reading aloud to a child make a difference, but the way parents read aloud matters. A book becomes a vehicle for using language—before, during, and after reading. In addition to reading aloud, engaging in probing conversations at home can help the child acquire the language skills needed to become a good reader.

Ways Parents Can Help Children Master Language

What	*How To*	*Why*
Engage in extended conversations at home.	• Ask child to reflect upon experience • Ask child thought-provoking questions about his experiences –complete descriptions of what happened –what was important	Helps child construct meaning from events
Read stories aloud interactively.	While reading a story aloud: • pause periodically and ask open-ended questions • expand on the child's answers • suggest alternative possibilities • pose progressively more challenging questions	Improves child's verbal expression
Discuss unknown words.	During reading or a conversation when reaching an unknown word: • Ask child if he knows the word • Ask child what clues there are to infer the word's meaning • Tell him the meaning, or look it up in the dictionary together	Develops child's vocabulary

Chapter Four

Understanding Alternative Approaches to Teaching Reading: The Whole Language and Phonics Controversy

> Controversy and confusion in the literacy field today center around how best to teach children to read. Specifically, the question is, should skills be taught directly in an organized and explicit skills development program as part of beginning-to-read instruction, or will students acquire these skills more indirectly by being read to, immersion in print, and learning skills in the context of reading for meaning—an approach known as whole language?[1]
>
> *Dr. Bill Honig, from* Teaching Our Children to Read

Educators have always debated the merits of teaching approaches. However, parents rarely participate in these discussions unless their child gets the short end of the methods stick. The current debate about reading education is an exception to this norm. Almost all informed parents know that educators disagree about how to teach reading. Very few, however, know who to believe or where to go for reliable information that will benefit their child. The popular press is bombarding parents with articles about the demise of children's reading and spelling skills and the conflicting opinions of professionals about how best to teach them. One of these articles appeared on the front page of the *Wall Street Journal* on October 30, 1996, stating:

> Spats over educational methods are hardly new. But few in the history of education have gone as public—or become as polemicized—as the battle over whole language.[2]

Popular press articles continue to describe and contrast two methods for teaching reading—phonics and whole language—and rarely discuss either the middle ground or the ways in which these approaches might complement one another. The press prefers to perpetuate controversy about the best way to teach children to read, because controversy sells. Articles, which have appeared in major newspapers as well as parenting magazines, describe educators as facing off in an emotionally charged battle over which approach to reading instruction is better. Although magazine and newspaper articles heighten a parent's awareness that reading methods are hotly contested, they usually provide skimpy descriptions of each approach, how one differs from the other, or what other alternatives there might be. Consequently, parents often remain uncertain of the issue and how to resolve it for their own children.

QUESTIONS PARENTS TYPICALLY ASK

- How do whole language teachers instruct children to read?
- How can I tell if my child's teacher uses phonics?
- Which approach is best? Is there a best approach?
- Can we tell which approach is best for my child?

When they hear from many sources that reading instruction is controversial and children may be struggling or failing to learn essential skills because of inappropriate instruction, proactive parents are likely to get involved and get informed. Educational reforms are under way in many schools, but parents may need to ask whether those reforms are in line with research-based practices. Until parents can count on schools to use effective, scientifically validated reading programs, they might have to ask pointed questions to get the information they want to know about the reading curriculum in their child's class.

The background information provided in this chapter enables you to ask important questions of educators and to evaluate the way reading is taught to your child. And if you're like me, you'll want to compare the instructional approach in your child's classroom against the "best practices" standards currently promoted by reading experts to prevent reading failure in the early grades and promote reading success all the way through school. I discovered myself that there is much more to reading than two ends of a methods continuum; there is a sensible middle ground, which includes a number of reading skills that must be taught well.

Is It Important for Parents to Know How Their Child Is Being Taught to Read?

Reading educators and classroom teachers in the majority of our schools are not yet basing practices on scientific research. Literacy instruction in American classrooms continues to reflect ideas about learning to read that have been disproven, especially the belief that children are best taught to read words "naturally," "in context," and by guessing on the basis of meaning, and the belief that direct teaching of word decoding and spelling is harmful. A 1997 publication of the National Right to Read Foundation claims that the whole language approach is used in approximately 85 percent of our nation's schools.[3] Objective evaluations of whole language practices, however, do not support its effectiveness. Although whole language has been described in theory by the professors who promote it, whole language in practice is difficult to pin down. Major reviews of research on whole language ideas and practices have concluded that there is no evidence the practices are more effective than the more balanced approaches they have replaced, and there is mounting evidence that they are less effective. In several recent, well-designed studies of classroom teaching, children receiving whole language instruction in first grade failed at a higher rate than children whose program included direct, systematic teaching of sounds, letters, and sounding words out, along with many other language and reasoning skills.[4] The gap between research and classroom practice is still wide.

Parents should know how reading is taught in their child's class and should know if the approach is working. Without such knowledge, parents can neither help nor advocate for their own child's educational well-being. Many studies have shown that children at risk for failure are affected dramatically by the instruction they receive from kindergarten on. These children show a predictable set of symptoms from the outset, which can be alleviated in most cases with informed teaching. Approximately one-third of children are not likely to read well unless they receive practice identifying the speech sounds in words and matching them with printed symbols; these children also need structured practice applying the sound-symbol links to reading and spelling. Some children, perhaps a third, can learn to read with any kind of organized method, because they can teach themselves a great deal from exposure to print. They sail ahead when surrounded by books and just figure out how reading works when enough practice occurs. Children in the average range generally do better when phonics and other language skills are taught systematically as part of a comprehensive reading program, but even these children vary in their needs. Whether your child thrives or suffers with a specific approach to reading instruction may be discovered or understood by you before anyone else.

The debates about reading instruction have had both positive and negative consequences. The good news is that experts from the research community have reached consensus on the essential components of effective reading instruction, although some questions still remain about the instructional methods that work best for certain children. Through various advisories, they have outlined what reading teachers should be doing to help the most children succeed. In California, for example, the Commission on Teacher Credentialing has designated and is going to evaluate prospective teachers on the knowledge and skills necessary to teach all components of reading. The bad news is that change comes slowly; it will take some time before the public can expect any consistent application of research into practice. This realignment of instruction toward research-based practice may occur (if it does) well beyond when your child has learned to read.

Can I Assume That Reading Is Taught Better in Public or Private Schools?

You cannot draw any conclusions about how well reading is taught based on whether a school is public or private. Some parents believe that public schools are subject to more regulation or legislation and this might mean that reading instruction will be scrutinized more carefully and therefore be better. Since authority over curriculum is decentralized in almost all states, this is not the case. California is one of the few states where there is some centralization over education. In other states decisions about curriculum are made by local school boards in each community. Even with centralized curriculum authority, there is no assurance that individual teachers in every classroom are well trained and implementing best practices.

Other parents assume that private schools have higher standards of quality, hire the best teachers, and offer the best education available. While some of these assumptions may be true for an individual school, there are plenty of private schools that have been, or still are, teaching reading without explicitly teaching skills. Sending your child to a private school is no assurance that the teachers use the best practices in teaching reading.

You need to be concerned about how reading is taught in your child's classroom, no matter whether your child attends a private or a public school.

How Can I Compare and Contrast the Major Reading Approaches?

Reading approaches can be contrasted in a number of ways, but the most significant appears to be the manner in which the "code" is taught to children. So-called phonics approaches also teach children how to read and comprehend; so-called whole language approaches do teach children something about how to read words. The differences, however, can be marked and have to do with emphasis, instructional strategy, the type of reading material given to children, and the way their errors are corrected. For simplicity, we can summarize these contrasts as follows:

Comparison of Two Approaches to Teaching Reading

	Phonics	*Whole Language*
Category Name	Code-emphasis	Meaning-emphasis
Order of Teaching	Parts-to-whole	Whole-to-parts
Instructional Strategy	Skills taught explicitly	Skills taught in context
Organization of Program	By sound pattern	By theme or meaning
Use of Literature	Stories selected to offer practice of phonics lesson	Stories selected for rich story plot and characters
Unknown Words	Teacher encourages child to sound it out	Teacher encourages child to guess from context and picture clues

What Is Whole Language?

The whole language approach, dominant since 1985, emphasizes two premises:

- The purpose of reading is to extract meaning from text.
- The skills needed for reading will be acquired from the experience of reading and need not be explicitly taught.

The first premise is not controversial. All educators agree that we read in order to gain information and comprehend the meaning in text. It is the second premise that is at the root of the instructional controversy. Whole language advocates believe that most children can read without explicit, systematic instruction in component skills. In fact, they believe that explicit skills instruction is not only unnecessary but potentially damaging because it can defeat a child's love of reading.

As the name *whole language* suggests, reading is taught in a manner that keeps language *whole*—or undivided into words, sentences, or sounds—and that uses the language of children's books. Whole language instruction is a good deal like the "see and say" methods of the 1950s, but with an emphasis on "authentic" literature. In pure whole language classrooms the children receive minimal and incidental instruction in how the alphabetic letters represent sounds. Whole language educators propose that children learn to read naturally from exposure to lots of reading, just like they learned to speak by being surrounded with speech from birth. The underlying assumption is that the child figures out the rules of the language on her own. Learning to read is viewed as parallel to learning to speak: it just happens in most children. It's an inductive approach; the child infers the sound-symbol correspondences from exposure to print and then applies that knowledge to figure out new words in stories that are especially motivating to read.

Dr. Ken Goodman, a leading advocate of the whole language movement, proposed in the 1970s that deciphering each word was not necessary for proficient reading. In his 1984 book, *What's Whole About Whole Language?*, he wrote:

> Readers are seeking meaning, not sounds or words. They may use their developing phonics generalizations to help when the going gets tough. If they are lucky enough not to have been taught phonics in isolation, with each letter equally important, then they will not be diverted from developing the strategies necessary to select just enough graphic information to get to the sense they are seeking.[5]

The curriculum in whole language classrooms typically centers around children's literature. As Dr. Jeanne Chall, whose 1967 seminal book documented the history of reading instruction, has said, "The focus is on reading right from the start. They read before they've been taught *how* to read."[6] Teachers frequently place a "big book" version of the story, which is an oversized copy of the book, on an easel so that all children can follow along as the words are read aloud. Children are expected to gradually recognize more whole words. When a child who is reading encounters an unknown word, she is encouraged to guess from context and picture clues; the strategy of sounding out the word is not taught or encouraged. The teacher may encourage the child to read the entire sentence for the gist of the meaning rather than to stop to analyze an unknown word. Sometimes the print is covered up to force children to guess, or the first letter alone is uncovered. Approximations of the target word are accepted by the teacher if they make sense.

The practice of teaching reading without first teaching children letters, sounds, and how to match them is not new. Other methods, which were popular during previous decades, were called the "sight" and "look-say" methods. Many of today's parents learned to read with the look-say method of the 1950s and 1960s, which used books featuring Dick, Jane, and Spot. In both the look-say method and the whole language method children learn whole words through repetition and memorization of words in stories. The widespread implementation of whole language during the 1980s marks the second time during this century that the pendulum has swung from one end of the code-versus-meaning continuum to the other.

What Is Phonics?

The phonics approach, if taught well, should emphasize learning and combining the unit building blocks of words and applying them to sounding out unfamiliar words. Children are explicitly taught that the alphabetic letters, and letter groups, correspond to distinct speech sounds. In education jargon, the phonics approach is known as code-emphasis, or code-based, referring to the alphabet as a code. In a classroom with a strong phonics program, the letter-sound correspondence is taught early in the reading curriculum and applied to simple stories with those patterns; literature is read aloud to the children until they can sound words out. At the beginning of first grade the teacher provides direct instruction about the relationship between the sounds and their spellings and teaches children how to blend sounds to make words. Children's literature is used as early in the curriculum as possible, but the stories children actually read are typically written so that the child will be successful sounding out words based on the sound-letter correspondences that have been taught. The stories the children read are deemed to have a "controlled vocabulary." The literature used to develop appreciation for reading must be read aloud initially.

The term *phonics* is a word with several meanings. It is used to refer to the following:

- an approach to teaching reading
- the system by which alphabetic writing represents speech
- the strategies children employ to sound words out

Phonics is only one of many language skills that are taught in a code-emphasis program, including the structure of syllables, the spelling and meaning of word parts (prefixes, suffixes, roots), and punctuation. Phonics approaches should also include well-designed instruction in comprehension, writing, vocabulary development, and literature appreciation.

Each approach to reading organizes and selects its supporting texts for specific and different purposes. Beginning reading books can be written for maximum interest, for maximum practice with "sight" words, or for maximum practice with phonics patterns. Should appealing literature be the basis for instruction, or should stories follow and provide practice with sound patterns after they have been explicitly taught? One argument that is made against phonics instruction is that it can replace or supplant good literature in the classroom, and children will not be motivated to read. Reacting to this caricature of code-based teaching, Dr. Jeanne Chall jokingly remarked, "Did you know that nobody read books before whole language?"[7] According to Dr. Chall, all traditional classroom reading methods have included literature, and any who omit it are not well-balanced or effective programs. Good literature may have to be read aloud to children until they are taught to

.words themselves, but good literature is the cornerstone well-designed language arts program for children. If a .mphasis program shortchanges literature or teaches skills in .onnected way, the program is not well designed. Even Noah W..bster's "blue book spellers" used over 100 years ago included some of the finest children's literature available at that time to reinforce skills.

To help you understand the differences between a phonics and whole language classroom we have included descriptions of a morning in two imaginary classrooms. (Where a letter appears between slash marks, pronounce the letter sound, not the letter name.)

A Morning in Two Imaginary Classrooms

A Whole Language First-Grade Classroom

When you walk through the door of this classroom the first thing that catches your eye is the arrangement of the room. There are learning centers with round tables throughout this room. The children's desks are arranged in clusters of four; when all the children are seated at their desks, about half of them would have their backs to the blackboard. There is a rocking chair in one corner placed on a large, soft rug. Behind the rocking chair is a bookcase filled with books. Each learning center table contains books and objects for the children to explore on a different topic. There are paperback copies of children's literature books and easy nonfiction books everywhere in this classroom; the variety of books is notable, as is the absence of multiple copies of any reading anthology. There are name labels taped to identify objects throughout the room.

When we enter the room the children are seated at the round learning-center tables engaged in separate activities. After a few minutes Miss V, a young teacher who has been at the school for three years, announces that she wants the children to gather on the rug for a story. She places a three-foot-by-two-foot copy of the popular children's story, *Clifford Takes a Walk*, on an easel beside the rocking chair. Once the children are seated and quiet, she opens the big book and asks if everyone can see it. She begins reading the story slowly while pointing to each word as she goes. After Miss V reads the entire story through, she takes a second large book and asks for a volunteer to read this story. A little girl volunteers and begins reading as Miss V points to each word. On the third page the girl hesitates because she doesn't know the word *pigeon*. Miss V points to the picture and asks if there are any clues on the page about what this word might be. The girl, seeing the picture of the pigeon, guesses the word. Miss V says "good" and the reading proceeds.

Following the group reading of the big books, the children assemble in their reading groups at the round tables. Each group is reading a different book. Children take turns reading aloud. Miss V divides her time among the four groups, listening to the reading as she circulates. While the children continue their reading we step out to the hallway and walk to the first-grade classroom next door.

A Phonics First-Grade Classroom

This room contrasts with the whole language classroom in some obvious ways. The desks are arranged in groups also; when the children are seated they each face the blackboard at the front. In fact, when we enter the room the children are seated at their desks all focused toward the blackboard at the front of the room. The teacher, Mrs. H, is talking about the consonant *t*, and the children are drawing the letter in the air in big sweeping motions. After several times practicing drawing the letter in the air she asks the children to choose a partner and lie down on the floor to make the shape of the letter. After the children have settled back into their chairs, Mrs. H then moves to the blackboard where she has taped a large poster board. She asks the children to think of all the words they know that begin with the sound /*t*/, and she records the list as each child anxiously wants to add a word to the list. Once this list is composed, Mrs. H then hands out a paper divided into six sections. She asks each child to write six words that begin with the letter *t* and then to draw a picture of that word in the square.

After the children finish their pages, Mrs. H directs the students' attention to the blackboard where she demonstrates the proper way to write the letter *t*. She then asks the children to practice writing the letter *t* several times on lined paper she distributes. After the handwriting practice, she asks all the children to come to the reading corner because they are going to read a book. She has written five words on an easel next to her rocking chair. Mrs. H first reviews five words that will appear in the story they are about to read together. She explains how to sound out the word *which,* noting that it has the sound /*tch*/ but does not follow the *tch* spelling rule as in *pitch, ditch,* and *stitch.* After distributing the books several children take turns reading the story round-robin style. When one boy reaches a word he doesn't know (*stop*), Mrs. H asks him to sound it out. He struggles, so she asks him, "What sound does *s* make?" He tells her the sound of each of the four letters and then pronounces them together, beaming with his success.

Historical Look at the Pendulum Swings in Reading Instruction

How Was I Taught to Read?

You and your children may both have been taught to read while the pendulum was on the meaning-emphasis end of the methods spectrum. Parents who remember Dick, Jane, and Spot books from first grade were probably taught with the look-say method, a whole word approach to teaching reading with strong similarities to whole language. From colonial times until the 1920s, when our grandparents and great-grandparents were in school, reading was always taught with a code-emphasis approach; first children were taught the letters and then they read words. Reading instruction gravitated away from code-emphasis from the 1930s to the 1950s during the advent of progressive education ideals. Finally in the late '60s, in response to public outrage at the drop in reading achievement, code-emphasis teaching came back, partially fueled by the popularity of the book *Why Johnny Can't Read.* Phonics was reinstated in most classrooms in the 1970s and early 1980s, a time when most of today's parents were in college and working. Then during the late 1980s whole language became the prevalent approach to teaching reading. We are the generation who not only were taught when phonics was out of vogue, but 30 years later our children are also learning to read without phonics.

How Did the Progressive Education Movement Affect the Teaching of Reading?

The progressive education movement, which began at Teachers' College at Columbia University during the 1920s, affected education profoundly with its philosophy of child learning. Progressive educators believed that children learn best when they are involved in an experiential, hands-on activity rather than in a teacher-directed lesson. Classrooms influenced by the ideals of progressive education are not organized with desks arranged in rows toward the teacher. Teachers typically do not stand at chalkboards lecturing to students who are taking notes. Progressive classrooms contain groups of children busily engaged in individualized projects, often initiated or chosen by the child. Students learn reading and math as part of multidisciplinary projects rather than in units where the focus is on teaching a single idea or skill. For example, in a multidisciplinary first-grade project on Japan, students might first read a story about a Japanese child and then complete a math exercise on adding Japanese currency. With the adoption of pro-

Reading Instruction: A Historical Timeline

1700s–mid-1800s	Children are taught to read through memorization of the alphabet, practice with sound-letter correspondences, and spelling lists. The prevailing texts used for teaching reading are the Bible and political essays.
Mid-1800s	Inspired by Jeffersonian democratic ideals, some educators attack phonics and urge a meaning-based approach to learning to read.
Late 1800s	All-purpose reading materials are replaced by graded readers designed to match a child's age and ability.
1930s–1970s	A look-say or whole word (not whole language) approach, exemplified by the "Dick and Jane" reading series, dominates reading instruction in schools. Instruction emphasizes comprehension.
1957	Rudolph Flesch's best-selling book, *Why Johnny Can't Read*, urges a return to phonics instruction. In a sharp political and emotional attack, Flesch accuses the whole word approach "of gradually destroying democracy."
1967	Jeanne Chall's book, *Learning to Read: The Great Debate*, is published. Chall continues to advocate for direct instruction in phonics.
Early 1970s	The Initial Teaching Alphabet (ITA), a phonetic alphabet, is used to teach reading in Great Britain and some school systems in North America.
1970s	The whole language philosophy, which has diverse intellectual roots in Australia, Europe, and North America, emerges. The philosophy promotes a meaning-based approach to learning to read.
Mid-1970s	Research on reading shifts from a focus on texts to an emphasis on how readers construct meaning.
1984	The National Academy of Education releases *Becoming a Nation of Readers*, a report on the status of research in reading education.

1988	Researcher Marie Carbo reanalyzes Chall's earlier research on reading, calling some of the data analysis into question. A lengthy research debate ensues.
1990	*Beginning to Read*, a landmark study by psychologist Marilyn Adams, analyzes the role of phonics in beginning reading programs. The book fuels controversy over the nature of reading instruction.
1994	Low reading scores on the National Assessment of Educational Progress (NAEP) in California lead to a pro-phonics backlash against the whole language movement.
Mid-1990s	Studies released by the National Institute of Child Health and Human Development (NICHD) of the National Institutes of Health indicate that children with reading difficulties benefit from explicit phonics instruction. Researchers believe the findings support phonics instruction for all students.
1995	California adopts two statutes known as the "ABC" laws, which require, in part, that the state board of education adopt instructional materials, including "systematic, explicit phonics, spelling, and basic computational skills."
1996	President Clinton launches the America Reads Challenge, a program to address national literacy concerns. Legislation corresponding with the initiative identifies reading instruction as a "local decision."
1997	The Clinton administration proposes a voluntary national test of fourth grade reading ability.
1997	Several California school systems are charged with violating the ABC statutes by using state funds to purchase nonapproved whole language instructional materials.
Late 1997	A study on the prevention of early reading difficulties, conducted by the National Academy of Sciences, is slated for release.
1997	Reading instruction continues to generate debate from local to national levels.

Halford, J. M. (September 1997), "Reading Instruction: A Historical Timeline," *Infobrief* 10, pgs. 4–5 (chart).

gressive ideals, educators began to focus more on children's learning processes than on the content of the curriculum to be learned.

Progressive education ideals did not develop overnight but were rather a natural outgrowth of a cultural shift in how children were viewed in our society. Historically children had been viewed as miniature adults who must be taught to behave as adults. The Romantics' view, which emerged during the early 1900s, proposed that children were not miniature adults and progressed through a series of mental, emotional, and social growth stages very different from adults. Further, the individuality of each child was celebrated. Once children were viewed as unique people who must be allowed to develop naturally, educators then began to question how children are taught. Educational methods began to emphasize children's natural readiness for learning and individual involvement in learning activity through self-expression and choice. If children needed to be children, we should not insist that they sit in desks in rows and learn exclusively through teacher direction. Thus the roots for the progressive education movement were planted.

E. D. Hirsch's recent book, *The Schools We Need and Why We Don't Have Them*, looks back across history and observes that during the 1920s several educational values and trends could be linked to progressivism:

- Experiential activities are superior to teaching a core curriculum of knowledge.
- Multidisciplinary projects are better than teaching distinct subject areas.
- Teaching socially valuable skills takes preference over intellectual knowledge.[8]

These trends had a significant impact on classrooms in our schools. Another educator, Diane Ravitch, describes classrooms of the 1940s in her book, *The Troubled Crusade:*

> Their common features were: centering the curriculum around basic areas of human activity, instead of traditional subject matter; incorporating subject matter only insofar as it was useful in everyday situations;

> stressing functional values such as behavior, attitudes, skills, and know-how, rather than bookish or abstract knowledge; reorienting studies to the immediate needs and interests of students.[9]

Since the emergence of progressivism, the teaching of reading in American schools has reversed positions twice. After many decades of teaching reading by instruction that emphasized the synthesis of component skills, instruction changed during the 1950s to the look-say method, which emphasized learning whole words by repeated exposure to them. After a major public outcry over low reading test scores, phonics was reinstituted in the 1970s. Yet during the 1980s the trend changed again away from the direct instruction of component skills. Both times during this decade when reading instruction veered away from a systematic skills-based approach, the philosophical underpinnings of the shifts were influenced by progressive ideals. During the 1980s whole language advocates cried for reading to be taught more "naturally" through immersing children in literature. They asserted that reading needs to be taught through meaningful activities or children will not appreciate why they are reading. Rather than teach reading as a separate subject, children read as part of multidisciplinary projects focused on topics such as foreign countries, animals, electricity, and so on. When viewed within this historical context, whole language ideals are understandable.

Teaching reading within multidisciplinary curriculum units, as advocated by whole language experts, was not a new idea in the 1980s when whole language emerged. The connection of whole language ideals to progressive philosophy is evident in the writings of one of the strongest proponents of whole language, Dr. Ken Goodman, in his 1986 book, *What's Whole in Whole Language?*

> Whole language teachers organize the whole of or a large part of the curriculum around topics or themes: What are the risks of nuclear war? Is water pollution a danger in our community? The history of our neighborhood. How to take care of hamsters. Nutrition in mice. They can be science units, social science units, literature units, or units that integrate all three, as well as the arts, humanities, and even physical education. A unit provides a focal point for inquiry, for use of lan-

guage, for cognitive development. It involves pupils in planning, and gives them choices of authentic, relevant activities within productive studies.[10]

Is Learning to Read Like Learning to Speak?

The degree to which the process of learning to read resembles learning to speak is hotly debated. Whole language theorists of the 1970s and 1980s observed that children learn to speak by hearing the language spoken in whole words, phrases, and sentences that are not artificially broken into sounds, syllables, or other bits. Extending logic without evidence, they also viewed the process of learning to read as parallel to the process of learning to speak. Dr. Goodman writes:

> Why do people create and learn written language? They need it! How do they learn it? The same way they learn oral language, by using it in authentic literacy events that meet their needs. Often children have trouble learning written language in school. It's not because it's harder than learning oral language, or learned differently. It's because we've made it hard by trying to make it easy. . . . But by isolating print from its functional use, by teaching skills out of context and focusing on written language as an end in itself, we made the task harder, impossible for some.[11]

Several decades of reading research, however, have clearly demonstrated that learning to read is neither natural nor easy for most children. It must be taught and learned through organized study and practice. Human beings took many thousands of years to develop alphabetic writing systems because the insight that sounds in words could be represented with letters was elusive and slow to develop when people first invented ways to write. Only 10 percent of the world's languages have even developed writing systems at all; writing systems are one of our most advanced creations. Humans are no more wired for learning to read and write than they are for learning to build automobiles. Because learning the written alphabetic code is inherently unnatural, children need coaching and practice to understand how the symbols work and to read them fluently. Human intellect makes reading possible for most people, but not without effort, instruction, and practice.

Why Is the Adoption of Whole Language Sometimes Referred to as a Movement Rather than a Teaching Approach?

We use the term *movement* to describe a shared belief system that motivates people to act together. The belief system may be based on compelling ideas, ideas that seem to have merit and that certainly have intuitive or logical appeal. Whole language became a belief system embraced by educators without evidence that it was effective, partly because educators usually do not make decisions based on evidence, and because it allowed teachers to change some practices that needed to be discarded. Dr. Goodman gives almost no specific information about exactly *how* to teach reading, but instead discusses a philosophy of education that claims:

- empowerment of teachers
- rejection of achievement testing
- arrangement of classrooms into learning centers
- integrated curriculum (integrating multiple subjects in a project)
- literacy as the means for gaining influence in society
- criticism of phonics teaching because it discriminates against lower-income children of diverse dialects

These statements represent the tone and substance of the whole language bible:

> Whole language teachers are accused of thinking they can make kids literate just by loving them.[12]

> Whole language teachers regard themselves as professionals. . . . They expect a degree of autonomy in their classrooms.[13]

> Whole language teachers understand that learning ultimately takes place one child at a time. They seek to create appropriate social set-

> tings and interactions, and to influence the rate and direction of personal learning. They are utterly convinced that teachers guide, support, monitor, encourage, and facilitate learning, but do not control it.[14]

In this philosophical treatise, the words *respect* and *power* appear frequently with regard to teachers' relationships with students and administrators. It is implied that teachers should be able to create their own reading program in their own way and that there is no established pedagogical standard of teaching reading to which teachers should be held accountable. While teacher empowerment is a worthy goal, teachers acquire it not through holding beliefs about child development, but through mastery of tools sufficient for the job at hand.

Does the Political Right Support the Phonics Approach?

In an article entitled, "How Whole Language Became a Hot Potato In and Out of Academia" in the October 30, 1996, issue of the *Wall Street Journal,* the writer reported,

> Organized back-to-phonics movements have sprung up in a number of states, California, North Carolina, Ohio and Texas among them. Robert Dole, ridiculing "modern education experts," has even made his disdain for whole language part of his presidential campaign.
>
> Meanwhile, whole-language proponents have rallied to the method's defense, accusing opponents of advocating a return to mind-numbing educational methods of the past, or worse, of being stooges for the Religious Right. Religious conservatives, indeed, have led some of the pro-phonics, anti-whole-language efforts, deriding whole language as yet another liberal assault on American education.[15]

Media articles on the reading debates mention frequently the alignment of political conservatives with "back to basics" education, including promotion of phonics instruction. Those who support inclusion of skills in the reading curriculum are accused of affiliation with the political right wing and the Christian Coalition, whose agenda includes many actions hostile to public education. Whole language proponents, on the other hand, claim to have a more liberal, democratic view of society and education's role in it. There is little truth to any of the generalities about politics and reading, however. Parents should note, for example, that the California Reading Initiative was passed unanimously by a bipartisan legislature; moreover, the chief mover behind it, state school board member Marion Joseph, is a liberal Democrat. Because leaders of both parties were concerned about the low achievement of children in California, education leaders from the entire political spectrum united to address the problem.

Most reading researchers who employ scientific methodology to investigate reading are not motivated by any political agenda. Furthermore, many are actually concerned that their findings have been misused by those who promote political agendas. For example, groups who espouse the replacement of public education with a voucher system often cite politically neutral reading research to promote their cause. Such misappropriation of information, however, does not deny its credibility or importance. The "back to basics" philosophy espoused by conservatives is not equivalent to the recommendations being made by experts in reading instruction, who emphasize that reading instruction can be improved in many ways from the methods of 25 years ago. Support for comprehensive, balanced, research-based reading instruction should be a bipartisan concern.

One of the most interesting aspects of the reading debates is their public nature. It is easy for parents to become concerned and involved if they suspect their child is not being well served in the fundamentals. The emotional intensity of parent advocates, in turn, gets the attention of the press; the press, in turn, tends to highlight controversy in its coverage of reading. To add interest, reporters will put a political spin on any issue. And so goes the "debate" and "war" of ideas, beyond reason or purpose.

Experts Agree on Best Approach

What Approach Do the Experts Recommend?

This simple question is deceptively complex. Because no reading method has ever worked equally well with all children, and some children fail to read no matter what instruction is employed, it should be restated as: what type of reading instruction works best with what types of students under what conditions and with what type of teacher? This is the research question being addressed by several major, long-term studies. Furthermore, experts will not agree on what "works best" until they agree on a definition of successful outcome and what measure will be used to evaluate it. Are children successful if they simply learn the skills, or must they also love to read independently? Even with the best teaching, how much will individuals differ in reading ability? We need to follow children for many years to know the consequences of early success and failure. Many reading-related skills need to be tested to get the whole picture about what works best.

Since the early 1960s several major studies, many more small studies, and several reviews of research have examined scientifically the issue of how to teach reading. As this book is being written, another major review is being published by a panel convened by the National Academy of Sciences. In a typical research design, standardized tests are administered before, during, and after reading instruction to well-defined groups of children. Then the results of the competing forms of instruction are evaluated. Dr. Marilyn Adams, under a U.S. Department of Education grant, conducted an extensive review of all reading research completed up to the time of her study in the late 1980s. Dr. Adams concluded that there is compelling evidence that children taught with systematic phonics instruction read better. Dr. Adams states:

> Collectively these studies suggest, with impressive consistency, that programs including systematic instruction on letter-to-sound correspondences lead to higher achievement in both word recognition and spelling, at least in the early grades and especially for slower or economically disadvantaged students.[16]

The same study concluded that when children received systematic phonics instruction, not only were their word recognition and spelling skills stronger, but their comprehension skills were at least as good as those taught with a meaning-emphasis approach. Several recent NICHD-sponsored studies have since shown that speech-sound awareness, letter knowledge, and phonics are indispensable components of effective early reading instruction. The issue is no longer whether phonics should be taught, but how it should be taught, to whom, when, and how long.

Dr. Bill Honig, the former State Superintendent of Public Instruction for California, argues in the conclusion of his book, *Teaching Our Children to Read,* that teaching children skills in learning to read is critical:

> An extreme whole-language approach—which assumes learning to read develops only through exposure to literature and print without the assistance of a systematic program to teach the skills needed to unlock the language code—does not foster this independence [of learning] for many children. Memorizing the large number of words used in technical and complex materials, as required by this method, is inefficient at best. By learning to decode and recognize phonemic patterns and sound/symbol correspondences, students will possess the tools to decipher new words as they encounter them and become fluent with a growing number of words.[17]

Dr. Honig was the State Superintendent of Public Instruction in the California public schools during the mid-1980s and played a key role in guiding the adoption of whole language in that state. His book, published in 1996, confirms his personal reversal of position on whole language. Dr. Honig now actively speaks around the country on behalf of skills-based reading instruction.

In many fields, a body of reliable, valid research results that converge on a major finding would resolve the debate, and the profession would move ahead to bring practice in line with new knowledge. It would be the responsibility of professionals who hold a license in the field to continually update their knowledge and improve their practices. In reading education, however, these findings have been met in some quarters with a mix of resistance and hostility. The most dedicated whole language educators even reject the idea that reading tests measure which children read better; in fact, the most orthodox whole language advocates say that children shouldn't be tested at all. They use this philosophical position to deny the value of objective evidence gathered through scientific research methods, and go their merry ways doing what they believe makes sense. So the debate continues.

Practical Ways to Tell What Approach Your Child's Teacher Uses

How Can I Tell How Reading Is Taught in My Child's Class?

Published materials distributed by the schools, including curriculum guides, can gloss over or simply not state clearly *how* reading is taught. These materials usually won't specify what evidence or rationale was used to develop the reading products the school has adopted. If reading educators rely on publishers to learn what they should know about reading instruction, they may get misinformation, outdated information, or conflicting information. It is therefore not surprising that parents who ask questions may unfortunately get incomplete or uninformed responses from schools about reading instruction. Although terms such as "balanced approach" are now well accepted and likely to be used, interpretations of those terms for instruction vary widely. The quality, balance, and organization of the program may be more or less good, and the program may or may not have been validated by objective studies, but districts usually do not make their decisions about the adoption of reading programs based on such criteria.

One parent who learned about the research supporting phonics asked a school administrator if phonics was taught in her child's school. The response of the district reading specialist in this good school district in suburban Chicago was, "Oh, our district never went completely to whole language like California. We use an approach which is a combination of both phonics and whole language." That statement seemed to be wise and defensible. Yet there are classrooms in that district that are teaching very little phonics and are almost completely whole language oriented. I know because my child was in one of those classes. My other child had a different first-grade teacher whose approach included systematic phonics, taught thoroughly and well. Note that these two classrooms are in the same school district with the exact same curriculum guidelines and under the same principal's supervision. There is no consistency in curriculum or strategy. The teaching approach in your child's classroom depends upon the views of your school district, but most of all on the viewpoint and training of your child's teacher.

The unanswered, obvious question for most observant parents is "Where is the quality control?" A mother of a child who was having trouble learning to read contacted me for information beginning in January of her daughter's first-grade school year. She was concerned that her child was having so much trouble learning to read and was falling behind. She decided that the first step was to have her daughter tested to determine if she had any learning disabilities which might be affecting her reading. By March she had completed an educational diagnostic evaluation which determined that her child did not have a learning disability. The psychologist who tested her daughter recommended a private tutor who uses a systematic phonics approach to teach reading.

Within three months of tutoring, her daughter was completely caught up in reading. We met in late June after the school year was over. This mother proudly showed me the reading, writing, and phonics material her daughter had completed in tutoring over the spring and early summer. After looking at papers that demonstrated a sequential and systematic approach to phonics instruction, I brought out my file with all my daughter's language arts papers from her first-grade class—a different first-grade class in the same school—and we spread them out on the dining room table. This mother was outraged that she was paying private tutoring fees for her daughter to get essentially the same instruction that my daughter received during first grade, while her daughter sat in another classroom not getting what she needed. I shared this mother's anger because my older child had had her daughter's first-grade teacher two years earlier, and we had to hire a private tutor for him as well.

How Do I Know If My Child Is Being Taught Phonics Well?

In a first-grade classroom that emphasizes the phonics approach, the systematic instruction of the letter symbol and its related sound will be evident. In addition to the teacher's description of classroom instruction, you can figure it out by looking at what is displayed around the classroom and the papers your child brings home. The following four sources will tell you what you want to know:

SOURCES OF INFORMATION ON HOW READING IS TAUGHT

- material displayed in the classroom
- the completed work sent home from school
- the teacher's newsletter to parents
- the reading series (basal reader) used in the classroom

At the beginning of first grade, determine if the teacher is focusing on the letter-sound connections. Look around the classroom for charts on the walls; if systematic phonics is a major component of the reading curriculum early in the year, there will most likely be charts of words that have selected letter sounds and evidence of reading and writing that uses those words. The words will be organized according to their sounds, not just their letters. For example, the letter *o* might head a list of *ox, otter, spot,* and *odd.* It should not head a list including *of, one, on, only, orange,* and *oat.* Although all correspondences will be taught in time, children should learn one major spelling for a sound and then move on when that is learned. Children who learn fairly easily will not be confused if two or three sounds are presented at once, such as */ă/* in *cap* and */ā/* in *cape,* as long as enough practice recognizing and spelling these sounds is given.

My daughter's first-grade teacher taught phonics; it was clear from the papers she brought home in her backpack—especially at the beginning of the school year. Every week there was work in her backpack that asked her to distinguish between two beginning consonant sounds and to paste pictures of words under the correct letter column. When I walked into the classroom during one of the first weeks of school, I saw a poster hanging from the corkboard strip over the blackboard with a list of words beginning with a consonant. The chart was handwritten, not preprinted, and looked as if the teacher had recorded words the students had generated. The teacher's newsletter to parents specifically mentioned the letter sounds that the class studied that week. Each week the teacher not only taught the sound of each letter, but also had students practice their handwriting of the letter, a skill all too often ignored in today's classrooms.

After completing consonants, the teacher then started working on the consonant blends and digraphs. There was an exercise for each blend so students always had a chance to practice what she had taught. Some of these exercises were very simple and could be done at home. One example was the exercise for the consonant digraph */sh/*. The teacher asked each child to take a blank piece of paper and think of six words to write and illustrate that begin with this sound. By early November, the class was studying the short vowels with a hand symbol for each one. Hand signals, rhymes and jingles, and gimmicks that call attention to the feel of the sound are all multisensory devices designed to help the child distinguish and remember the sounds.

At the very beginning of the year the children spent little classroom time individually reading because they hadn't been taught enough letter sounds. Throughout the first two months of first grade the emphasis during reading instruction was on the systematic teaching of phonics. The one exception to this was that the class read as a group using a big book to develop the children's sight vocabulary of common nonphonetic words. This use of big books is quite different from using big books with the expectation that the children are memorizing all the words. Small reading groups were created in late October or early November to give children a chance to practice and to accommodate the different levels of readers. The teacher read to the children throughout the entire year, typically reading books that contained rich vocabulary beyond the children's own current reading level.

Parents frequently ask for practical, concrete suggestions about how to tell what approach their child's teacher is using. One way to tell is to look at the teacher's weekly newsletter, typically sent home with your child on Fridays. Below you will find excerpts from a newsletter that describes phonics instruction. Following this list are actual parent newsletters written by two first-grade teachers in the same school during late October/early November.

EXCERPTS FROM PARENT NEWSLETTER OF TEACHER'S COMMENTS ABOUT PHONICS AND READING INSTRUCTION

Week of September 30

- We reviewed the /*ks*/ sound and practiced writing capital *X* and lowercase *x*.
- We wrote two sentences on the chalkboard, and we had to edit them for errors in capitalization, punctuation, and spelling.
- We practiced writing capital and lowercase *D*, *F*, *B*, and *V*. We also thought of words that begin with the sounds.

Week of October 7

- After sharing our weekend activities, we talked about the /*sh*/ digraph and thought of words with that sound.
- We practiced writing capital and lowercase *K* and *Z* after our opening and show-and-tell activities.
- Some of us had small-group reading time, while the rest of us did some activities with words that belong to the *-at* family (*mat, bat, hat,* etc.).
- Our first project of the day was to edit some sentences that were written on the chalkboard.
- After reviewing the /*sh*/ sound, we had small-group reading time.

Week of October 14

- We wrote in our journals and then practiced writing capital and lowercase *G*.

- We talked about the *ch* digraph and named words that have the */ch/* sound.
- We practiced writing capital and lowercase *P* and *J*, reviewed the */ch/* sound, and had small-group reading time.
- We worked collaboratively on word families (*-an, -ad, -am, -ag*) and then had small-group reading time and center time.
- Most of the morning was spent doing reading work activities and meeting in small groups to read.
- Since the word *sunflower* is a compound word, we brainstormed a long list of other compound words (we just started a unit on sunflowers).

Week of October 21

- After our opening activities, we reviewed the *-at*, *-ag*, *-am*, *-an*, *-ack*, *-ad*, and *-ap* word families and discovered that every word had a short */ă/* sound. We then brainstormed other words that have a short */ă/* sound.
- We practiced writing the capital and lowercase *Y, Z,* and *Q*.
- We thought of words that begin with the */q/* sound. We noticed that every *q* word started with *qu*.
- As we came into the classroom, our morning message asked us to look around the room for words that have the short */ă/* sound. (We found a lot of them.)
- We did our reading activities and had small-group reading time.
- We hunted for compound words in the classroom.
- We spent some time spelling consonant-vowel-consonant (CVC) words.
- After our opening activities, we had our reading and writing time.
- After we edited some sentences, we read several poems about spiders.

Newsletter from Whole Language First-Grade Classroom

- To help us get in the mood for Halloween we read a story called *In a Dark, Dark Wood.* After rereading it a number of times, the students illustrated their own books, making sure the text matched their pictures. Then they practiced reading it in a spooky voice to one another!!! We also decorated our own dark, dark house (our puppet theater transformed!!!) and even added a dark, dark box, into which we put all kinds of spooky things.
- Our student teacher created a fun math activity for the class. She made a pumpkin for each student with a "slide" containing number sentences. The students had to depict the number sentences in spooky pictures, rather than in numbers.
- We met with our second-grade learning buddies to share some stories that each class wrote. The second grade read their *12 Days of Halloween* songbook and other stories. We read our *Dark, Dark Wood* stories, *Ten Black Dots* books, and *How Many Bugs in a Box?* books. Afterward we learned a funny song called "Witch's Brew." Each team then created a recipe for their own witch's brew!
- We strengthened our understanding of word families by working in groups to practice word sorting with the word families we have learned.
- Each student received an individual mini-pumpkin to decorate. Before decorating them, however, we performed a few experiments on them! First the students predicted if their pumpkins would sink or float and then put their pumpkins in a tub of water to test out their predictions. We discovered that all of the pumpkins floated. Then they weighed their pumpkins on a balance scale, using teddy bear counters as their unit of measurement. Finally, we predicted if our big classroom pumpkin

(continued on page 108)

Newsletter from Phonics First-Grade Classroom

Monday

We started writing in our "new" journals today. We wrote about our weekend activities. We reviewed the short /ă/ sound by spelling some CVC (consonant-vowel-consonant) words. We talked about short /ĭ/ and brainstormed words with that sound. We met with partners to discuss what makes a cat "good" and/or "bad." Afterward we shared our ideas and made word webs with the information. We then read the book *The Good Bad Cat*. We started a geometry unit in math. We talked about solid figures and counted the faces and vertices of each one. After we read *The Berenstain Bears* and *Too Much Junk Food*, we discussed the things we need to do to stay healthy. We also looked at a food pyramid and named the food groups that are important to eat each day.

Tuesday

During our opening activities, we discussed "election day"—what that means and the importance of it. After doing a short /ĭ/ activity, we had small-group reading time and work time. In math, we reviewed the solid figures and then went on a "shape search." We looked for objects in the classroom that are cubes, cones, rectangular prisms, spheres, and cylinders. After reading the book, *Bread, Bread, Bread*, we discussed foods in the grain food group. We found pictures of grain foods and wrote about our favorite food in that group. As a follow-up to our Halloween candy homework, we added up the total amount of candy all of us received altogether—2,146.

Wednesday

Our day began with the reading of a "fun" book about vegetables entitled, *June 29, 1999*. We looked for pictures of vegetables

(continued on page 109)

(continued from page 106)

would sink or float. The vote was 17–4 in favor of the pumpkin sinking. Were we surprised when it actually floated!!!

- Before cutting our Halloween pumpkin we predicted how many seeds would be inside. Our predictions ranged from 25 to 600. After taking out the seeds we worked as a team to count them. Each student received a cup of seeds and glued them in groups of 10 to a strip of paper. Then we counted the strips by counting by 10s. Each time we got to 100, we started over again. When we were finished we found out that our pumpkin had 700 seeds!!!
- On Halloween we played a fun bingo game. Our bingo cards contained many of the words we have been learning in our reading. They contained color words and lots of high-frequency vocabulary. Afterward the students got to eat their candy corn and goldfish markers. YUM!
- After reading a lot of October poems and songs, each student illustrated an October poem. This will become part of a collection of illustrated poems. Each month we will add a new poem to our collection.
- We wrapped up the month of November by recording our favorite October memories in our classroom memory big book. Each student wrote about his/her favorite memory of October and illustrated it. At the end of the year these pages will form each student's own memory book.

Reminder: Halloween homework and shoe boxes with "recyclables" are due on Monday!!!

(continued from page 107)

and fruits, named specific foods in each group, and wrote about the vegetables and fruits we like best. We also sorted a variety of food pictures into the dairy group and the meat, poultry, eggs, and nuts group. We discussed the results of the elections. We also did some reading activities, had small-group reading time, and reviewed the */ch/* sound.

Thursday

We started the day with our November assembly in the auditorium today. After our opening activities and show-and-tell time, we wrote sentences. We edited them for capitals and punctuation marks. We also reread *The Good Bad Cat.* Each of us chose the name of a specific pet and wrote and illustrated something good that the pet does as well as something bad it does. In math we looked for solid figures in a picture and matched specific parts of a shape to the whole figure.

Friday

When we came into the classroom today, we discovered an "abandoned island" that has a river, streets, and railroad tracks. There was a sign on it that said the island was free to anyone who wanted it. We discussed many reasons as to why there were no buildings or people. We decided to "take" the island. We started thinking about the possibility of "building" a community on it. We discussed what a community is and what a community needs. Afterward we spelled words that have short */ă/* and short */ĭ/* in them. We also had reading time. We continued learning more about the food groups. We named foods that are in the milk group and the meat, poultry, eggs, and nuts group. We also wrote about our favorite foods in each of these groups.

Show-and-tell next week: Choose a food you like and give three clues, including its food group.

The whole language classroom sounds like great fun. However, there is a very important foundation missing in reading instruction, which seriously impairs some students' ability to learn to read. You can see from these two newsletters that in the phonics classroom the emphasis early in the school year is on studying letters and letter-sound correspondences. During the first month of school the phonics teacher told parents in the newsletter which letters were studied that week, that the class had talked about words that began with those letters, and practiced their handwriting of both upper- and lowercase letters.

In addition to studying the parent newsletter and observing the classroom, you can also evaluate whether the reading textbook used in your child's classroom supports phonics. Over the years the textbook publishers have swung from meaning-emphasis to code-emphasis, with most of the major publishers still on the meaning end currently. Dr. Patrick Groff, Professor of Education Emeritus at San Diego State University, wrote an article for the March 1997 newsletter of the National Right to Read Foundation. In this article he expresses his dismay that most of the textbooks approved by the California Board of Education in December of 1996 do not meet the criteria established by the California Reading Initiative. He proposed that these textbooks were accepted because of the lobbying pressure brought by these large publishers, in whose materials school districts were already heavily invested. According to Dr. Groff the reading series can be categorized as follows:[18]

Phonics-Based	***Whole Language–Based***
Open Court by SRA	Harcourt Brace
Metra	Houghton Mifflin
Science Research Associates (SRA)	Literacy Tree (Rigby)
Total Reading	Macmillan
	Scholastic
	Scott Foresman
	Silver Burdett
	The Sunshine Series (Wright)

This analysis of textbooks was of the editions available in late 1996. Parents need to use caution in interpreting this analysis because publishers issue new editions frequently, and many of these programs already have supplements designed to fill gaps in previous editions. Many other phonics-emphasis programs exist that were not submitted for state adoption in California, such as the Slingerland and Spalding approaches. With the trend toward more direct and systematic instruction of skills within the meaning-emphasis approach, later editions released by these same publishers might position the reading series in a different category from the editions Dr. Groff analyzed.

Is All Phonics Instruction Equally Effective?

A mother of two daughters—a fourth-grader and first-grader—was dismayed that her older child, who had received almost no phonics instruction, was a terrible speller. This mother, determined that her younger child receive better instruction, asked the school to use more phonics instruction in first grade. She had spoken to her daughter's first-grade teacher early in the school year and was promised more phonics. After a couple more months of still no systematic phonics, this mother met with the principal. The principal defended the teacher's practice by insisting that the teacher *was* teaching phonics. However, this parent was informed enough to point out to the principal that she believed it was not systematic phonics. The principal gave the parent a book to read that discussed a reading curriculum that this school endorses. The parent followed up with a letter to the principal disputing that the word games, which were incidental to the primarily whole language focus of instruction, were *not* the systematic phonics she was seeking.

In short, all that goes by the name "phonics" is not equally effective. Two of the key characteristics about phonics instruction that parents need to know are the distinctions listed in the chart on the following page.

A common warning of whole language textbooks and materials is that phonics taught in isolation is bad. That is, it is wrong, meaningless, and possibly inhibiting to children to teach them the specific sounds in isolation (for example, the sound of *x* is /*ks*/). Sounds are to be inferred from reading itself. Otherwise, the

Ways to Describe Phonics Instruction

Criteria	*Definition*
Implicit vs. Explicit	• whether sounds are taught by themselves (in isolation) or in the context of words • whether sound-symbol correspondence is taught explicitly or left for the child to infer from the patterns in words (implicit phonics)
Systematic and Sequential vs. Random	• sound patterns taught systematically—with a predetermined, logical sequence—or sounds taught in random sequence, as they come up in words children naturally use

warning goes, children may conclude that reading has no purpose or meaning. So, in a whole language class, you might see the teacher present a line from a familiar story and ask the children to guess what letters go in the blanks: M__ __nb__ __m w__s a m__nk__ __. (Moonbeam was a monkey.) The teacher would not say, the /*u*/ sound is sometimes spelled *oo,* as in *moon, racoon,* and *spoon.*

The whole language version of phonics is not only contextualized, it is implicit. In implicit instruction, phonics is learned only after or during story reading, not as a separate lesson component. Under such conditions, there is usually no direct teaching of individual sounds. An implicit, nonsystematic phonics lesson might occur if the teacher is concentrating on literature, selects a word in a book the class is reading, and spontaneously writes a list from a word family. Then she might ask the children to figure out how to read another word with the sound-symbol correspondence buried in the whole word. She would not, however, take the sound out of the word or dwell on word lists.

Phonics instruction may be systematic or random. Word families (*hutch, clutch, crutch*) can be used in either way. My older child's teacher who emphasized whole language used the books *Chicka Chicka Boom Boom* and *Ten Black Dots* during the second or third month of first grade. These stories were used for integrated math and language arts projects. A list of words that had the same beginning sound was placed on a chart as one activity from one of these stories. This phonics lesson was an ancillary activity where the real focus was on reading the stories aloud together and creating books based on the alphabet and number themes of the stories. It struck me as strange that in the fall of first grade, children were asked to read the words "skinned-knee D and stubbed-toe E and patched-up F," all of which appear in the story *Chicka Chicka Boom Boom*. There were too many sound spellings to learn at once, and not enough practice provided reading words with just those sounds. My son practiced and practiced at home with our copy of this picture book so that he could read it successfully at school when the entire class read the story aloud. He had to memorize the words to read it; the sounds were too many, too fast to learn. Many young children are overwhelmed in just this way. Aren't we sending children the message that they are supposed to be able to read these words themselves even though they have not really been taught how?

Reading researchers who have extensively compared different approaches usually conclude that the phonics lesson must be explicit and systematic to benefit most children. In one recent summary, a former state superintendent who has done his homework concludes:

> *However, these symbol/sound skill-strands must not become so jumbled with other strands that students miss the point,* as is currently the case with much classroom instruction that stresses integrated language arts activities and attempts to deal with skills on the fly or haphazardly. Nor should skills be taught in such an isolated and rote manner that students fail to connect skill understanding with the actual practice of reading.[19]

Explicit teaching of phonics requires planned, sequenced instruction of the spellings for individual sounds and their patterned use in words. The teacher needs not only to present the sounds and their common spellings in a logical sequence, but also to assess whether the children in the class are developing proficiency with what they have been taught as they are asked to read and write.

Recent evidence also supports the superiority of explicit instruction in phonics over implicit instruction, although some implicit, organized programs work satisfactorily for students who do not have serious reading problems. These programs emphasize word families in a logical order and do provide ample practice in specific patterns. While some children can learn this way, more children learn when there is an explicit, systematic component in teaching, and the skills are then linked to fluent reading. Especially for children with learning disabilities, with linguistic differences, and children of poverty, systematic, explicit teaching of these skills gets children off to a good start. Children can learn to notice the entire printed word and to read through it, sounding it out, without using guessing as their primary strategy.

How Do I Know If My Child Needs More Phonics?

You will know if your child falls into the group of children who need systematic phonics to learn to read if your child:

- is not able to sound words out
- does not recognize words if they are taken out of context

If whole language instruction is given to children who should be taught decoding deliberately, they will find the task of learning to read an incomprehensible mystery based on chance, picture clues, and rote imitation. A child who cannot translate print into sound will find reading to be laborious and such a difficult task that he will begin to dislike or avoid reading. Sounding out the word is the last strategy he will try, when it should be the first. Such children fall behind immediately in first grade, and their problems should be noticeable by the middle part of first grade, if not before.

I watched one of my children struggling to learn to read. Unfortunately it was my oldest child, so it was not as obvious to me that something was wrong as it might have been with my second child. When my son reached an unknown word, he couldn't figure it out. His eyes would begin searching the pictures to see any object that began with that beginning consonant, and then he would guess. Studying the letters in the unknown word, or sounding it out, was the last strategy he would try. If we asked him to sound it out, he was generally unsuccessful for all but the easiest consonant-vowel-consonant words.

There are ways you can tell if this is happening to your child (see the table on p. 117).

If My Child Is Already Reading, Does She Need Phonics?

Children who are already reading at the beginning of first grade do indeed benefit from sequential and systematic phonics instruction if it is fast paced and active. If it is lively and well paced, instruction in phonics and word structure increases a child's ability to recognize letter patterns and to appreciate the relationship between spelling and meaning. A child's spelling improves substantially when explicit instruction in phonics occurs early in first grade. You will notice that your child's writing will display her heightened sensitivity to the separate sounds in words. Children usually begin writing words with only the beginning consonant and ending consonant sound. The next step of development typically is the inclusion of consonants and vowels in the middle of the word. Long vowel spellings and consonant blends such as *dr, nt,* and *st* are generally learned a bit later. Throughout the primary grades, good readers will write better after word study that includes letter-sound correspondence, syllable patterns, word endings, and odd but high-frequency spellings (*would, could, should,* etc.).

Current research indicates that even children who learn to read easily benefit from direct teaching of vocabulary, spelling, word structure, sentence structure, and so forth, as long as the focus on reading good literature is maintained and the pacing is appropriate. Dr. Bill Honig defends the importance of skill instruction even for the children who will learn to read easily:

> Even the 60% to 70% of children who come to school already supported by rich literary experiences, and who eventually will learn to

read under any instructional system or philosophy, need supportive skills instruction. Without this support, many will end up reading significantly below their potential in later grades.[20]

Why Do Some Children Learn to Read Easily with Whole Language?

Experts believe that nearly one-third of children will learn to read well regardless of the approach used to instruct them. These children may have a strong innate ability to link speech sounds to letters and to remember what they see in print. They may need very little instruction of any kind in order to figure out how to read. When placed in a whole language classroom, they make the implicit translations between speech and print without much visible effort and are very comfortable focusing on the meaning and themes of the lesson. The brains of good readers who learn in spite of the teaching they receive appear to be "wired for language." These children are in fact learning phonics, but in many cases they figure it out on their own and can teach themselves new patterns as they are encountered.

What Approach Do the Experts Advocate Now?

What experts are advocating is not a simple return to old-fashioned ideas about reading or an emphasis on basic skills alone. No credible expert champions the return to workbook phonics that was disconnected from literature and writing. Most leaders in reading research agree that direct, logical, and explicit teaching of basic skills is a necessary component of reading instruction, which daily should focus on comprehension and appreciation of literature. Documents such as the California and Texas reading advisories outline that all reading programs should include instruction components that are enumerated on the basis of research about how children learn to read and what successful children know. They are emphatic about the use of activities and literature to provide meaningful practice of skills, but also encourage teachers to spend equal time on reading for understanding, enjoyment, and enrichment. They all note the important contribution of parents' home reading to children's literacy development.

How to Observe If Your Child Is Struggling in Learning to Read

What to Do	*What You Will See*
Observe your child's reading for signs of struggle.	Watch what she does when she comes to an unknown word. Can she figure out the word by studying the letters? By the end of first grade, is she beginning to see letter chunks in words (i.e., *ick, ed, tion, re*)? Although beginning readers are often slow and methodical, they can usually give a sensible response and do not avoid trying to read through the words. For example, if your child reads the word *was* as */w/ /ă/ /z/*, she is using the desirable strategy. If she reads *was* as *with* or *yes*, there may be a problem.
Listen to your child.	My son complained that reading was so hard. He asked why he was the first one in his class to finish a math worksheet, yet was in the lowest reading group.
Ask specific questions of the teacher.	Ask your child's first-grade teacher which reading group she is in. Find out if the teacher thinks she is a strong, average, or below-average reader.
Compare what your child is doing versus a younger child.	A red flag for me was realizing what tasks came easily to my daughter, who was two and a half years younger. When I saw how quickly she was learning the sounds of letters compared to my son, I began to ask more questions.
Observe how your child likes to read aloud to you.	If your child resists reading aloud to you at home or complains that it is hard, begin your search to find out why.

California continues to reform its approach to reading with a coordinated set of laws on teacher licensing, classroom instruction, instructional materials, and continuing education for teachers. Because this effort, known as the California Reading Initiative, includes a complete rethinking of reading instruction from the whole language policies of 1987, it is an example for the rest of the nation. A reading task force, appointed by the California Department of Education to guide the necessary changes, advised that reading for the early elementary years be taught in a "balanced and comprehensive approach," which includes both teacher-directed instruction in skills *and* activities that are literature-based. An initial report of this task force, which served as the conceptual basis for a series of laws, states the following:

> It was determined that a balanced and comprehensive approach to reading must have:
>
> 1. a strong literature, language, and comprehension program that includes a balance of oral and written language;
> 2. an organized, explicit skills program that includes phonemic awareness (sounds in words), phonics, and decoding skills to address the needs of the emergent reader;
> 3. ongoing diagnosis that informs teaching and assessment that ensures accountability; and
> 4. a powerful early intervention program that provides individual tutoring for children at risk of reading failure.[21]

After the task force agreed upon these guidelines, separate committees were formed to develop blueprints for reading instruction, teacher training, and programs for early intervention for students having difficulty learning to read. The curriculum committee defined a list of seven components that must be part of reading instruction (see the following charts). In addition to specifying components of a balanced curriculum, the committee suggested what skills a child needs to have mastered in each grade level from preschool through third grade. Sample learning activities to develop these skills were also described. Subsequently, after another year of work by a committee on standards, the grade-level expectations were adopted as statewide performance standards for elementary children.

The newly adopted performance standards are available to the public. Parents who wish to see this publication can order a copy either by calling (800) 995-4099 or by downloading it from the Internet from the California Department of Education Web site: http://www.cde.ca.gov.

1. From the left menu bar select—State Board of Education
2. Then select—Policies & Program Advisories/Reading Program Advisory

How Important Is Writing and Correct Spelling?

Writing is a critical component of a good reading or language arts program. The originality and personal communication emphasized in writing programs has been a valuable step forward in language arts instruction. Spelling instruction, however, helps and does not hinder children's creativity and desire to write. When young children try to write words they have not yet memorized or studied, they may discover the speech sounds in those words and become more aware of the letters in the words when they see them in print. "Invented" spelling is desirable in kindergarten and early first grade but should not be a substitute for formal spelling instruction from mid–first grade onward. New laws in California specify that spelling and writing skills should be taught in elementary language arts, and that letting children invent spellings in lieu of an organized spelling program is a practice of the past.

What Is the Current Status of Reading and What Needs to Happen in the Future to Avoid Another Pendulum Swing?

Parents *do* need to be informed and inquisitive about the reading instruction occurring in their schools. Although rhetoric in reading is changing to include the words "balanced and comprehensive," practices still vary widely. The debate may seem to be diffused, but there are still no national or state standards to which reading programs are held. A large gap remains between the recommendations of researchers and classroom practices. Educators tend to do whatever they want when they are neither held

SEVEN INSTRUCTIONAL COMPONENTS OF READING CURRICULUM[22]

Phonemic Awareness

Research confirms that for a child to be able to learn to read, she needs to understand that words and syllables are composed of strings of separate speech sounds. One-fifth of the children depend upon explicit instruction in this area to develop an awareness of speech sounds. Instruction in phonemic awareness needs to occur in preschool through first grade. Examples of activities to develop this skill include listening to and generating rhymes, clapping syllables in a word, identifying words that begin with the same speech sound, and substituting one sound in a word to make a different word.

Letter Names and Shapes

Before a child can benefit from instruction in the letter-sound correspondences, she needs to recognize and know the shapes and names of letters. Preschools and kindergartens should offer many activities to reinforce letter recognition.

Systematic, Explicit Phonics

Children taught systematic and explicit phonics early in their reading instruction become better readers. Optimum benefit is achieved when children are directly taught the letter-sound correspondences where principles and rules are emphasized and clarified. It is best if the phonics is systematic in that it starts with the simplest consonants and a few vowels and builds to the more complex speech sounds. Children have the opportunity to learn directly about individual speech sounds, then blend them together, and practice them in words including word families. Practicing with meaningful reading is critical, but it is best if the reading is with text where they are able to decode the words from what they have already learned.

Spelling

Invented, or temporary, spelling is a tool in the early years for children to think about the sounds in words. Systematic, formal instruction in correct spellings should begin in first grade and continue throughout the years. Instruction needs to focus on the patterns of letters in words, teaching children the regularities of our language.

Vocabulary Development

Research shows that the majority of the new words a child learns are learned by reading them in text. All children should be read to as much as possible for developing vocabulary. Beginning in kindergarten words should be taught in a context and by providing the definition of the new word.

Comprehension and Higher Order Thinking

Children need to have achieved a level of fluency and broad vocabulary before they can fully attend to the meaning. Once they reach this proficiency, direct instruction in comprehension strategies is recommended. Beyond this instruction the best activity for developing comprehension is for the child to read a variety of genres, both fiction and nonfiction.

Appropriate Instructional Materials

The best instruction uses a variety of reading materials. At every stage reading aloud is important. In kindergarten big books are particularly effective for teaching how print is read, especially stories with predictable or familiar text. Instructional reading should be a part of each program. Instructional reading occurs when a child reads material that stretches her reading capability in either the words contained, the genre, the story structure, or the message to be comprehended. All programs should also emphasize independent reading time where the child reads materials in which she can correctly read 95–100 percent of the words on her own.

accountable for knowing and using research-based practices nor supported in doing so. Whole language practices continue in many schools in spite of the fact that not one well-done study exists that shows the superiority of this approach when it is compared to approaches that teach the alphabetic code explicitly. There has been a series of reports on reading sponsored by the U.S. Office of Education and the National Institutes of Health of which most teachers are still unaware. A National Academy of Sciences panel report was just released in the spring of 1998. In spite of more information about reading than we have ever had before, it is not likely to be used until reading scores fall, or until parents mobilize to express their dissatisfaction with the status quo.

Some school districts may be aware of the research advisories but continue to invest in short-term or cursory training for teachers that will not make a great deal of difference in overall performance in reading. It is an unusual district that adopts a comprehensive program for prevention of reading failure, provides sufficient, continuous training for teachers, and expects all staff to be invested in addressing the needs of children.

Evaluations and standards should stabilize the swinging trends in reading education, but as long as decisions are based on romantic ideals about child-centered learning instead of on objective measurements and systematic teaching, we are likely to stay awash in untenable ideas. As Dr. Jeanne Chall said in her November 1996 speech to the International Dyslexia Association's international conference, "Nobody's stupid in this race. If they can't see it, it is because they *won't* see it your way."[23] Dr. Chall compared the current movement to fashion trends in women's clothing. This year it's a return to the classics. Next year, who knows? But teachers and children hardly benefit from frequent shifts of allegiance to one method or another.

The romantic view of children dies hard with many defenders holding the fort. Whole language proponents remain convinced that meaning-emphasis approaches that dig right into literature develop children who will love reading more than skills-based instruction that teaches them to learn how to read the words. Although at the end of first grade children may express a love of reading with whole language, the enthusiasm is short-lived if they cannot make their way through an unfamiliar book. Children who are taught skills do better than children who are not taught skills; but within this principal, there are more and less effective ways of accomplishing the objective.

This time we need to get it right. We need as a society to endorse the principles of teaching that are supported, help teachers know those principles and the studies that support them, and expect teachers to stay current with the best practices in order to have a professional license. Every other profession does the same. There is less chance of philosophical pendulum swings to adversely affect children if teaching is a well-grounded discipline. It is critical that teacher training programs develop a strong commitment to the whole spectrum of knowledge and skills that make a good teacher.

Talk of "balance" in reading instruction is not enough. Each component must be taught well. Most children can learn to read if they are taught how to read the alphabetic code; this skill in turn depends upon letter knowledge, vocabulary, verbal memory, and awareness of the speech sounds in words. None of these elements should be left out of an early reading program. Simultaneously we are cheating our children if these elements are taught as separate, unrelated skills, if children do not read every day, if they do not hear literature read to them every day, and if we do not actively teach comprehension skills and strategies from the outset. Those who want to bring phonics back to the classroom have a supportable agenda, but it is not enough to overlay some phonics instruction on whole language methods without revising the practices that did not work. Substantive, systemic change is necessary before most of our elementary students will be assured success.

CHAPTER FIVE

How Does a Child Learn to Read?

> If we want children to learn to read well, we must find a way to induce them to read lots. . . . And so the circularity of the situation is extremely important: If we want to induce children to read lots, we must teach them to read well.[1]
>
> *Dr. Marilyn Adams, from* Beginning to Read

In Chapter 2 we urged you to be involved in your child's experience of learning to read, so that you can support and monitor his progress. To be effective as a coach or teacher, you must understand how children learn to read. From that foundation will come insight into how your child is doing and what actions on your part will be helpful.

Is Reading Easy or Difficult to Learn?

A fundamental idea to keep in focus is that reading is one of the most complex things a human being does. Humans could speak for about thirty thousand years before they devised systems to write and read, and literacy continues to be an elusive goal for most of the world's people. To read, we must translate a visual symbol system into speech, and translate speech into meaning; all this must take place very rapidly so that we have mental space to think about and learn from what we are reading.

If you already read well, it may seem contradictory to emphasize that reading is difficult. You may be able effortlessly to look at the text on the page and make sense of it. However, our own sense that reading is effortless is not a reliable indicator of what it takes for our brain and senses to accomplish the task. When the reader's eyes scan the symbols on the page many circuits of the brain fire off to interpret these figures as letters and translate letters into words. Additional, neighboring connections in the brain extract meaning from the words represented by the letters. Most of this activity takes place on the left side of the brain in 95 percent of the population, although circuits on the right side are also active. Furthermore, circuits in the front and the back of the brain must work in concert with one another when we read. In saying that reading is complex, we mean that many areas of the brain are actively employed and that fluent reading requires many networks of brain cells to work together.

Second, learning to read can be extremely challenging for some children, even though they are of normal intelligence or better. Infants are born with brains that are "wired for language," and they learn how to talk naturally by being exposed to the language of their caregivers. But they don't learn to read through contact and interaction in the same way they learn how to talk; in order to read, most children need to be taught a range of component skills. If you are aware that most students have to work at reading, and that intelligence alone will not guarantee success at reading, you may be more sensitive and patient while your child is learning to read—your child's first and most important academic challenge. Understanding the process will better prepare you to know when reading seems more difficult than it should be, or when to be concerned that your child is falling behind.

Assuming that reading is complex and difficult, we will begin this chapter with an overview of what experts study and know about how someone learns to read. Although much is known about the mental activity of proficient reading, there is much more to be learned about how individual children differ from each other. Some children induce the rules of the language by exposure to it, while others need explicit instruction in everything from letter-sound associations to spelling rules. Some children read quickly, others never seem to establish a habit for anything. Luckily, scientists are beginning to understand why such differences occur, and with the right tests, kindergarten children who are likely to have difficulty can be flagged.

Before your child begins to learn to read, however, you may not be able to predict whether it will be easy or difficult for him. The following information may help you know what to expect.

How Experts Study Reading

The current understanding of skilled and beginning reading has converged from many different fields of research. Educators, psychologists, medical scientists, and neuropsychologists (psychologists who study how the brain governs behavior) have all studied different aspects of reading, with complementary discoveries occurring on a number of research frontiers. An overview of the areas of research is provided below.

AREAS OF READING RESEARCH

- what the eyes do while reading and what eye movements can tell us about the workings of the mind
- what areas of the brain work sequentially, or in tandem, while reading
- what is different about good and poor readers as they process the print on the page
- what measures can identify the children who are "at risk" for reading difficulty
- which approaches to teaching reading work best for all children and for the struggling readers
- the degree to which hereditary and environmental factors play a part in learning to read

---

Eye Movements

Reading is silent and covert, which makes it more difficult to study. Scientists who study reading must infer what is going on in the brain. The most significant external manifestation of silent reading is the movement of the eyes. With the help of new technology that enables computers to track, record, and analyze eye movements, cognitive researchers have made many discoveries over the past 15 years or so. Eye movement research has provided some helpful insights, including:

- descriptions of what we look at when we read
- what interferes with fluent reading
- how reading changes with the kind of text we are reading
- what we do when we have not read something accurately

Beyond doubt, this research confirms that we look at every letter in almost every word as we read. Beyond doubt, reading is a print-driven process; comprehension depends on processing specific, clear, complete information about the words on the page.

Studying the eye movements of good and poor readers has led to further insights about what the brain is doing during reading. Good readers (like you) may seem to skip over words or letters; you may think when you are reading that you are not really looking at all the letters, and that you are detecting words based on perception of a few letters or the word's general appearance. That impression is not true. Good readers are simply faster at seeing all the letters in a word and are less prone to making mistakes in their perception of those letters. They scan print thoroughly, just like a computer scanner would, but they don't have to expend much attention or mental energy to do it. Good readers appear to use a "sounding out" strategy only when they meet up with a strange name or unusual word. They learned to read whole words quickly, because the match between spoken words and written symbols was never difficult for them in the first place; they are fluent decoders who do not get "hung up" to identify a word as much as poor readers. They can read faster and more accurately; therefore, they comprehend more than students who expend all their mental energy deciphering what the print is saying. The eye movements of poor readers may seem to be irregular: poor readers may look back more often or have trouble following the line, but these problems are a symptom of a more basic problem, not the cause of reading difficulty.[2]

Brain Studies

With the advent of noninvasive brain scanning techniques, scientists can now watch the brain activity of a person while reading. These techniques enable experts to understand which areas of the brain are activated while reading or performing tasks that enable reading. In this research a person inside a fMRI (functional magnetic resonance imaging) machine is asked to repeat words, determine which two out of three words rhyme, or read a passage. The researcher can then see the bright red areas of activation that signal which areas of the brain are working while completing each task.

Even with brain scanning, no one can tell exactly *what* the brain is doing in order to be able to read—just which parts of the brain are activated during a task. It is clear, however, that the language centers of the brain, in the middle on the left side, are less active in poor readers, and that reading is essentially a language skill.

Psychological Studies of Good Readers and Poor Readers

In addition to eye movement and brain activation studies, many other researchers have compared skilled and unskilled readers and drawn conclusions about what they do differently. Skilled readers are compared with poor readers to see how groups perform on tasks such as word recognition, language analysis, syllable identification, rhyming, pattern recognition, and pronunciation of nonsense words.

Many studies conducted over several decades have yielded a fairly complete outline of the psychological and linguistic competencies that characterize a successful reader. Again and again, the results of well-designed research have shown that linguistic skills, especially those that have to do with awareness and production of speech sounds, are central to reading competence. Reading does not depend as much on intelligence, background knowledge, experience with books, or visual-perceptual skills as we once thought. It does depend on specific language abilities, many of which can be learned in school.

Prediction of Reading Problems

Even today, many children who have trouble with reading in first or second grade are not identified until they have experienced several years of frustration. However, recent studies have shown that reading failure is avoidable if children who demonstrate warning signs are identified in kindergarten. Early identification of reading difficulty, in turn, has led to successful early instruction that prevents problems in all but the most dyslexic children. Early identification is possible because research beginning with preschoolers and kindergartners has consistently shown the benefits of testing them in a number of areas:

- speech sound awareness (phoneme awareness)
- knowledge of letters
- speed in naming series of objects, colors, numbers, and letters
- vocabulary
- familiarity with print

Children who are low in these areas are at risk for reading failure; children who receive remedial instruction in these areas are more likely to succeed.

Honing in on Instruction

Our understanding of how children learn to read has progressed exponentially in the past couple of decades because two powerful forces have promoted funding of this research:

- societal concerns about the general cost of reading failure
- the passionate advocacy of parents and educators who serve students with learning disabilities

Over 85 percent of individuals with school-identified learning disabilities experience difficulty in learning to read. Children tend to fall along a continuum in the degree of ease of learning to read: those who are designated "disabled" are simply the farthest out on a continuum of reading ability. One prominent research group at Yale estimates that 17 to 20 percent of the school population has significant reading impairment, although only 5 percent will continue to have serious disabilities if they receive well-designed instruction.[3]

Research has not focused only on those with reading problems; in order to understand reading failure, researchers have had to understand normal reading development and proficient reading behavior. The effort to find measures to predict which children will read easily and which are "at risk" for difficulty pushes experts to understand better the precursor skills that need to be in place for a child to be able to read easily. In evaluating which type of instruction works best with children with learning disabilities, experts gain knowledge about the various instruction techniques that might work for all children.

Heredity and Environment: Two Influences on Reading

It is widely understood that reading problems often run in families. Geneticists are documenting this tendency from studies of twins raised separately and apart, and studies of several generations within families. Ever since reading disabilities began to get the attention of the medical profession in the 1930s, scientists have suspected that reading is, in part, an inherited skill. If a parent is a poor reader or poor speller, it is common for one or more children in the family to have reading disabilities as well. What modern science has discovered is that critical linguistic skills are "in the genes," specifically the ability to detect the sound structure of words. If all environmental conditions are favorable for reading, then individual differences in reading ability can be attributed more to the influence of inherited traits than to teaching. However, if environmental conditions are unfavorable—such as no books in the home, no one who reads in the home, and/or poor teaching—then differences in reading ability can be attributed more to the influence of the environment than to heredity. Spelling ability is highly influenced by heredity or a specific genetic predisposition; it is true, to some extent, that good spellers are born. However, it is also true that better spellers are made by better teaching.

Who Is Conducting This Research and How Do We Know That It Is Reliable?

The research on reading is primarily occurring in university or clinic settings throughout the United States, and to a lesser extent in other countries, including Canada and England. Fortunately today there is some quality control over research efforts here in the United States, although that has not always been the case historically. Much of the seminal research in speech processing, language learning, brain imaging, genetics, and instruction of reading has been funded by the federal government under a division of the National Institutes of Health (NIH), the National Institute of Child Health and Human Development (NICHD). Additional studies have been carried out under the U.S. Office of Education and through private funding.

NICHD's involvement in reading research began with the initiation of a research program in 1965, about the time the nation turned its attention to improving the well-being of children with medical, psychological, and educational problems. The growth in attention to reading problems corresponded with the launch of the field of learning disabilities in our country in the late 1960s. The first studies were small-scale investigations of speech processing and its relationship to reading and writing. The funding for research was limited at first until the mid-1980s when a congressional act called the 1985 Health Research Extension Act charged the NICHD to improve the quality of reading research. Funding has jumped dramatically during the last decade, and in the last five years has included large-scale, long-term studies of reading instruction for well-defined groups of children.

During earlier decades the field of reading enjoyed little consensus because the research was limited in scope and sophistication. Studies were unreliable: the results could not be counted on from one setting to the next. Studies were not reproducible: research was not capable of being replicated because basic research problems were not solved. Because of conflicting results from poorly designed studies, it was impossible to make definitive statements about the causes of reading difficulties, the factors that predict which children are at risk for failure, or the instructional practices that worked the best for certain types of children. The NICHD research program is particularly credible because it requires the highest standards of scientific methodology, implementation, and review.

CURRENT RESEARCH POLICIES AT THE NICHD

- Projects are funded by a peer review process involving a panel of researchers who are not competing for the specific project.
- Research is designed to test competing theories against one another instead of proving or disproving one theory at a time.
- Projects are of long-term duration (average length of eight years) enabling conclusions about whether children outgrow deficits over time and whether early instructional practices in reading affect later reading achievement.
- Strict sampling procedures are enforced to ensure large samples of children representing all subgroups of the population for IQ levels, ethnic groups, income levels, etc.
- A large number of researchers are involved in any one project to reduce the possibility of researcher bias.
- Similar questions are investigated across several research centers.
- Conclusions are endorsed after findings are replicated or converge across multiple researchers and settings.

All of these practices assure the public that the conclusions reached from projects that are funded and overseen by the NICHD are of the highest scientific credibility.

Currently the NICHD is coordinating the work of over 100 researchers in education, psychology, and medicine in 18 research centers across the country.

What Is Known About How Skillful Readers Read

What Are the Hypotheses About How People Read?

Several key hypotheses about how skilled readers read have emerged over the past several decades. Because skilled readers read so quickly and effortlessly, several explanations of their remarkable speed and efficiency are possible. One set of hypotheses that has been tested in numerous ways, and generally rejected as untrue, is that skillful readers:

- recognize whole words without examining the individual letters
- go directly from print to meaning without studying each word
- use context to anticipate words, thereby reducing the time needed to study words

The drive to determine if these hypotheses were correct was fueled by the highly politicized debate about how reading should be taught to children. If skilled readers recognize words as wholes rather than by examining all the individual letters in the word, then perhaps children should be taught from the outset to read whole words. If context is all important to recognizing words, then teaching children the skills of breaking words apart into syllables and separating prefixes and suffixes from roots would seem to be a waste of time. This basic issue about the mental processes involved in skilled reading was at the crux of the phonics versus whole language debate, as articulated in this quote from Dr. Marilyn Adams:

> Skillful readers' processing of text seems far too fast and efficient to be based on letterwise processing of its print. Similarly each of these hypotheses has been transported to the educational domain with the same well-intentioned motivation: If we could release children from letterwise processing of text, we could expedite their graduation into efficient, skillful readers.[4]

What Conclusions Have Been Reached?

From studying eye movements, researchers conclude that a reader's eyes make thorough, but rather jumpy, movements across the text, hopping across some text and fixating on other places. The majority of the time is consumed in fixation time. The study of these fixation times led to major insights about how readers decipher words. Remember the electric typewriter you used to type your term papers in college before personal computers made typewriters obsolete? The electric typewriter's ball spun across the line creating text. But it didn't flow at a continuous pace; the ball stopped at some points spinning around and hesitating before moving on. Imagine the eyes of a reader moving in this way, left to right across a line of text, hesitating for a while, then flowing down the line again.

Researchers have reached consensus that skilled readers:

- read almost every word, skipping only a few words like *and* and *the*
- read every letter in every word
- perceive letters in chunks, not individually

These findings seem to contradict the apparent fluency and ease with which good readers scan and interpret a text. In fact, researchers who were involved in designing and conducting numerous studies on reading did not believe their findings at first. Dr. Marilyn Adams, who was one of those researchers, often describes how disappointed she and her colleagues were to discover that reading was not a "psycholinguistic guessing game." Concluding that the favored hypotheses of the 1970s were in error, she summarized the scientific consensus as follows:

> As appealing as each of these hypotheses may have been, none is correct. It turns out, instead, that skillful readers visually process virtually every individual letter of every word as they read, and this is true whether they are reading isolated words or meaningful, connected text.
>
> Even while the individual letters of text are the basic perceptual data of reading, they are not perceived one by one, independently of each other. Instead, their efficient and productive perception depends additionally on ready knowledge of words—their spellings, meanings, and pronunciations—and on consideration of the contexts in which they occur.[5]

Therefore, we know that skilled readers don't skip across a sentence, focusing only on the words important for the content. Although they spend more time on some words than others, they read essentially every word. They also process the individual letters in the words, even when they use context or other clues to help. The use of context may enhance the speed of recognizing the word, as will familiarity with the word; however, skilled readers appear to perceive words at the level of individual letters in order to successfully read the text.

Is It Important to Recognize Words Quickly?

Rapid and automatic recognition of words is a critical skill for expert reading. In order to read well, the reader must recognize words quickly and accurately. Educators use the term "decode" to refer to the process of translating from the letters on the page to pronouncing, or recognizing, the word. Stopping to figure out unknown words wreaks havoc, not only on reading speed, but also on reading comprehension. If children read too slowly, they cannot maintain sufficient momentum to remember what they just read. Beginning reading is like learning to ride a bike: if you ride too slowly, you fall off.

Hypotheses About Skillful Readers Compared to Research Results	
Hypotheses	*Research Results*
Skillful Readers:	*Skillful Readers:*
• recognize whole words without examining the individual letters	• read virtually every letter in every word, perceiving letters in chunks—not individually
• go directly from print to meaning without studying each word	• read almost every word, skipping only a few words like *and* and *the*
• use context to anticipate words, thereby reducing the time needed to study words	• rely little on contextual information because word recognition skills are so rapid, automatic, and efficient

How Do Skilled Readers Recognize Words So Quickly?

The question of *how* skilled readers read so quickly has inspired researchers for many years.[6] We know that skilled readers recognize words at such a swift pace and expend so little effort on basic word identification that the reader's attention can primarily be focused on extracting meaning from the passage. There are several things skilled readers do that increase the efficiency of their reading:

- recognize letters in groups, or chunks
- break words into syllables with little conscious analysis
- use their knowledge of how words are spelled to read by analogy (recognize words because they look like known words)
- employ their knowledge about the way a written text is structured
- activate their extensive vocabulary

Each of these skills is examined in the following sections.

1. Grouping Letters

Researchers know that skilled readers view letter sequences in chunks, even beginning in first grade, as soon as they are exposed to print and learn the sound-letter correspondences. Although at the very beginning they may focus on one letter at a time, they quickly learn to perceive several letters grouped together as a unit that corresponds to a sound, syllable, or part of a syllable, such as *ung* or *atch* or *eigh*. Because skilled readers are familiar with so many words, they not only recognize high-frequency words, but they also recognize high-frequency letter combinations. For example, a skilled reader may process the letters *th* as a unit rather than separately because a skilled reader knows that a *t* is more likely to be followed by an *h* than just about any other letter, and the *th* combination corresponds to one speech sound. The most repetitive patterns in print are the ones learned most easily.

2. Breaking Words into Syllables

Good readers quickly break a long word into syllables; they "see" where the syllable breaks are likely to be in reading a new word. They are familiar with common letter combinations, such as the doubled consonants in the middle of words like *middle,* and are aware of syllable breaks in the spoken word. Because they know which letter patterns occur frequently together within a syllable, and which letters are likely to be adjacent at a syllable boundary, they can see the break between syllables more readily. For example, a good reader reads *cagwitzpat* as */cag/ /witz/ /pat/*. The break between the *g* and *w* is likely because these letters do not occur side by side within the same syllable. There are no words in English spelled or pronounced *agw*. Once a reader perceives a syllable, he begins searching the memory for a word that matches those letters, simultaneously beginning to sound out the letter combinations. This is sometimes referred to as "reading by analogy to known patterns."

Segmenting words into syllables occurs during visual scanning, not afterward. As a skilled reader focuses on a word of text, he perceives the letters almost instantly. As the reader perceives the letters, he also simultaneously clusters the letters into chunks that he knows appear frequently in words. Adams refers to this as the "overlearned knowledge about the sequences of letters" in words.[7]

Skilled readers appear to possess an excellent knowledge of orthography, which may be the foundation of their incredible speed and efficiency in attacking text. This same knowledge of orthography drives their expert ability to instantly break long words into roots and their surrounding prefixes and suffixes, as in words such as *countermandatory*.

3. Knowledge of Word Spellings

Because skilled readers are familiar with so many words and have a good eye for the spelling of words, they use this knowledge to recognize words quickly. Careful analyses of English orthography have shown that the letter sequence of *dr* is forty times more likely to occur than the sequence of *dn*. Skilled readers intuitively know that *dn* rarely occurs together, and so they are more likely to anticipate a syllable break between these two letters. Examples of words containing the letters *dn* at a syllable boundary include *midnight, baldness,* and *kidnap.* The more knowledge a reader has of the spelling of words, the easier it is to recognize a word when it appears with a prefix or suffix.

4. Knowledge About Written Text

In addition to employing their "overlearned knowledge" about high-frequency letter patterns and spellings of many words, skilled readers use other knowledge about written text. Because of their experience reading, they possess an understanding about sentence structure and how thoughts are communicated in paragraphs. They use this knowledge of the positioning of subjects, verbs, and descriptive clauses in sentences to anticipate words as they are reading.

5. Knowledge of Word Meanings and Pronunciations

A reader is instantly recognizing letters, breaking them into chunks, and beginning to look for matches with words he knows. While all this is occurring another process is working simultaneously—the process of testing to see if the words make sense. The mind searches to see if there is a word stored in the long-term memory that matches the letters recognized from the text. A person with a larger vocabulary, spoken as well as written, can process text more quickly and efficiently. Sometimes a reader "hears" the sounds of the word pronounced mentally to help sort through the memory for a word that matches the letters on the page. This internal pronunciation is especially useful in exploring alternative pronunciations of an unknown word.

There is an intriguing paradox about learning to read. In order to read fluently and efficiently you need to quickly recognize words. Yet the way to achieve rapid word recognition is to study the letters in words repeatedly, so that letter chunks, syllables, and whole words will become part of the repertoire of words you recognize automatically. The paradox is that the process of breaking the word apart and studying it on a letter by letter basis is exactly what ultimately allows you to become automatic in reading that word and not have to study it letter by letter later. This may be no different than many other things we learn. In order to play a flute sonata fluently you have to break it apart and practice several measures slowly over and over again until eventually your fingers can fly over the notes almost automatically. Overlearning and repeated exposure leads to automaticity in playing a musical instrument, as practice with phrases and patterns leads to automaticity in reading words.

Does a Reader Recognize Any Words Automatically?

If word recognition is key in reading, does the reader have to decode each and every word—that is, go through the process of breaking the "code" of the alphabetic letters—in order to read every word? Or are there any words that a reader can automatically recognize? Skilled readers do automatically recognize some words, as follows:

> Fortunately, any word that is highly familiar will be mapped directly, instantly, and effortlessly from sight to meaning. Yet, this can happen only to the extent that the word's unique, ordered sequence of letters has been learned and overlearned through experience.[8]

How Many Words Can a Reader Recognize Automatically?

Do skilled readers recognize words so quickly because there is a limited number of words that appear over and over again? Researchers have analyzed the print of books for adults and children to see how many words appear repeatedly and what percent of the text these few words represent. In one study of words in the schoolbooks of children in the third through eighth grades, the researchers counted the number of times each word occurred and reached the following conclusions:

- 109 words represented 50 percent of the text
- 1,000 words represented 75 percent of the text
- 5,000 different words represented 90 percent of the text

The last 10 percent of the words in the sampled text were 80,000 words that occurred very infrequently.[9]

Thus, the overwhelming majority of the words in print are a few very common words that appear repeatedly. Because skilled readers know these words well, they can very quickly recognize them and know their meaning. However, the less common words are most often the "content" words: the adjectives, adverbs, nouns, and verbs that carry specific meanings and shades of meaning, and that may be the key to understanding the text. These are the words least likely to be known and most likely to be sounded out or decoded by analogy to other known words. For example, in this book the words *orthography* and *automaticity* and *phonology* are infrequent words that must be decoded by many people reading this book. The meanings of the concepts discussed, however, depend upon the reader's understanding of these words.

How Do Readers Learn the Meaning of New Words?

Word recognition is faster when the reader knows or anticipates the meanings of the words being read. It is helpful to have a large vocabulary, but how does someone acquire it? Experts have been intrigued with the question of whether a child learns more new words from instruction at school or from his independent reading.

How many new words per year do children learn, and do they learn them from instruction or by figuring them out themselves? Experts estimate that a school-age child learns 3,000 words per year, which is more than 8 per day.[10] Researchers do not believe that this increase in vocabulary can be ascribed to classroom instruction. Therefore, the experts conclude that although vocabulary instruction in school is useful in increasing a student's word knowledge, children learn more new vocabulary words from context while reading independently than from what happens in the classroom. But the caveat is that a child only learns a word if he focuses on the unknown word and its characteristics rather than skipping over it. Children need to learn to piece together clues from the context to develop a prediction about what an unknown word means. The other caveat is that only children who read independently will be expanding their vocabularies in this manner.

See the list of 150 words on page 143 to learn which words appear most frequently in your child's schoolbooks.

Do Skilled Readers Internally "Hear" the Words as They Read?

One of the few points of disagreement among researchers is whether or not skilled readers "hear" the pronunciation of the words mentally. Most likely, skilled readers can directly access a word's meaning by looking at the letters and do not recode the words into speech. Once a reader has read a word many times, he may be able to retrieve the word's meaning automatically without using the sound/letter system to sound it out mentally, thereby further speeding up the recognition process. However, good readers can at any time fall back on their knowledge of the sound-letter correspondence system to check a word or decode it.

Most researchers agree, however, that connecting letters and letter patterns to sounds is an essential step the first few times a word is read until the spelling pathways are established in the mind. That is why decoding ability and phonemic awareness are so essential in learning to read. One is unlikely to be a good reader without success at sound analysis and phonic blending.

List of 150 Most Frequent Words in English Schoolbooks According to the American Heritage *Word Frequency Book*[11]

the	but	into	long	also
of	what	has	little	around
and	all	more	very	another
a	were	her	after	came
to	when	two	words	come
in	we	like	called	work
is	there	him	just	three
you	can	see	where	word
that	an	time	most	must
it	your	could	know	because
he	which	no	get	does
for	their	make	through	part
was	said	than	back	even
on	if	first	much	place
are	do	been	before	well
as	will	its	go	such
with	each	who	good	here
his	about	now	new	take
they	how	people	write	why
at	up	my	our	things
be	out	made	used	help
this	them	over	me	put
from	then	did	man	years
I	she	down	too	different
have	many	only	any	away
or	some	way	day	again
by	so	find	same	off
one	these	use	right	went
had	would	may	look	old
not	other	water	think	number

What a Child Must Know to Be Ready to Read

Before a child will benefit from reading instruction—even phonics—some key skills must be in place. Three skills appear to be more critical than all others, including how much a parent has read to his child:

1. awareness about print and how a book is read
2. knowledge of the names of the letters
3. awareness of the speech sounds in words (phonemic awareness)

Children are keen observers. In their everyday lives they are surrounded by print on street signs, cereal boxes, *Sesame Street*, and in picture books. Usually, without even being told, they realize that print comes in many shapes, sizes, and colors and can be found on a huge variety of mediums—everything from metal coins to newspapers to neon signs. Preschoolers from enriched homes also know before entering school that adults are reading the print in books (not telling the story from the pictures), that there's a right-side-up way to hold a book, and that the pages are turned from left to right. They may also realize that the set of symbols called letters in print compose words which are separated by white spaces. The preschooler who is aware of books and print may even realize that words come in many lengths. This child may even have observed that it's often the words that take the longest to say that look the longest in print.

Most children can identify and name the majority of the letters of the alphabet by the time they enter school. The process of learning the alphabet usually begins at home when the child is taught to sing the alphabet song. This is a great first step because through repeated singing of the alphabet song, the child knows the names of the letters before trying to attach visual representations of the letter forms to the names. Because the letters in our language system are abstract and so many letters are easily confused, recognizing and naming the letters in the alphabet are tasks that require careful visual attention. Researchers believe that letters are not remembered as a holistic shape, but rather by the spatial relationships of the curved and straight lines. The importance of knowing the letters for being able to learn to read is well documented. Experts have concluded that a child who cannot recognize and name letters is seriously impaired in learning letter sounds and recognizing words.

Print awareness and knowledge of letters develop more naturally from the everyday life of a preschooler than the third skill that is a prerequisite to reading—the awareness of the speech sounds or phonemes in our language. Over the past 10 years one of the most highly researched areas of reading is phonemic awareness; several hundred studies have been devoted to understanding what it is, why it is important for early reading, and whether it can be taught directly. Further, the research has investigated whether direct teaching will improve reading and spelling, what kind of teaching works best for whom, and under what conditions.

Recent sophisticated studies with kindergarten children and older poor readers have shown that phonological skill (ability to identify, sequence, substitute, and move around the sounds in words) is the single best predictor of a child's ability to learn to read easily. That is, if school personnel gave only one type of test to kindergarten children in order to find out who was at risk for reading failure, they would find the most children most reliably by testing for phoneme awareness and other aspects of speech-sound processing. Usually there is time to do more than one type of test, so in practice teachers do not need to rely on only one indicator of possible problems. The potential to find children who will not respond well to early reading instruction is even greater if other assessments are employed—especially tests of print knowledge, vocabulary, speed of naming, and general language proficiency. The scientific findings are compelling and should be understood by anyone who works with young children on academic skills.

Phoneme awareness is simply the ability to hear and manipulate phonemes—the smallest unit of speech that distinguishes one word from another. Our alphabet represents phonemes, but somewhat indirectly, often using letter combinations to spell. Let's analyze three common words—*song, little,* and *educate.*

The word *song* has four letters, but three speech sounds, and the speech sounds may differ according to regional dialects. The word *little* has six letters, but four discernible sounds, and the second *t* is not spoken by American people the way it looks in print or the way it exists in the abstract. That is because the phonemes exist

Representations of Three Words

Alphabetic Level	*Phonemic Level*	*Phonetic Level*
s o n g	*/s/ /aw/ /ng/*, or */s/ /o/ /ng/*	*/s/ /aw/ /ng/*, or */s/ /o/ /ng/*
l i t t l e	*/l/ /i/ /t/ /l/*	*/l/ /i/ /d/ /l/*
e d u c a t e	*/e/ /d/ /y/ /u/ /k/ /a/ /t/*	*/e/ /j/ /y/ /u/ /k/ /a/ /t/*

only in theory—they get transformed as soon as they are combined into spoken words, and when they are combined, they are often changed a bit from the way we might pronounce them when they are spoken alone. The word *educate* is also not written the way it sounds. In the abstract, there is a */d/* in the word, because it comes from a Latin root, *duc-*, which means to lead. However, when we pronounce the word, the */d/* is changed by Americans to a */j/*, quite automatically. Our spelling system is also determined by the meanings of words, what language they came from, and what part of speech they are.

Developing the ability to hear and recognize phonemes turns out to be quite difficult for many people, both adults and children. A child initially hears spoken language as ideas, or units of meaning. Later he becomes aware that these ideas can be segmented into words: that "It's time to put on your pj's and go to bed" is not all one connected unit, even though it may be repeated as a unit on occasion. The awareness of words as separate units develops partially through exposure to print, and seeing the spaces we place between the words. Awareness of syllables develops in three- and four-year-olds, mostly through rhymes, wordplay, songs, and imitative production of longer words. Finally, awareness that words are composed of individual speech sounds develops easily in some children, but with more effort and instruction by others. At about age

Development of Phonological Skills

Typically Mastered by This Age	*Skill*
3	• recitation of rhymes • rhyming by pattern • alliteration
4	• syllable counting (50% of children by age 4)
5	• syllable counting (90% of children by age 5) • counting phonemes (<50% of children by age 5)
6	• initial consonant matching • blending 2 to 3 phonemes • counting phonemes (70% of children by age 6) • rhyme identification • onset-rhyme division (segmenting initial and final sounds in a word)
7	• blending 3 phonemes • segmentation of 3 to 4 phonemes (blends) • phonetic spelling • phoneme deletion (take a sound out of a word and recombine sounds)
8	• consonant cluster segmentation (such as *st, cl*) • deletion within clusters (separate *s* and *t* in *st*)

five, children begin to be able to take sounds from words, compare initial and final sounds, rhyme, and blend word pieces together. Awareness of sounds is critical for reading because the alphabetic writing system we use corresponds, albeit indirectly, to phonemes.

At home, many brief, fun interactions can help develop awareness of words, syllables, and speech sounds. Reading nursery rhymes to a child, making more rhyming words, and deciding if words rhyme are believed to be excellent ways to point out the sounds in words. For many children, rhyming is natural, easy, and fun. Others who have little idea of the concept, even with ample modeling and exposure to examples, may be showing an insensitivity to language. Try these activities:

- clapping the number of syllables in names
- substituting beginning sounds in names
- repeating longer or novel words found in stories
- singing songs that emphasize rhyme and alliteration, such as "Willaby Wallaby Woo" and "Down By the Sea"
- playing word games such as asking the child to say *cat* without the /*k*/ or *meat* without the /*m*/ to develop phonemic awareness

There are many simple activities parents can do at home that may help direct children's attention to the speech sounds in words. (See Chapter 6 for more information.)

Key Components of Early Reading Instruction

Research over the past 20 years has led to major conclusions about how good readers read well and how children learn to read. Because of convergent findings on basic issues in reading, the NICHD was justified in broadening its research effort to include the examination of questions about effective reading instruction practices in the early years (primarily kindergarten and first grade). Although it is still early in the cycle of some of these intervention research projects, there are some preliminary findings that point to the importance of some basic instructional principles. These principles have already been incorporated into the California Reading Initiative and are supported by other policy documents that are based on reviews of research. These instructional policies are listed below.[12]

1. After Screening Children, Begin Teaching Phonemic Awareness at an Early Age (Kindergarten).

In one study of 1,400 kindergarten children, the researchers observed whether the teachers included any phoneme awareness instruction in their lessons. They found that children who were "at risk" for failure were much more likely to be good readers at the end of first grade if their teachers had called attention to sounds and syllables in kindergarten. Other studies have compared approaches to instruction and determined that children who score low on screening tests learn the skills more readily if they are taught directly. That means that for 10 to 20 minutes per day the teacher is helping children through activities that develop phoneme awareness at the appropriate level. For children in the average range, who are not early or natural readers, wordplay, practice with sound matching, sound separation, and sound blending, and simultaneous instruction in letter-sound relationships is likely to enhance success. It is still a question for research how many children benefit from systematic, direct instruction—and how many can do well with a less systematic approach.

Proactive parents need to determine if their child's kindergarten instruction includes rhyming, syllable clapping, breaking words apart, and putting them together. Although most kindergarten teachers teach the alphabet, not all have lessons designed to raise awareness of sounds in words. Many kindergarten teachers include a "letter of the week" activity that focuses on each letter, but not necessarily the identity of sounds in spoken words. For example, if a kindergarten teacher is on the letter *j* and includes *jelly* in the daily snack, and asks children to bring objects to school including *jacks*, *jump rope*, and a toy *jeep*, the children may not have learned that *judge* begins and ends with the same sound and that sound is /*j*/.

More examples of activities that develop phonemic awareness include:

ACTIVITY AND DESCRIPTION

Substituting the Phonemes in a Word
Ask the child to think about what word is left if the *s* is dropped from the word *sit.* What if the first sound in *it* is changed to *a*?

Sound Matching
Do the words *mice* and *men* begin with the same sound? Which word in a list starts with a different sound (*mat, mom, bat, milk*)?

Sound Blending
The puppet likes to say words in pieces. Can you help him say the whole word together? *Ti ger. Pan da. Chris to pher. St eel. W i n d.*

(See Chapter 6 for more information on phonemic awareness tasks.)

2. Teach Each Sound-Spelling Correspondence Explicitly. Because many children cannot easily or accurately recall sound-letter correspondences when they must apply them in reading whole words, it is best if the instruction is explicit and systematic. In some of the most effective early reading programs, the instructor teaches children the sounds with a key word (*/g/* is the sound in *goat*), a story, and rhymes that use the sound repeatedly. The children practice identifying, separating, and blending the sound into words. Then they read and write sentences with the letter-sound correspondence used liberally in the text.

3. Teach Frequent, Highly Regular Sound-Spelling Relationships Systematically.

Because some letters make two sounds (like the soft and hard sounds of letters *g* and *c*), and because many sounds are spelled with letter combinations (like *ph* and *oa*), children need to learn a whole system of correspondences beyond the individual letters of the alphabet. There are between forty and fifty speech sounds in English, depending on the linguistic analysis cited, and several hundred ways to spell them. The most frequent can be taught in an orderly, sensible way, with emphasis on those that are most useful and common, so that children can read almost any new word they encounter.

4. SHOW CHILDREN EXACTLY HOW TO SOUND OUT WORDS.

The most effective early reading programs show children how to read through a word, sound by sound, and to rely on this strategy as the first one they try. The programs also teach the use of context and meaning to check whether a reading makes sense. For example, if a child sounds out the word *was* as */w/ /ă/ /z/* the context should help the child alter his or her pronunciation and to continue reading with meaning.

5. USE CONNECTED, DECODABLE TEXT FOR CHILDREN TO PRACTICE THE SOUND-SPELLING RELATIONSHIPS THEY LEARN.

It is a basic principle of learning that we must practice new skills until they are learned. The most effective programs have readers for children that contain a high percentage of words that can be sounded out using the skills the children have been taught. The number of sight words, such as *and, the,* and *you*, is kept to a minimum at first and gradually expanded with a few at a time as practice is provided.

6. READ ALOUD AND SURROUND CHILDREN WITH INTERESTING, HIGH-QUALITY BOOKS.

While children are at the early stages of learning to read, they can understand oral language that is much more complex than what they can read themselves. Knowledge of word meanings and familiarity with the language in books is gained when teachers and parents read aloud to children from books at their interest level. While children are learning to read, they can learn about the world that opens up to them through reading and continue to acquire vocabulary, background knowledge, and an acquaintance with the more complex language of books.

Stages of Reading Development

How Does Reading Continue to Develop After the Learning-to-Read Years?

Dr. Jeanne Chall, head of Harvard's reading department for many years, first proposed that learning to read occurs in stages. Dr. Chall emphasized that understanding a reader's development across time helps guide educators about what to teach, when to teach it, and what methods to use in reading instruction. Her 1983 book entitled *Stages of Reading Development,* helped to put arguments about reading methods in perspective. Learning to read is a long-term process, she argued, which necessitates passage through six major stages, each of which is a prerequisite for the next.

Today it may be harder for parents and educators to observe these stages than it used to be historically. Dr. Chall points out that the one-room schoolhouse teachers of years ago had a better perspective on reading development than today's teachers who spend years teaching one elementary grade. The teacher of the early twentieth century often understood the steps a child would take in learning to read because she watched individual children progress across the grades. Today's parents have fewer sources of information about their child's reading progress because families are smaller and extended family members may live far away. It is easier in larger families, with children in stair-step increments of age, to see that a child's reading development isn't on track. Today's families, smaller in size and with less access to the perspective of extended family members, have fewer guideposts for how their child is doing. As Dr. Chall has stated:

> With smaller families and greater mobility, parents now have a poorer base against which to measure the reading development of their children. Grandparents and aunts and uncles used to help provide the larger memories.[13]

Dr. Chall's six major stages of development have been elaborated and refined by others, but remain a helpful framework for parents to understand reading development. The stages are shown in the table on page 154.

"Reading," then, is not the same thing for a young child and an adult. Although the mastering of skills from one stage continues as the reader moves to the next stage, the skills are progressive and sequential; success at "reading to learn," for example, depends upon successful mastery of basic decoding. Individuals with reading disabilities, most of the time, have not successfully completed the stage of decoding or mastered the prerequisite stages for successful decoding. Their inaccuracy in word reading interferes with their ability to read fluently and comprehend connected text. Dr. Chall's framework indicates why it is important to read to older poor readers who should be in the "reading to learn" stage. Without the exposure to text, they are likely to fall farther behind in vocabulary and knowledge of concepts learned from books—the tasks that are generally mastered by students at a particular grade level.

Dr. Chall's Stages of Reading Development		
Stage	*Ages/Grades*	*Skills*
0—Pre-reading	Ages 6 months–6 years	• Has knowledge about books • Recognizes letters • Insight about words—phoneme awareness • Conventions of print
1—Initial Reading, or Decoding	Grade 1—beginning Grade 2 Ages 6–7	• Learns the code • Recognizes sight words
2—Confirmation, Fluency, or Ungluing from Print	Grades 2 and 3 Ages 7–9	• Acquires fluency in reading • Consolidates skills learned in stage 1
3—Reading for Learning New Information	Grades 4–8 Ages 9–14	• Reads to learn • Relates print to ideas • Reads materials with one viewpoint • Reads text limited in technical complexity • Reading is more efficient than listening
4—Multiple Viewpoints	High school Ages 14–18	• Reads materials with multiple viewpoints • Able to deal with layers of facts and concepts added to previous knowledge
5—Construction and Reconstruction	College and beyond Age 18 and beyond	• Constructs knowledge from reading • Depends upon analysis, synthesis, and judgment • Constructs knowledge on high level of abstraction • Creates own "truth" from "truths" of others

ADVICE FOR PARENTS

- ***Read aloud*** to your child often and continue this practice even after he begins reading. Reading quality literature and nonfiction books helps expand your child's vocabulary. Children with more extensive listening vocabularies have an easier time deciphering unknown words, because they have heard the word before and know its meaning.
- ***Play a word game a day*** with your preschooler. Use the time you spend with your toddler singing nursery rhymes, looking at the letters on a stop sign, comparing the names of his favorite cereals in the supermarket, and playing games with magnetic letters on the refrigerator as you cook dinner. Focus on the unique shapes of the letters, and on the sounds they make.
- ***Practice reading.*** Developing readers need to read, read, and read to become more skilled.
- Help your kindergartner and first-grader to ***focus on letter patterns*** in words. Seize any opportunity you can to focus your child's attention on letter patterns in words ("look at how *fat, cat,* and *sat* all have the same last two letters").
- Encourage your child to ***sound out words*** because he needs to study the letters in words to develop automatic word recognition. If your child can't sound out unknown words by the middle of first grade, look into whether he has had enough phonics and enough practice using the skills in reading decodable books.
- ***Don't wait*** to get extra help if your child is not on track during the "learning to read" stage. Children who fail to master sequential skills during preschool through second grade are very likely to stay behind in reading unless intensive instruction is provided. The quantity and diversity of text children must read multiplies tenfold beginning in third grade and it doesn't diminish. Although older students who are poor readers can learn with the best instruction, it becomes more difficult to provide that help as students get older. Do it now!

Part Two

What You Can Do to Help Your Child

Chapter Six

Preschool and Kindergarten

My Child Has Always Been Verbally Precocious. Does Her Ease in Learning Language Mean She Will Find It Easy to Learn How to Read?

Children with excellent verbal skills do not necessarily learn to read easily. Learning to read involves substantially different processes from learning to speak. Before your child can read the words on the page she needs to have an adequate understanding of letter-sound correspondence. For the majority of children the process of connecting a speech sound to each letter takes some effort, and, for many children, takes explicit training and practice. Many children who struggle in learning to read have excellent oral vocabularies that will aid comprehension. Once the child receives training in linking speech sounds to letters, her strong oral vocabulary is an asset in reading fluently. A child with a robust vocabulary can more quickly recognize a word in print if it is already part of her oral vocabulary. Not only does a large vocabulary speed up the process of recognizing the word, but it also helps the child move fluently through new information in a book. About half of total comprehension ability depends on knowing individual word meanings.

The Importance of the Early Years

How Early Does a Child Begin to Learn Language?

From the day of birth, your child's brain is receptive to learning language. Children learn to speak by being surrounded by speech. They just naturally absorb it. By a child's first birthday she begins to name a few things like ball, doggie, bottle, or cup. By 18 months most children have a vocabulary of at least 20 words. Somewhere around age two they have a vocabulary of more than 200 words and are speaking two-word phrases. During the third year a child should be speaking three- and four-word sentences containing verbs and pronouns (i.e., I, me). Learning to read and learning to speak are subsumed by different brain circuits that are specialized for each function. These circuits overlap but are not identical.

Scientists tell us that the brain develops through experiences. The effect of early experiences on language development is explained in *Newsweek*'s 1997 Special Report on the Child:

> Experience counts in building vocabulary, too, and at a very young age. The size of a toddler's vocabulary is strongly correlated with how much a mother talks to the child, reports Janellen Huttenlocher of the University of Chicago. At 20 months, children of chatty mothers averaged 131 more words than children of less talkative mothers; at 2 years, the gap had more than doubled, to 295 words. "The critical factor is the number of times the child hears different words," says Huttenlocher. The effect holds for the complexity of sentence structure, too, she finds. Mothers who used complex sentences (those with dependent clauses, such as "when . . ." or "because . . .") 40 percent of the time had toddlers who did so 35 percent of the time; mothers who used such sentences in only 10 percent of their utterances had children who did so only 5 percent of the time.[1]

In fact, your child's brain development during the first three years of life includes much more than the maturation of the language centers. Scientists have made major breakthroughs recently in understanding how the brain develops and how a child learns. *Time* and *Newsweek* magazines each wrote a cover story or special report during 1997 to cover this important news. The first three years of life are now viewed to be more important than previously thought. We now know that the neural circuits of the brain continue to develop after the child is born—they're not determined by the time of birth—and that what a child experiences helps to determine how the connections in the brain form. In the nature-versus-nurture continuum, this discovery reinforces the importance of nurture, or environment, on what the individual's capabilities ultimately will be in life.

Newsweek's special report highlighted the shift in scientists' understanding of brain development. In this article the author quoted from a report released 15 years earlier that stated that neuroscientists once believed that "by the time babies are born, the structure of their brains [had been] determined."[2] But by 1997 researchers knew that was wrong. In a cover story of *Time* magazine in February 1997, entitled, "How a Child's Brain Develops," the author explains how the brain of a child at age two has twice as many synapses, or connections, as an adult brain. The child's brain also consumes twice as much energy as that of an adult. It is also amazing that the highest density in synapses, or nerve connections within the brain, occurs at age 2 and continues until around age 11 when it begins to decline.

Your habits of talking and listening will make a difference in your child's language development. By conversing with your child throughout the day while you are together, you are helping her learn language. This discussion can occur during the simple experiences of your everyday life. Fancy toys and field trips are not necessary to stimulate language. You can enrich your child's understanding of the world by talking to her about what you are doing—while doing the grocery shopping, measuring ingredients to prepare dinner, or sorting the recycling materials into the recycling bins. Even the experience of watching television can be a source of discussion instead of a replacement of it. Some good habits are shown in the following chart.

Ways to Help Your Child's Language Develop	
Recommended Habit	*Example*
Rephrase and extend your child's words.	*Child:* That's a doggie. *Parent:* Yes, it's a Doberman pinscher!
Ask a clarifying question.	*Child*: That's a man. *Parent*: Tell me more about the man you saw.
Model more complex vocabulary or sentence structure.	*Child*: See my building. *Parent:* Yes, I see the tall skyscraper you built with lots of windows so people can see the view of the city.
Ask "open-ended" questions.	*Child*: I like that story. *Parent*: What was your favorite part of the story?

Some recommended activities are provided below.

ACTIVITIES TO DEVELOP ORAL LANGUAGE[3]

Meal or Snack Time

Encourage "curiosity questions," such as what the food is made of and where it is grown. Meal time is often one of the only times during the day when a child engages in interesting conversations with an adult. It can be a time to describe events, interpret the significance of what happened, and be exposed to new vocabulary.

Sharing

Tell your children your personal stories. Talk to them about things that are important to you or that interest you. Share your uncertainties and how you will address difficult questions.

Pretending
Encourage pretend playing. Make sure your child has long, uninterrupted periods of time to engage in complex pretend play. Don't discourage your child's "self chatter" during this time. Provide props and be an audience if your child wants to perform a play.

Time to Talk
Turn off the car radio and talk with your child while you are riding in the car. Set aside a regular time during the day to talk privately with your child—whether it is as she arrives home from school, at the dinner table, or before bed. Listen to how she expresses her ideas and help her with her vocabulary.

Field Trips
Take your child to new places. Every trip to the zoo, the library, the museum, or even the grocery store is filled with opportunities to learn new vocabulary.

Wait Time
Support your child's efforts to communicate complex thoughts by waiting patiently while she puts her ideas together. Suggest words as needed. Let your child control the subject of the conversation. Compliment your child's efforts to use new words.

What Does My Child Need to Know to Be Ready to Read?

There are three types of information a child needs to know to be ready to read. They are:

1. Print Awareness
    - knowledge that people read the text, not just look at the pictures

- awareness of how to read a book—right side up, starting with the first page and continuing to the end; the left page is read first, and the text is read from left to right
- understanding that words are units separated by white spaces

2. Knowledge of the Alphabet
   - being able to recognize and name all the letters

3. Phonemic Awareness
   - knowing the speech sound which corresponds with each letter

How Does My Child Become Familiar with Print?

Beginning at an early age children are exposed to print in their everyday lives. While your child is strapped in the car seat on the way to the grocery store, she sees the stop sign at the corner. Once inside the store she sees the word *Life* written in large, bold letters across the top of some cereal boxes. She notices the word *Pepsi* in the familiar royal blue and red lettering boldly displayed on the billboard while driving to a relative's house. While watching *Sesame Street* on TV she sees letters and words. And, while you read Eric Carle's wonderful story, she sees "Do you want to be my friend?" repeated on page after page.[4] Print is everywhere in your child's environment—on signs, T-shirts, food boxes, books, television, and even on children's linens. All this exposure to print provides the opportunity for a child to begin studying letters well before receiving any instruction from the adults in her life.

Beyond being aware of the print surrounding her, a child needs to understand some concrete concepts about how a book is read before beginning to read. If you ask three-year-old children what an adult is reading in a book, the majority will point to the pictures.[5] After all, that's what your preschooler is "reading" in the book. Your child may assume that you are making up the story from looking at the pictures and that those symbols surrounding the pictures are just extraneous decorations on the page.

Ways to Help Your Child Develop Print Awareness

What Your Child Needs to Know	*What You Can Do to Help*
Words are read, not the pictures.	Point to the printed words as you read aloud.
Words are read across the page from left to right.	Follow along with your finger as you read.
A book is read turned "right side up," and pages are turned from right to left.	Ask your child to open the book to the first page for you. Ask her to turn the pages.
Words are composed of letters.	Make a sign for your child's door with her name. Show your child the letters in her name. In books show your child that the white space separates the words.
Each letter has a capital and small letter form and can be written in many fonts.	Although children are generally taught the capital letters first, it helps if they have an awareness that there are two forms for each letter. Take one letter (for example, an *A*) and point out all the different sizes and shapes of *A*s.

Advice and Activities for Teaching Your Child the Alphabet

How Important Is It for Me to Teach My Child the Alphabet?

The importance of a child being able to name and recognize the letters has long been misunderstood by parents. For many years parents have believed that they had to do two things to prepare their child for school:

1. teach their child the alphabet
2. read, read, read to their child

It *is* important for your child to know the alphabet as accurately as possible before she enters school. She needs to instantly and effortlessly recognize all the letters so that she is prepared to dedicate all her attention to other tasks, such as learning the sound associated with each letter or how to write it correctly. However, although she may know the alphabet and you have read to her, she may not have the precursor skills to be able to read easily. These are necessary, but not sufficient, conditions to learn to read. Also important is phonemic awareness, which is the ability to recognize and manipulate the separate speech sounds in words.

Even though there are several skills that your child needs to read, knowing the alphabet is certainly one of those skills. One of the most important things your child needs to accomplish during kindergarten is to learn the sounds associated with letters. Knowing the alphabet can help make learning the sounds easier for your child. Imagine how difficult it would be to try to remember the sound of the letter *z* if you are trying to remember what that letter symbol is called. It is much easier to associate a sound with a letter if you already know the name of the letter—knowing the alphabet is almost like having an anchor for each sound. Additionally, since many of the letter names closely relate to their sounds, learning this sound-symbol relationship is easier for a child who already knows her letters before receiving instruction in the sounds.

Should I Teach My Child the Letter Names or Shapes First?

Most educators recommend teaching the skills in the following order:

ORDER TO TEACH ALPHABET SKILLS

1. Names	Recite the ABCs.
2. Shapes	This is a *B*.
3. Sounds	This is a *B* and it says "buh."

Therefore, before you begin working with the magnetic letters on the refrigerator door or blocks with letters, it is best to start by singing the alphabet song together. The name of the letter is the one thing that never changes; the letter shapes come in upper- and lowercase and many different fonts, and the letters can make different sounds depending upon which letters surround them. The letter name is constant.

The next step after singing the alphabet song is to introduce the printed letters. You can do this through reading aloud some of the ABC books such as *Chicka Chicka Boom Boom*.[6] Purchase a set of plastic letters so your child can feel the shapes of each letter and begin to differentiate them. Put salt, sand, or cornmeal in a tray and let your child trace letters with a finger. Have your child skywrite the letters with big sweeping arm motions. Sculpt letters in the bathtub bubbles or with clay. Play a game where you call out a letter and then your child has to lie on the floor and position her arms and legs in that letter's form. Adding the kinesthetic-tactile sense is an extremely effective way to help your child. Maria Montessori, a well-known early childhood expert, recognized the importance of incorporating the kinesthetic-tactile sense for children to learn. Most Montessori preschools use sandpaper letters to initially introduce the shape of each letter to preschoolers.

It's best to teach the capital letters first because they are more distinguishable than lowercase letters. Capital letters are harder to confuse or reverse.

Should I Teach My Child to Write the Letters?

Although there are some good reasons for children to write letters as preschoolers, you will want your child to develop good habits of letter formation when she is physically ready. Don't even start having your child try to write the letters until she has good control of her finger muscles. When you do begin to coach writing the letters, start by having your child use a thick crayon, pencil, or marker. Writing is an effective way for you to observe if your child has noticed the differences between the letters. Even though writing reinforces attention to letter form, it is not possible for many children to control a pencil well before kindergarten. Many need help developing finger strength and dexterity during kindergarten. Many children benefit from writing large on surfaces that are fun to touch—finger paints, chalkboards, or sand trays.

When Should I Begin Teaching My Child the Alphabet?

Teaching your child the alphabet is a process that usually takes a couple of years. Although you will proceed at whatever pace is appropriate for your child, a general guideline follows:

Ways to Help Your Child Develop Alphabet Skills

Age	*Skill*	*Activity*
2–4	Letter naming	• Sing ABC songs. • Read ABC books.
4–5	Letter recognition	• Use plastic letters. • Read ABC books. • Form letters in clay, papier-mâché, bubbles, sand, etc.
5–6	Letter sounds	• Read rhyming books. • Do word activities involving recognition of beginning, ending, and rhyming sounds. • Match pictures of objects to letters.

We have surveyed educators' books and conferences in search of activities parents can easily do at home to help teach the alphabet to their preschooler. The first activity, *Counting, Matching, and Naming Letters*, described on the following page, is excellent. It was developed by educators at a teacher training institute in Houston, Texas, called the Neuhaus Education Center. This activity has been very effectively used in preschools and kindergarten classrooms. Parents love this activity because it is fun, simple, and requires very little investment in special materials. It will help you teach your child to recognize the letters. The second activity focuses on learning the sequence of the alphabet. The third activity is a variation that continues to reinforce the alphabet.

Activity 6.1—Counting, Matching, and Naming Letters[7]

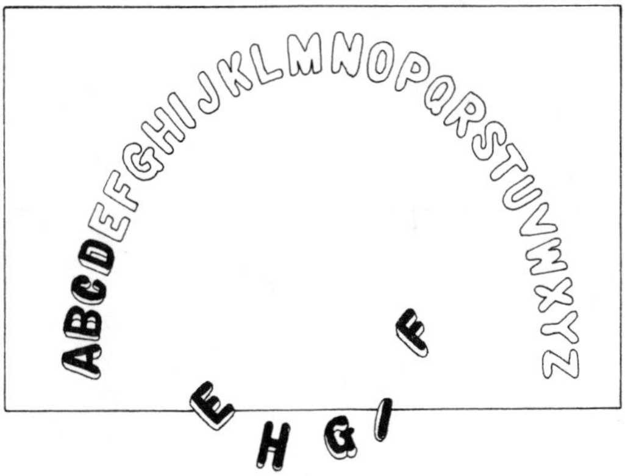

What You Need

- Set of plastic alphabet letters—preferably capital letters
- Mat that you make on an 11" x 17" piece of firm paper. Trace the plastic letters and fill them in, in an arc shape, so that the plastic letters will fit over the letters written on the arc. The arc should extend from the lower left to the lower right corner.

What You Do

- Ask your child to count how many letters there are.
- Then ask your child to place the plastic letters on the matching letters on the arc of the mat.
- Teach her the name of each letter, introducing about four new letters per day. For example, "This is the letter *A*."
- After she can differentiate the letter shapes and has been taught the names of each letter, ask her to say the name of the letter as she places it in position on the arc.
- Repeat often, until your child can recognize each letter, place it over the corresponding symbol on the arc on the mat, and say the name of each letter. Generally, it takes several weeks for a child to master all the letters.

Activity 6.2—Learning the Sequence of the Alphabet[8]

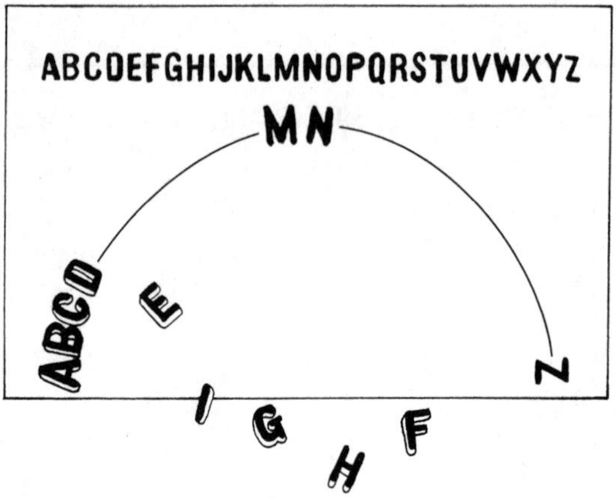

What You Need

- Set of plastic alphabet letters
- A slightly different mat made on an 11" x 17" piece of firm paper. List the letters in order in a straight line across the top to provide a reference for the child. This time, instead of the letters composing the arc, draw a line to form the arc. Then provide three "anchors" by writing the letter *A* at the lower left corner of the arc, the letter *Z* at the lower right, and *M* and *N* at the midway point at the top of the arc.

What You Do

- Ask your child to take the plastic letters out of the container and place them right side up in the center of the arc.
- Then ask her to find the *A* and place it.
- Next find the *Z* and place it, followed by the *M* and *N*.
- The child then begins with *B*, then *C*, and so on, placing all the letters in order along the arc.
- When your child has finished sequencing the letters, ask her to check it by touching and naming each letter, starting with *A* and moving to *Z*. The alphabet across the top of the mat can serve as an additional reminder.
- Repeat this activity frequently until the child can place all the letters in the proper order within two minutes. Generally, it takes several weeks for a child to master this task.

Activity 6.3—Guess the Letter[9]

Note: Wait until the child can successfully identify, name, and place the letters on the arc within the two-minute, suggested time before playing this game.

What You Need

- Two sets of plastic alphabet letters—preferably capital letters
- Two 11" x 17" mats with or without the letters filled in on the arc
- Two brown paper bags, or cloth bags, big enough to hold the letters

What You Do

- This is a game that two children can play together or you can play with your child. The object is to try to correctly identify and name the letters based on feeling them without looking. The winner is the first player to fill in all the letters on her arc.
- The first player reaches into a brown paper bag and feels a plastic letter without looking at it. If she can correctly name it, then she gets to place it on the arc on her mat and choose another letter. She continues choosing letters until she makes a mistake.
- Once a mistake is made, the turn rotates to the next player.
- The player who successfully identifies and places all the letters on her arc is the winner.

Additional Activities to Help Your Child Recognize Letters

Here are two additional activities to help your child recognize letters. These activities are included in a publication of the U.S. Department of Education following the release of their study, *Becoming a Nation of Readers.* The focus of this brochure is on what parents can do to help prepare their child for reading. These activities are simple and can be done with materials you probably already have around your house.

Activity 6.4—Letter Scrapbook[10]

What You Need

- Spiral binder
- Old magazines to use for cutting out pictures
- Scissors
- Glue or glue stick
- Marker

What You Do

- Label the top of each page with a letter of the alphabet.
- Ask the child to cut out pictures from the magazines of things that begin with each letter.
- Ask the child to paste the pictures on the appropriate pages of the notebook.
- Label the pictures for your child so that this book becomes a handmade picture dictionary of things your child has chosen.

Activity 6.5—Snakey Letters[11]

What You Need

- Modeling clay or cookie dough

What You Do

- Roll pieces of the clay or dough into snake-shaped pieces for your child to use.
- Help your child form the pieces into the shapes of letters.
- If you have used cookie dough, make sure that the letters with enclosed circles (i.e., *o*, *b*) have plenty of space inside the circle before baking. This will assure that the circles will not close up when baked.

What Is Phonemic Awareness and Can I Help My Child Acquire It?

One of the most important things researchers have learned about reading during the past 20 years is the crucial role of one skill in determining how easily a child learns to read—phonemic awareness. As defined in Chapter 5, phonemic awareness is the ability to hear and manipulate phonemes, the smallest meaningful unit of speech.

Educators frequently encourage parents to read nursery rhymes to their children. Rhyming is considered an important indicator that a child is developing good skills that are prerequisite to learning to read, and a first step toward awareness of speech sounds. In order to be able to hear that two words rhyme, a child must attend to the way the ends of words sound (not their meanings), and ignore the different beginning sounds.

When a child doesn't have a good sense of sounds, letters, and their connections, she may be showing early signs of a learning disability. Not only are dyslexic children consistently poorer in phonological awareness tasks than normal readers, but this weakness in language awareness predicts very well how easily first-graders will learn to read. As Dr. Joseph Torgesen, a leading researcher in phonological awareness, explains:

> The strong predictive power of phonological awareness tests in kindergarten is important for the early identification of dyslexia, because it indicates that it is possible to identify children for early intervention even before reading instruction begins.[12]

Phonological awareness is "necessary, but not sufficient" to become a good word reader. Besides being able to notice, think about, and manipulate sounds in words, a prospective reader also needs to use that knowledge to read words, recall extensive vocabulary, remember background knowledge about the word, and use strong thinking skills.

The other major breakthrough in reading research over the past few years is that for most children who have difficulty, phonological awareness can be stimulated through direct training. This is great news because it means that even for children who enter school with deficiencies in their understanding of speech sounds, appropriate kindergarten and first-grade curriculums can develop this key skill for reading readiness for most children.

How Do I Know If My Child's Phonological Awareness Skills Are "on Track" Developmentally?

Dr. Torgesen has outlined what a child whose phonological skills are developing normally will be able to do by grade level.[13]

CAPABILITY OF CHILD WITH APPROPRIATE PHONOLOGICAL SKILLS

By the End of Kindergarten

- identify whether two single-syllable words rhyme
- think of a word that rhymes with another
- when reading a target word and a list of three words, identify which of the three words begins with the same sound as the target word
- when reading three words, identify which one begins with a different sound from the other two

By Midway in the First Semester of First Grade

- look at words with two letter sounds (phonemes) and blend the sounds together to figure out the word (i.e., *in, on, at, bee*)
- say what word remains if a given sound is dropped from the beginning or end of a three-phoneme word (i.e., say *cat* without saying the */k/*—*at*)

By the End of First Grade

- pronounce separately the sounds in two-phoneme words (*sh-oe; b-oy*)
- pronounce separately the first sound in longer words (*h-oneysuckle*)
- blend together the sounds in three-phoneme words (*m-e-n*)

Songs, Games, and Activities to Develop Your Child's Pre-Reading Skills

Can I Help My Child Develop an Awareness of Speech Sounds?

Yes, there are some activities that you can do that help draw your child's attention to speech sounds. Although we recommend that you do these activities, these alone may not be enough to develop adequate skills for your child to be prepared for reading. Hopefully these activities will supplement what her preschool and kindergarten teacher is also doing in the classroom.

The first two activities are useful for developing your child's awareness that sentences are composed of separate words, and words are composed of syllables. The next activities and songs help your child develop an awareness of the different sounds in words. The first activity is rhyming. The following several activities involve distinguishing the sounds in words. Children generally find it easiest to hear and segment the beginning sound of a word. The ending sound is usually the next one the child becomes conscious of, and the middle sound is the hardest. Tasks that involve identifying and separating the sound are easier than separating a specific sound and substituting another sound in its place.

Activity 6.6—Counting Words in a Sentence[14]

One precursor skill for learning to read is to understand that sentences are composed of separate words. In this activity you will ask your child to move an object (a block, a Lego, a button, etc.) for each word she hears in your sentence. Then she will count the objects and tell you how many words there are in that sentence.

What You Need

- 5–7 objects—blocks, coins, and so on

What You Do

- You say a sentence.
- Ask your child to repeat the sentence. As she says each word, show her how to move one object for each word to position the objects in a line.
- Then ask her to count the objects. That is the number of words in this sentence.
- Increase the number of words in the sentence as she understands the task.

Sample Sentences:

The dog barks.
A cat scratches.
The brown dog sleeps.
The big horse jumps.
A fish can swim fast.
A cow jumps over the moon.
The police officer tells the cars to stop.

Activity 6.7—"Un-Compound" That Word[15]

This activity builds the ability to play around with pieces of words, in this case compounds, by taking parts away. You will ask your child to say the word that remains when she deletes one syllable, or word, from the compound word.

What You Do

- You say a compound word.
- Ask your child to repeat it.
- Then ask your child to say what word remains if you omit one portion.
- Your child pronounces the word that is left.

Examples:

cowboy	Say it again without the boy.	cow
outside	Say it again without the out.	side
grasshopper	Say it again without the grass.	hopper
jellyfish	Say it again without the fish.	jelly
zookeeper	Say it again without the zoo.	keeper
rattlesnake	Say it again without the snake.	rattle
cupcake	Say it again without the cake.	cup
dishwasher	Say it again without the dish.	washer
horsefly	Say it again without the horse.	fly
baseball	Say it again without the base.	ball
campground	Say it again without the ground.	camp

Activity 6.8—Hearing Rhyming Words[16]

Being able to hear whether words rhyme is an important skill that verifies that your child is hearing and differentiating the speech sounds in words.

What You Do

- Say each pair of words below and ask your child to repeat them and tell you if the words rhyme. They rhyme if all the sounds are the same except the beginning sound.
- Start down the first column for the easiest pairs, followed by the middle, and then the right column.
- Do a few at a time—not all at once.

go / top	tip / lip	nose / rose
in / lap	lamp / camp	sock / soup
yes/ my	rest / test	tie / by
mad / sad	fox / box	spoon / moon
cat / rat	shoe / sit	man / mop
rip / bag	red / ran	dress / mess
out / pig	my / by	round / pound
pig / big	mice / nice	back / boss
run / sun	ten / top	moss / boss
hit / sit	fix / mix	rain / train
ten / pen	tall / toe	sail / trail
hop / mop	light / bite	hair / here
sing / ring	cup / pup	hear / cheer
pit / mitt	fair / pair	mind / find
red / bed	sad / sleep	light / fight
pill / hill	day / say	inch / itch
get / let	leg / peg	kid / slid
him / but	tree / bee	live / give
map / lap	now / nap	like / lick

Activity 6.9—Picture Sort by Initial Consonant Sound[17]

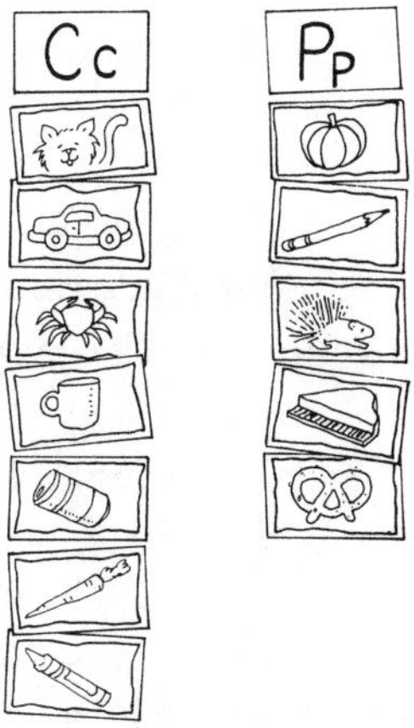

This activity draws your child's attention to the sound of the initial consonant in the words.

What You Need

- Cards with pictures of familiar objects (e.g., snake, dog, cat)
- Cards with letters that correspond with initial consonant sounds of the picture cards

What You Do

- Sort the pile of picture cards so that you use only the pictures that correspond with the letters you are going to use this time.
- Put two letter cards out as column labels.
- Say the letter sound.
- Take one picture card for each sound and position it under the column heading.
- Hand your child one card at a time and ask her to say the word. You need to make sure she is calling the picture by the name you expect (i.e., *rabbit* instead of *bunny*).
- Ask her to position the card in the appropriate column to match the sound of the beginning consonant.
- Ask her to repeat all the words in the column to check that the card is in the right place.
- After your child is proficient with two columns, increase to three and then to four columns. Once she has mastered this, you can add a miscellaneous or "?" column for anything that doesn't fit.

Remember the song we sang as children called "The Name Game"? For each person's name you sing a series of sounds. For example, using the name Nelson, it goes something like this:

Nelson Nelson Bo Belson
Be Bi Bo Belson
Nel–son

Another common song using alliteration and rhyming is "Willaby Wallaby Woo" from the collection *Singable Songs for the Very Young* by Raffi, a popular singer and songwriter for children (Raffi, 1976). You can sing this song using all the names your child knows. A sample verse goes like this:

Willaby Wallaby Wee, an elephant sat on me.
Willaby Wallaby Woo, an elephant sat on you.
Willaby Wallaby Wustin, an elephant sat on Justin.
Willaby Wallaby Wanya, an elephant sat on Tanya.

Both of these songs, along with the ones given in the activities that follow, help your child not only to segment one sound away from the rest of the word, but to substitute another sound in its place.

Activity 6.10—Picture Match Song[18]

Note: The purpose of this activity is to help draw your child's attention to the letter sounds at the beginning of words. You may either ask the child the question or sing the verses of the song, if you and your child enjoy music.

What You Need

- Series of pictures of familiar objects (e.g., snake, dog, cat)

What You Do

This song is sung to the tune of "Jimmy Crack Corn and I Don't Care." Sing the first four lines saying the sound of the letter instead of the letter name. In the example below, where the */d/* appears say the sound rather than the letter name. Wait for your child to hold up a picture of an object that begins with the letter sound you have requested.

Do you have a */d/* word to share with me?
Do you have a */d/* word to share with me?
Do you have a */d/* word to share with me?
It must start with the */d/* sound.

After your child holds up the picture (in this example, of a dog), then you sing this response:

Dog is a word that starts with */d/*.
Dog is a word that starts with */d/*.
Dog is a word that starts with */d/*.
Dog starts with the */d/* sound.

Continue by singing the verse, substituting another letter sound corresponding to the beginning consonant of a picture you have given your child.

Children do not need to recognize the alphabet letters in order to play this game, since the sound of the letter is emphasized in this game—not the letter name.

Variation: You can play this without pictures while sitting in the car or waiting in a doctor's office. The child would look around the room to find an object that begins with the sound you have requested.

Activity 6.11—Board Game for Initial Consonant Sound[19]

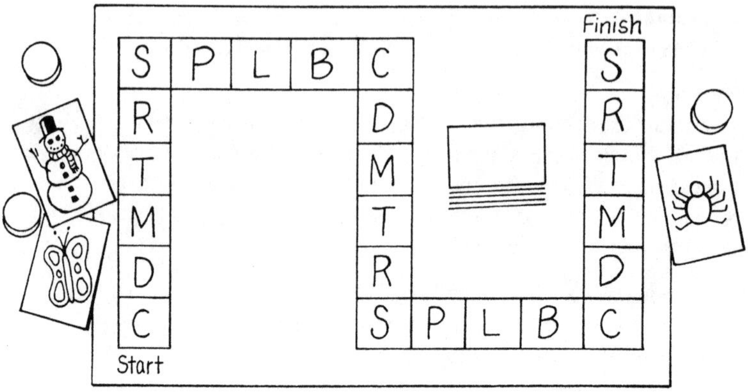

This game is fun to play and easy to make, especially once you already have the picture cards completed. It requires your child to think about the initial consonants in words.

What You Need

- Cards with pictures of familiar objects (e.g., snake, dog, cat)
- Poster board with a game outline similar to that of Candy Land, but instead of colors on each square, write initial consonant letters that correspond to the picture cards
- Markers for number of players

What You Do

- Decide which player goes first.
- Player picks a card from the deck and moves her marker to the square with the consonant that corresponds with the beginning sound of the word on the picture card.
- Next player picks a card, looks for the consonant for that picture, and moves her marker.
- Continue alternating turns.
- Player who reaches the end first wins.

Activity 6.12—Name That Sound Song[20]

The purpose of this activity is to help draw your child's attention to the letter sounds at the beginning of words. You may either ask the child the question or sing the song, if you and your child enjoy music.

This song is sung to the tune of "Old MacDonald Had a Farm." Where a letter appears with slash marks (i.e., */d/*), pronounce the letter sound, not the letter name.

What's the sound that starts these words:
Turtle, *time*, and *teeth*?
    (wait for a response from your child)
/t/ is the sound that starts these words:
Turtle, *time*, and *teeth.*
With a */t/*, */t/* here, and a */t/*, */t/* there,
Here a */t/*, there a */t/*, everywhere a */t/*, */t/*.
/t/ is the sound that starts these words:
Turtle, *time*, and *teeth*.

What's the sound that starts these words:
Daddy, *duck*, and *deep*?
    (wait for a response from your child)
/d/ is the sound that starts these words:
Daddy, duck, and *deep.*
With a */d/*, */d/* here, and a */d/*, */d/* there,
Here a */d/*, there a */d/*, everywhere a */d/*, */d/*.
/d/ is the sound that starts these words:
Daddy, *duck*, and *deep*.

You can continue using any three words beginning with the same letter sound.

Activity 6.13—Change That Sound Song[21]

This activity focuses your child on the sounds in our language by substituting new sounds in place of the original ones in familiar songs.

This song is sung to the "Someone's in the Kitchen with Dinah" section of the song "I've Been Working on the Railroad."

I have a song that we can sing
I have a song that we can sing
I have a song that we can sing
It goes something like this:

Fe-Fi-Fiddly-i-o
Fe-Fi-Fiddly-i-o-o-o-o
Fe-Fi-Fiddly-i-ooooo
Now try it with the */z/* sound!

Ze-Zi-Ziddly-i-o
Ze-Zi-Ziddly-i-o-o-o-o
Ze-Zi-Ziddly-i-ooooo
Now try it with the */br/* sound!

Bre-Bri-Briddly-i-o
Bre-Bri-Briddly-i-o-o-o-o
Bre-Bri-Briddly-i-ooooo
Now try it with the */ch/* sound!

Che-Chi-Chiddly-i-o
Che-Chi-Chiddly-i-o-o-o-o
Che-Chi-Chiddly-i-ooooo
Now try it with the / / sound!

You can continue using any sound. After you have suggested the sounds a number of times and your child has caught on to the process, your child can suggest the next sound.

Activity 6.14—Silly Sounds at Old MacDonald's Farm Song[22]

Another song you can use for this same activity is "Old MacDonald Had a Farm." It goes like this:

Old MacDonald had a farm
Ee-igh, ee-igh, oh!
And on this farm he had some cows
Ee-igh, ee-igh, oh!
With a moo-moo here, and a moo-moo there
Here a moo, there a moo, everywhere a moo-moo
Old MacDonald had a farm
Ee-igh, ee-igh, oh!

Old MacDonald had a farm
Bee-bigh, bee-bigh, boh!
And on this farm he had some cows
Bee-bigh, bee-bigh, boh!
With a moo-moo here, and a moo-moo there
Here a moo, there a moo, everywhere a moo-moo
Old MacDonald had a farm
Bee-bigh, bee-bigh, boh!

You can continue using many other sounds (i.e., See-sigh, see-sigh, soh!). You may want to use the same animal verse after verse and change the sound only, initially. After your child is comfortable changing the sound each verse, then you can also change the animal.

Activity 6.15—Change That Word[23]

Success with sound substitution at this level is usually a sign that children are ready for beginning reading and spelling. The three sections of words below are in order of difficulty—beginning sound, ending sound, and middle sound. Be sure to say *sounds*, not letter names.

What You Do

- You say the word.
- Ask your child to echo it (repeat after you).
- Then ask your child to change one sound to another one. (Use plastic letters or letter blocks as a variation to further support the activity.)
- The child pronounces the new word.

Examples:

lip	Change the */l/* to */s/*	sip
tap	Change the */t/* to */n/*	nap
lip	Change the */l/* to */h/*	hip
man	Change the */m/* to */p/*	pan
rag	Change the */r/* to */b/*	bag
lad	Change the */l/* to */b/*	bad
tell	Change the */t/* to */s/*	sell
melt	Change the */m/* to */b/*	belt
band	Change the */b/* to */l/*	land
kit	Change the */k/* to */p/*	pit
sand	Change the */s/* to */l/*	land
hid	Change the */h/* to */k/*	kid
bee	Change the */b/* to */tr/*	tree
go	Change the */g/* to */sn/*	snow
dot	Change the */t/* to */g/*	dog
bus	Change the */s/* to */t/*	but
tap	Change the */p/* to */n/*	tan
sent	Change the */t/* to */d/*	send
sell	Change the */l/* to */t/*	set

Words below all use short vowel sounds:

hot	Change the */o/* to */a/*	hat
bed	Change the */e/* to */a/*	bad
stick	Change the */i/* to */a/*	stack
pick	Change the */i/* to */a/*	pack
lip	Change the */i/* to */a/*	lap

Activity 6.16—Name Those Sounds Song[24]

The most difficult task in working with speech sounds is to isolate all the individual sounds in a word. This is different from identifying the letters—it is identifying the individual speech sounds, or phonemes, in a word.

This song is sung to the tune of "Twinkle, Twinkle, Little Star."

Listen, listen
To my word
Then tell me all the sounds you heard: *race*
/*r*/ is one sound
/*a*/ is two
/*s*/ is last in *race*.
It's true.

Listen, listen
To my word
Then tell me all the sounds you heard: *coat*
/*k*/ is one sound
/*o*/ is two
/*t*/ is last in *coat*.
It's true.

Thanks for listening
To my words
And telling all the sounds you heard!

Although this song is ideal for words with three speech sounds, or phonemes, one possible adaptation for words with two sounds is as follows:

/*g*/ is one sound
/*o*/ is two
And that is all in *go*
It's true.

Why Invented Spelling Is Positive at This Stage

Should I Correct My Kindergartner's Spelling?

This is one of the most common questions parents ask. Most schools now encourage kindergarten and early first-grade children to write words the way they sound and not worry about correct spelling. Parents are concerned that their child will learn to spell words incorrectly if they are told that any way they write a word is fine. This practice is frequently called "invented spelling" or "phonetic spelling."

Experts think it is important for young children to experiment with spelling until they understand that sounds in words are spelled consistently in print. Invented spelling encourages a child to begin writing without having to be accountable for correct spelling. You will notice that your child's writing may show the beginning consonant sounds first, then other significant consonant sounds, and finally the vowels appear when the child is tuned in to all sounds in a word. It is easy for you to see what letter-sound correspondences your child knows when you look at her writing. Children use letter names to derive sounds at this stage so they might write *kr* for car or *yt* for want.

Although phonetic spelling is a useful first step at ages 4–7, parents are justified in being concerned when a child continues to spell words incorrectly for too long. We recommend that adults encourage correct spelling, sometimes referred to as "book spelling," for selected words no later than the middle of first grade, and preferably sooner. The time to expect correct spelling is when the child begins weekly spelling lists. Most schools begin formal spelling lists by the middle of first grade. These lists should include the words that appear in children's books most frequently. Hopefully these lists will be derived to illustrate spelling patterns as well as high-frequency, non-phonetic words. After a child has had a word on a spelling list, then she should be held accountable for spelling it correctly. Many second-grade teachers use a personal dictionary or poster list that includes the words the child is expected to spell correctly. The child can add her own new words to this dictionary and use it whenever she needs to look up a word.

Throughout the early elementary grades children are usually encouraged to write words in any way for first drafts of their creative writing. However, by third grade they should be expected to correct the spelling of all their final drafts.

Recommended Commercial Products

Are There Any Commercial Products Available That Can Help My Preschool Child Prepare for Reading Instruction?

Yes, there are some good products that can help your child develop knowledge of letter sounds and the alphabet. A company named LeapFrog produces a series of talking toys that emphasize the alphabet and the sounds of the letters. These products were developed with the assistance of Dr. Robert Calfee and Kristy Dunlap, early learning experts at the Stanford University Graduate School of Education. Their original product, Phonics Desk, is shaped like a plastic tray with spots to hold removable plastic capital letters. The child can press the letter when it is in its place and hear the letter's name. There are also word cards with pictures to position in a slot. After the child puts the correct letters on the card, the word is pronounced. Later LeapFrog products also say the letter's sound and ask the child to press the letter, and ask the child to press the correct letters to make a word it pronounces.

When my children were between ages three and six, I searched for products that were games for developing pre-reading skills. Two of our favorites were dice to create words and tiles with words to create sentences. Whenever we went to a restaurant for dinner, I would grab one of these games on my way out the door. While we were waiting for our food, we would all join in and try to create sentences with word tiles. Once one person had created a sentence, the next person would vary it by changing one or several words. Sometimes we would take a timer and see who could create the longest sentence during their turn.

Some recommended products are described below.

Recommended Commercial Products

Name of Product	*Company*	*Description of Product*
Phonics Desk Create-a-Word Traveler	LeapFrog LLC 2608 Ninth Street Berkeley, CA 94710 (800) 701-LEAP www.leapfrogtoys.com	Family of products that emphasize learning letters, letter sounds, and words. Products are geared for different ages. Different shapes appeal to different ages—from Phonics Bus for toddlers to Animal "boom box" for up to fifth-graders.
Smart Cubes	Mighty Mind Leisure Learning Products, Inc. 16 Division St. West Greenwich, CT 06830 (203) 531-8700	Series of five games that come in a plastic jar with 10 dice each. Child rolls dice and creates words from five beginning letters or blends and five word endings.
Lots O'Tiles	Educational Insights 16941 Keegan Ave. Carson, CA 90746 (800) 995-4436 www.edin.com	Sets of plastic square tiles with either letters or words. Helps child recognize common words. Child constructs sentences using tiles.

How Should I Respond If My Preschooler Pretends to Read a Book?

Many parents recall the first time their child pretended to "read" a book to someone else—their preschool class, a sibling, or a stuffed animal. When my son was three years old his favorite book was Virginia Lee Burton's *Mike Mulligan and His Steam Shovel.* At bedtime, night after night, he picked this book off his bookshelf for us to read to him. One day he came downstairs carrying the book and announced to me that he was going to take it to preschool and read it to his class. And that is exactly what he did. His teacher told me afterward that during circle time he sat in a chair and "read" the entire story to the class, practically verbatim. Of course, he wasn't actually reading the book. He had memorized the story from all that repeated reading and was able to retell it by being prompted from the pictures.

Pretend reading should be encouraged at this age. There's no need to clarify with your child that she is not actually reading. Celebrate her accomplishment and join in the excitement. This gives her practice turning the pages properly, moving from left to right, and following along with the story plot. The pride she feels helps inspire her interest in learning what reading is all about.

Recommended Books to Read Aloud to Your Child

Can You Recommend Some Good Books to Read to My Preschool and Kindergarten Child?

As emphasized earlier in this book, your role in helping select good books is important. That applies to books you read aloud as well as books your child reads to you once she begins reading. Our list of recommended books in Appendix 3 is provided to help you in selecting quality children's literature. These books have good stories and rich vocabulary and include some classics children love. This list was compiled based on our personal experience as well as research on medal winners and books that appear in many other lists. I wish that someone had simply given me this list of 50 picture books, each of which is a must to either purchase for your home or check out of the library to enjoy with your child. This list appears in Appendix 3 so that you can tear it out and take it to the bookstore or library, or pass it out to relatives for gift ideas.

CHAPTER SEVEN

First Grade

What to Expect When Your Child Begins Reading

Can I Expect My Child to Begin Reading During First Grade?

Most children do begin reading some time during first grade. You may feel excited yet uncertain about what to expect and how to help, especially if this is your first child. Learning to read is actually a process that occurs across the preschool and early elementary grades. As discussed in previous chapters, many of the skills that must be in place before your child can learn to read occur during the preschool years. Your child must:

- understand that print relates to spoken words
- learn the letters of the alphabet
- associate distinct sounds with individual letters

- recognize some frequent words by sight
- be able to figure out unknown words

Even when your child has mastered all these skills and is interested in reading, it will most likely take him the better part of a year to progress from the simplest Dr. Seuss books to short chapter books, such as the *Frog and Toad* books.

In some ways watching a child learn to read resembles watching a child learn to ride a bike. With both reading and bike riding, individual skills are learned over a long time. One day your child will pull all the individual skills together and finally ride that bike. However, before taking that first solo ride down the sidewalk on a two-wheeler, he went through a series of approximations to integrate all the skills together. Your child had to know how to pedal at the appropriate pace, how not to lean too far to one side or the other, and how to remember to look ahead instead of down. He had to do these things without thinking too hard or he'd slow down and fall off.

How did your child learn those skills? When your child was two or three years old he rode a small tricycle. After mastering the tricycle you got him a two-wheeled bike with training wheels. He learned how to control the speed of the bike and how to maneuver around the bumps on the sidewalk, while the training wheels did the work of keeping the bike level. Even after you took the training wheels off, you ran along beside your child's bike, letting go for brief periods of time, until he got the feel of how to balance the bike.

As with bicycle riding, reading skills are acquired gradually over several years. One major difference between them is that there will not be a visible defining moment of accomplishment in reading, as there is when your child rides a two-wheeled bike for the first time. Some of your child's progress will be obvious, and some of the steps you will not be able to see until he demonstrates the skill to you. Just as in bike riding, you can play a significant role in helping your child learn to read.

Will My Child Just Start Reading One Day?

In general, you will see a very gradual development in reading achievement rather than an abrupt jump. There is often a period lasting anywhere from a couple of weeks to a couple of months when your child is on the verge of reading beginning books. He seems to know all his letter sounds, has known the alphabet for a year or more, recognizes a sizeable number of frequently occurring words by sight, and seems ready to read. However, he may be struggling to pull it all together and figure out how to relate the sounds to the words rapidly enough. You may remember feeling that way about his bike riding, also—it seems like he *could* do it, but he just doesn't.

In spite of the gradual nature of this process, you may observe some breakthroughs along the way. The first time your child reads a Dr. Seuss Beginner book, such as *Hop on Pop*, believe me, you and your child will both feel as if he is reading. It *is* exhilarating for both of you! Many parents can vividly describe a moment that their child began "really reading" and details about which book and where this event occurred.

Although it occurred several years ago, I can remember as clearly as if it happened yesterday the moment my son had that "aha" experience of feeling that he was finally reading. One evening after dinner he stood before me with a book in hand, *Play Ball, Amelia Bedelia*, and told me he wanted to read this book. I remember cringing because I thought it would be too difficult for him. But because he was a reluctant reader, I didn't want to do anything to squelch his interest in reading. We were standing in a back porch adjacent to my office where I was searching for a file. There was no furniture in this room, so we sat down on the carpeted floor and he began to read the first few pages. Because it was clear that he was determined to try reading this book, I held onto my side of the book and devoted my full attention to giving him whatever help he needed. He loved the double meanings in this story where the silly housekeeper was interpreting baseball expressions literally. He rolled back and laughed when the housekeeper picked up the plate when the children told her to "steal" second base. It took him about 45 minutes to read this small book. He just couldn't stop reading, even though it was an extremely laborious task for him. The memory will stay with me forever—of sitting on the floor in that musty porch watching my son slog his way page by page through this short story, laughing, growing in excitement with the realization that he *could* read that book.

Be ready to spend extra time listening once your child gets really determined to learn to read. Don't be surprised if he wants to read to you more frequently and for longer sessions once he starts to read. Give your child the extra time needed to finish a story, because the feeling of success motivates him to try other books. And most importantly, take your cues from your child about when he is ready to move forward—don't push him.

Watching my second child learn to read was a completely different experience from watching my first child. Because I had already helped one child learn to read, it was easier for me to see her passing through the stages. In addition, because she learned to read during the summer when I was her only reading coach, I was watching all her reading experiences. I could see how many times she saw a sight word before being able to recognize it instantly, how quickly she could sound out unknown words, and when she understood how to search for words hidden in compound words. It seemed more clear to me which books she was ready for, so selecting the appropriate books was not as difficult as with my first child. Even though my role in helping her was easier, she still sat teetering on the cusp of reading for almost six months. One thing that was harder for me was to wait for her to be ready to take the next step. There were moments when I thought she was ready to try more difficult books, but she didn't want to do it. After waiting through one of these lags until she was ready, she would take off at a fast pace. Remember, let your child establish the pace. Don't push.

When your child experiences one of these breakthroughs, share the excitement together and emphasize what an accomplishment he has just achieved. Point out what a great job he did in reading that book and how little you helped him. Soon he will be announcing proudly to you how little you helped him read other books. Mention how he never could have read that book all by himself a few weeks ago. Celebrate with a trip to the ice cream shop, just like you might celebrate a home run in a baseball game.

Parents are important cheerleaders for children's progress. But there are two additional roles that are very important for parents to play at this point in a child's reading development.

HOW YOU CAN HELP YOUR CHILD AT THIS STAGE

- Select appropriate books.
- Coach your child while he reads.

Advice on How to Select Appropriate Books

How Do I Decide Which Books My Child Is Ready to Read?

One of the most important roles you play is choosing books that are at your child's reading level. Unfortunately, choosing successful beginner books is not that easy. Some reasons for this difficulty are:

- the levels indicated on the books aren't consistent among publishers (i.e., a Level One book in one series may be closer to a Level Two book in another series)
- public libraries frequently color code easy reader books by level of difficulty, but often the range of difficulty within one category is too large
- it is difficult to find an abundant supply of the very easiest early reader books

To demonstrate how the levels vary among publishers, we have taken excerpts from two books—both are Level One—published by different companies.

Excerpts from Level One Books from Different Publishers

	My Pal Al *by Marcia Leonard*[1] *(The Millbrook Press Real Kids Readers)*	Do You Like Cats? *by Joanne Oppenheim*[2] *(Bantam Doubleday Dell Bank Street Ready-to-Read)*
Page 1	Al is my pal.	Do you like cats— short-haired sleek cats, playing-hide-and-seek cats,
Page 2	His fur is red.	slink-around-the-house cats, pounce-and-catch-a-mouse cats?
Page 3	He likes to sit up on my bed.	Do you like long-haired cats—cats with bushy tails and tufts, cats with paws of silky puffs?
Page 4	He is not big.	Short fur, long fur—what kind of cat do you prefer?
Page 5	He is not small.	Would you like a tabby cat, all striped in gray and black?
Page 6	He is not fat or flat or tall.	Or would you choose a calico, with patches on its back?
Page 7	He does not bark.	How about a Siamese, born as white as snow?
Page 8	He does not purr.	Did you know that Siamese change color as they grow?
Page 9	But I can pat his soft red fur.	Would you pick a tail-less Manx? A silvery Russian Blue?
Page 10	I sing to him.	A gray Maltese? A red Burmese? Is one of these for you?

Because of the inconsistency among publishers in determining reading levels, you will need to preview your child's books. Some quick tips are provided below.

How to Review a Book for the Beginning Reader

Visual Review	*Content Review*
Font Size • most children prefer type that is larger than a standard 12-point font Number of Words per Page • less than 10 words per page Pictures • interesting • provide clues about unknown words, as well as about the story	Vocabulary • Skim two or three pages to see if the vocabulary is at the appropriate level of difficulty for your child. Punctuation • Look for books with few punctuation marks, except for periods. • Quotation marks are confusing to children just learning to read.

Don't be surprised if for every beginning reading book you select you reject at least two others as inappropriate. Even with such a high rejection rate, this process doesn't take long because it takes less than 30 seconds to review each book.

Is There an Objective System to Determine the Reading Difficulty of Books?

One system that scores and ranks the difficulty of text is the Lexile Framework. The system, developed with funds from the NICHD, was designed to match appropriate books to children's reading levels. The difficulty of text is measured by looking at sentence length and the difficulty of the vocabulary, based on how frequently the word is used. In addition to calibrating the reading difficulty of text, this system can also be used to assess a student's reading level as measured by a comprehension test. School systems use the software to assess the reading level of students, measure the difficulty of reading materials, and produce individualized reading lists for students.

Interpreting a child's reading level can be confusing and is frequently misunderstood. When a second-grade child scores at a reading level of 4.5, it means that he reads as well as a fourth-grader who is halfway through the year would read that second-grade material. It doesn't mean he reads fourth-grade material as well as a midyear fourth-grader.

Because children read at varying levels, it is difficult to recommend books by grade level. Since this book has chapters by grade level, we have recommended books for each level. If your child reads at a higher level than the average child, then you will need to look ahead to the next grade. Because of the individual variability in reading level, the company that distributes the Lexile system designates an overlapping range. Here's their recommendation of how to link the Lexile scores to grade levels:

Relationship of Lexile Readability Scores to Grade Levels

Grade Level	*Lexile Score*
Kindergarten and First Grade	0–400
Second Grade	300–500
Third Grade	400–700

The Lexile score is included on our recommended reading lists because it provides reliable information for parents about the readability of books.

I'm Having Trouble Finding Really Easy Books for My Beginning Reader.

Finding books that are just right for your child at this very earliest reading stage can be frustrating. Two great sources for beginning readers are your child's classroom and the library. Consider asking your child's teacher if he can bring a book home overnight. Educators have access to lots of easy early reader books through education distribution channels, but few of these publishers distribute their books to parents. Most kindergarten and first-grade classrooms have a supply of these small, very easy books. Since your child needs lots of books for this stage and may only spend 10 to 15 minutes reading each book, next try the library. A child who is determined to learn to read may be reading 20 to 30 of these books per week; he will rarely reread the very easiest beginner books, because the stories are generally not captivating enough to reread.

You might try joining a children's book-of-the-month club. Most clubs will mail you a catalog, and you can choose either the set of books recommended for your child's age or select others.

Lists of Recommended Books for Three Stages of Early Reading

Can You Recommend Some Books for My Child to Read?

To be able to recommend books we need to describe the reading level of the child, and then match the appropriate level of text so the child can read successfully. For purposes of recommending books, we have divided the first year of learning to read into three stages. The chart on page 202 provides an overview of our definitions of these stages.

First Stage—Emergent Reader

During this first stage of beginning to read, it is important to select books that assure your child's success. Although there are some excellent books distributed through educational channels, they are not included in this list because they are not readily available to parents. Following are four categories of books for the beginning reader, all of which are available in bookstores:

1. Dr. Seuss's Beginning Reader books
2. Easy readers published by children's book publishers
3. Picture books
4. Controlled vocabulary early reading books

Description of Beginning Readers by Stages

	First Stage	*Second Stage*	*Third Stage*
Name of Stage	Emergent Reader	Beginning to Read	Early Reader
Type of Books	Easy-to-read	Easy-to-read	Early chapter books
Words per page	5–10	10–20	30+
Other Characteristics of Text	• large type font • no quotations • no contractions • limited punctuation	• some quotations • limited contractions	• fewer pictures • more varied punctuation

1. Dr. Seuss's Beginning Reader Books

It is amazing how one of the very first books many children read is a beginner Dr. Seuss book. It's easy to understand why. Children experience success in reading these books, they are widely available, and children love them. In Dr. Seuss's *Hop on Pop,* each page introduces new words, two at a time, and highlights the words first before using them in very simple sentences. Since the words are part of the same word family, it is easier for the child. For example, on the first page the words "up" and "pup" are shown in large capitalized letters. Below the words is the simple sentence "Pup is up." This book introduces 50–60 easy words, and incorporates other basic verbs, adjectives, and pronouns to make sentences.

After finishing *Hop on Pop,* try *Go, Dog Go!* The story in this book is more interesting. We suggest reading it second because it requires knowledge of some vocabulary words, and the words are not introduced and highlighted as deliberately as in *Hop on Pop.*

These beginning Dr. Seuss books have all the characteristics of a good book for the emergent reader, as listed below:

- few words per page
- large type size
- easy words
- no quotes
- no contractions (i.e., *can't, aren't, won't*)
- frequent repetition of new words
- unknown words that can be sounded out
- pictures with clues about the unknown words (e.g., there is a picture of a pitchfork the first time this word appears in the story)
- interesting story that will be captivating to the child (including some humor)

2. Easy Readers Published by Children's Book Publishers

Next, try some Level One books from the Easy-to-Read series published by children's book publishers. Many of these books are available at public libraries, as well as, at bookstores. There are at least nine series of these early reader books. Some of the most common are listed in the table below.

Common Early Reader Series

Series Name	*Publisher*
Puffin Easy-to-Read, Puffin Books	Penguin Books USA
All Aboard Reading	Grosset & Dunlap
Step into Reading	Putnam & Grosset Group
Hello Reader!	Random House
Little Bill Books (Bill Cosby)	Scholastic, Inc.
Dial Easy-to-Read	Scholastic, Inc.
I Can Read Books	Penguin Books USA
Ready-to-Read	HarperCollins
Bank Street Readers	Macmillan

As demonstrated earlier in this chapter, you will need to look at the difficulty of the text instead of assuming that all publishers level their books with the same methodology. My children found the Puffin Level One books to be the easiest. We then followed with some All Aboard Reading and Bank Street Readers books.

3. Picture Books

Some of the picture books your child outgrew a couple of years ago are great as early readers. It's fun to bring these books out again and allow your child to enjoy them in a different way. One of the proud moments for him will be the accomplishment of reading a book to you that he remembers you reading to him so many times before when he was a toddler.

Not all picture books have an easy enough vocabulary for your child to read successfully at this stage. Try books that have a lot of repetition and deal with colors, numbers, or days of the week—all vocabulary your child needs to master, some of which are non-phonetic sight words to be memorized. Some easy picture books are:

- *Brown Bear, Brown Bear, What Do You See?,* by Bill Martin, Jr., and Eric Carle
- *Goodnight Moon,* by Margaret Wise Brown
- *Ten Black Dots,* by Donald Crews

Although these books may contain some more difficult words, if your child remembers the catchy rhyme, he will breeze through it without much coaching from you.

4. Controlled Vocabulary Early Reading Books

There are two varieties of controlled vocabulary books:

1. Phonetically controlled vocabulary, which includes only words with sounds that have been taught or sight words previously introduced. The stories are written around carefully selected words that correspond to the building of knowledge about phonics.

2. Controlled vocabulary through frequency of use. Dick and Jane books would be included in this category, since they introduce new words, some of which are not phonetic, but repeat the word frequently so the user learns it through repetition.

One controlled vocabulary sequential series of early readers that is commercially marketed to parents is a series known as "Bob" books that are distributed by Scholastic. These books are packaged in boxes with eight small books, approximately 4 x 6 inches in size, labeled by numbered order. Each small book contains a colored softcover and usually 12 pages of text. The words always appear at the same place on the page (on the bottom of the page) written in script-like lettering with black-and-white sketched drawings above the words. As an example, the second book in set three introduces the long vowel combinations *oe, ou,* and *ai.* Not only are the words controlled, but the consistent placement of text and the simplicity of the illustrations allow the child to focus on the words with limited distractions.

One complaint about sequential controlled vocabulary books is that the stories are sometimes dry. Because the number of words that can be used in the very earliest books is so limited, the stories are not as interesting to children who have been listening to picture book stories read to them that contain more complex characters and plots. However, for a child who is desperately trying to learn to read and experiencing frustration, the feeling of success can override the limited story development. If your child struggles with some of the books suggested earlier in this chapter, try some phonetically controlled vocabulary books.

Some books are written with a very intentional vocabulary using only words that are easy for the beginning reader to read, yet are not dry. An example of a decodable book, which contains words carefully selected to match the phonic patterns the child is more likely to be familiar with, is *The Sunset Pond* by Laura Smith. A few lines from this book demonstrate the careful selection of words:

Bud jumps in the pond and swims fast to get the stick. He huffs and puffs as he grasps it and swims back to Matt.

As the sun slips past the hills in the west, the pond glints red and pink. A duck lands on the pond and drifts in the sunset.[3]

You can see that this vocabulary is rich and graphic, yet these words can be sounded out by the child.

Recommended Book List
First Stage—Emergent Reader

Title, Author, Publisher, and Description	*Lexile Score*
Dr. Seuss Beginning Reader Series	
Hop on Pop by Dr. Seuss (Random House, 1963) This book uses word families (*house* and *mouse*, *pat* and *sat*) to present a limited vocabulary to a beginning reader. The book introduces two words at a time, with illustrations to show ways to incorporate the words in very simple sentences.	157
Go, Dog Go! by P. D. Eastman (Random House, 1961, 1989) What makes this such an excellent beginner book is the introduction of so many of the most common words. The child is exposed to relational words (*in* and *out*, *up* and *down*, *big* and *little*, *under* and *over*), as well as the use of punctuation marks, such as quotation marks and question marks. The author was able to tie this all together in a story about dogs meeting and having a party together.	<10
Easy Readers Published by Children's Book Publishers	
Rex and Lilly: Playtime by Laura Krasny Brown (Little, Brown, 1995) This book is fun and cute, and most children love it. The vocabulary is fairly easy. The pictures are great. There are more words on the page than the Harriet Ziefert books that follow, so you may want to try them first.	30

Cat Games by Harriet Ziefert (Penguin, 1988) This book has two chapters, each a very simple story about cats and dogs playing hide-and-seek. Each page has very few words, lots of words are repeated, and the pictures are appealing for a child. The simple vocabulary makes this a good beginner book.	124
Harry Goes to Fun Land by Harriet Ziefert (Penguin, 1989) Harry, the hippo, goes to a carnival with his grandfather and enjoys the rides and food. If your child likes this hippo, there are several other books about Harry set in different locations.	182
A New House for Mole and Mouse by Harriet Ziefert (Penguin, 1987) Mole and Mouse enjoy trying out the bathtub, the piano, and the bed in their new house. However, they have to wait for someone to ring the doorbell to be sure it also works just fine.	163

Second Stage—Beginning to Read

After your child is able to successfully read the level of books in the First Stage, try moving to books where the type is somewhat smaller and there are more words per page. Try the Level One books from Grosset & Dunlap's All Aboard Reading series and Random House's Step into Reading series.

Appropriate books for this stage of reading will contain quotations and a wider variety of punctuation marks. It may help to briefly explain these to your child as he reads. The more difficult concept to explain is contractions. Many of the Level One books actually fit into this stage of reading. There are also a larger number of picture books that are great to try now, including *Do You Want to Be My Friend?* by Eric Carle and the *Curious George* books by H. A. Rey. Some of the Dr. Seuss books, including *Green Eggs and Ham* and *The Cat in the Hat,* may be at the right level for your progressing reader at this point. For a more complete list, see Appendix 3.

Recommended Book List
Second Stage—Beginning to Read

Title, Author, Publisher, and Description	*Lexile Score*
Dr. Seuss Beginning Reader Series	
The Cat in the Hat by Dr. Seuss (Houghton Mifflin, Random House, 1957, 1985) The list of all the things the cat holds on his umbrella and balances at once provides lots of vocabulary words for your child to practice.	150
Green Eggs and Ham by Dr. Seuss (Random House, 1960) Children love the rhyming and repetition of this silly story about Sam, who after much refusal finally tries green eggs and ham and likes them. The book is long enough that you may need to break it into several reading periods. But the vocabulary is simple enough and offers lots of words from word families (*house* and *mouse*, *goat* and *coat*, *rain* and *train*, *box* and *fox*) and is full of relational words (*here*, *there*, *everywhere*).	<10
One Fish, Two Fish, Red Fish, Blue Fish by Dr. Seuss (Random House, 1960, 1988) This book contains many common words your child needs to know (*wish*, *many*, *know*). All the silly names for the creatures rhyme with another word on the page (*Gump bump*, *Zans cans*, *Nook book*), which is great practice at sounding out unknown words.	260
Easy Readers Published by Children's Book Publishers	
Ice-Cold Birthday by Maryann Cocca-Leffler (Putnam & Grosset, 1992) A snowstorm interrupts a girl's birthday party. Her father's creative solution of writing a birthday message in the snow in the family's front yard saves the day.	140
Five Silly Fishermen by Roberta Edwards (Random House, 1989) Children love this silly story about five fishermen who think they have lost one friend when the fisherman forgets to count himself. This is a great book for this stage!	57

What a Hungry Puppy! by Gail Herman (Putnam & Grosset, 1993) After finding an old shoe and sock, a puppy named Lucky finds a bone, only to have to surrender it to a big dog who is thankful that Lucky found his bone for him.	66
Danny and the Dinosaur by Syd Hoff (Scholastic, 1958; HarperCollins, 1986) This is a brilliantly written book that my children loved! It's about a dinosaur who comes alive and explores the city with a boy named Danny.	100
Picture Books	
Clifford the Big Red Dog by Norman Bridwell (Scholastic, 1963, 1985) Bridwell writes this book so that it is engaging for the toddler as a read-aloud, yet contains simple enough vocabulary for the emerging reader to read. Almost all of the Clifford books are simple enough for your child to read at this stage.	260
Goodnight Moon by Margaret Wise Brown (Harper & Row, 1947, 1975) This charming book, which infants love to hear over and over again, is wonderful for the emergent reader. Your child will be able to read most of it without help because of the repetition, the rhyming, and the wonderful pictures. Your child will even enjoy searching for the mouse on each page, once again.	250
The Very Hungry Caterpillar by Eric Carle (Putnam & Grosset, 1969) The middle section of the book, in which each day the caterpillar eats one food, is easiest. Some of the words for all the foods the caterpillar eats on Saturday, plus words such as *stomachache*, will require a little coaching, but overall it's worth a try. Also try Eric Carle's other picture books, such as *The Very Busy Spider* and *Do You Want to Be My Friend?*	200
Brown Bear, Brown Bear, What Do You See? by Bill Martin, Jr., and Eric Carle (Holt, 1983) This is one of the best picture books for the emergent reader. The vocabulary is easy, with a limited number of words, and the picture clues are fabulous. The child will begin to recognize the names of the colors as the bear always says what color each animal he sees is (and of course the picture reveals the color). Your child will expect the repetition of the title question followed by the animal described by color.	N/A

Third Stage—Early Reader

Once your child makes it to this stage, there are so many more interesting books for him to read. Here are some of the changes you will observe, which cause the books for this stage to be more captivating:

- characters are more interesting
- plot has more substance
- stories are told in several chapters
- multiple books are available about a character
- stories include conversations using quotes

You can usually find at least one character your child really likes. Whether it's Peggy Parish's Amelia Bedelia, Arnold Lobel's Frog and Toad, James Marshall's Fox, or Else Holmelund Minarik's Little Bear, your child is almost certain to become fond of at least one of these characters. This fondness will motivate your child to read more. Once your child finds one character he likes, then feed this interest by providing as many books as possible on this same character. My son and I both loved Frog and Toad, so you can imagine how stunned I was when my daughter didn't like them at all. After several false starts we finally found a character my daughter enjoyed. She loved Amelia Bedelia. A description of one book in each of these series is provided in the chart on pages 211–212.

My children stopped being interested in reading picture books once they reached this third stage.

Recommended Books to Read Aloud

As discussed in Chapter 3, it is important to continue reading aloud to your child while he is learning to read. While a child is learning to read, his listening level far exceeds his reading level. By reading stories aloud that captivate his interest in increasingly more developed characters and plots, you are stimulating your child's desire to be able to read those stories himself. In addition to

Recommended Book List
Third Stage—Early Reader

Title, Author, Publisher, and Description	*Lexile Score*
Easy Readers Published by Children's Book Publishers	
Penrod's Pictures by Mary Blount Christian (Macmillan, 1991) Penrod is an adorable porcupine who has lots of adventures with his friends, including Griswold Bear. Penrod is generally an optimistic and enterprising character.	N/A
The Meanest Thing to Say by Bill Cosby (Scholastic, 1997) This new series of early readers by Bill Cosby is wonderful, not only because of its cultural diversity, but also because Mr. Cosby tackles important value issues in these books. The vocabulary makes them a little more difficult to read than some of the others in this list.	350
Frog and Toad All Year by Arnold Lobel (HarperCollins, 1976) Most early readers love the tender friendship and fun adventures of these two friends, Frog and Toad. These stories are warm and entertaining. Also try *Days with Frog and Toad* and *Frog and Toad Together.*	210
Fox on the Job by James Marshall (Penguin, 1988) When Fox needs a new bike, he gets a series of jobs to earn money. Fox discovers some jobs he is not well suited for when he insults the women customers as a shoe salesman and messes up the delivery of pizzas. He finally finds a job that is perfect for him.	140
Little Bear by Else Holmelund Minarik (HarperCollins, 1957, 1985) The mother bear's sensitive way of relating to her baby is wonderful, as are the pictures by Maurice Sendak.	370

(continued)

Recommended Book List
Third Stage—Early Reader *(continued)*

Title, Author, Publisher, and Description	*Lexile Score*
Amelia Bedelia by Peggy Parish (HarperCollins, 1963, 1991) On Amelia Bedelia's first day of work as a maid, she follows the list of her new employer literally. This literal interpretation leads her to spread dusting powder on the furniture, draw a picture of the drapes, and dress the chicken with clothes. Also try *Play Ball, Amelia Bedelia.*	120
Mr. Putter and Tabby Pour the Tea by Cynthia Rylant (Harcourt Brace, 1994) These are wonderful books about an older man named Mr. Putter and his touching relationships with his pets. Also try another series by this author about Henry and Mudge. *Henry and Mudge in the Family Tree* has the lowest Lexile score among this series.	270
Oliver Pig at School by Jean Van Leeuwen (Penguin, 1990) Ms. Van Leeuwen writes this wonderful series about Oliver Pig and his many friends. Their adventures include scenes which capture the attention of children.	340
Other Books and Picture Books (see Appendix 3 for more)	
Down on the Funny Farm by P. E. King (Random House, 1986) When P. J. Funnybunny decides he doesn't like being a bunny, he goes to live with seven different kinds of animals. After realizing that he doesn't like to sleep all winter with the bears, can't fly with the birds, and doesn't like to work like the beavers, he is happy to return home and appreciate being a bunny. Early readers enjoy the fluency they feel due to the amount of repetition.	212
Curious George by H. A. Rey (Houghton Mifflin, 1941, 1969) Your child will thoroughly enjoy reading this story about the monkey who is curious about everything and manages to get out of lots of tight spots. Also try *Curious George Rides a Bike* and *Curious George Goes to the Hospital.*	400

exposing him to good literature, you are directly increasing your child's vocabulary by reading aloud to him. As you are reading to your child, be aware of new vocabulary words that appear in the story. Stop at the end of a sentence and ask your child if he knew what a word meant. If he doesn't, define the word for him and then reread the sentence.

You may notice somewhere around ages five to seven that your child needs something more than picture books; you will sense that the stories are not holding his attention as well as they used to when he was a preschooler. At this point, begin reading books that have more developed characters and plots. Generally these read-aloud books will have few pictures. It's good practice for your child to create mental pictures, or visual images, while listening. This is an important comprehension skill, which he will need beginning in second grade, when he reads chapter books that contain few illustrations.

Start with books, such as *Winnie the Pooh,* where each chapter contains an entirely new story. Since the characters remain the same, your child will grow to love Pooh or Roo. You can read a new chapter each night, and it is not necessary for your child to remember what happened from the previous few nights to fully enjoy the story. Try reading some of the Grimm's fairy tales to your child at this stage. My children also enjoyed stories from *The Children's Book of Virtues* by William J. Bennett. The individual chapters about virtues and fairy tales are just the right length for this age, and the topics may lead to a discussion about an important value such as honesty.

Once your child is accustomed to listening to stories without pictures, then try a relatively short book in which the plot is developed throughout the book. When selecting books to read aloud, choose books that are about two years above his reading level. Skip the books he will soon be able to read himself (like *Frog and Toad,* and etc.) so that the stories will be fresh and fun when he reads them himself.

At this stage my daughter loved to listen to books from the American Girls Collection, written by various authors. This collection contains a series of five or six books about five different

Recommended Book List
First Grade—Read-Aloud Books

Title, Author, Publisher, and Description

Books Where Each Chapter Is a Story

The Children's Book of Virtues by William J. Bennett
(Simon & Schuster, 1995)
This book contains timeless stories and poems from Aesop and Native American and African folklore edited to be appropriate for children and including exquisite illustrations by Michael Hague.

The World of Pooh by A. A. Milne
(Penguin, 1926, 1954)
Each chapter contains a separate story about Winnie the Pooh from *Winnie the Pooh* and *The House at Pooh Corner.* Illustrations appear every few pages.

Short Chapter Books

American Girls Collection by various authors
(Pleasant Company, various dates)
A series of five or six books about each of five different girls. Each girl lives during a different time in American history. The stories about each girl provide historical information about life in the United States during that time period.

Longer Chapter Books

Mr. Popper's Penguins by Richard and Florence Atwater
(Little, Brown, Scholastic, 1938, 1966)
Mr. Popper receives a penguin as a gift from a friend. After struggling to decide how to make ends meet, he begins performing with a family of 12 penguins.

Pippi Longstocking by Astrid Lindgren
(Viking Press, Viking Penguin, 1950, 1978)
Pippi is an amazingly strong girl who lives alone and is mature beyond her years in age. She is silly and fun and has loads of adventures.

The Boxcar Children by Gertrude Chandler Warner
(Albert Whitman, 1942, 1950, 1969, 1977)
This first book in a series of over 60 books introduces the story about four children who are orphaned, yet are very enterprising in earning money and fixing up an abandoned boxcar to live in. They later live with their grandfather and continue to demonstrate their creativity through solving a new mystery in each book.

Charlotte's Web by E. B. White
(Harper & Row, 1952, 1980)
This enchanting story about a spider named Charlotte, who befriends a pig named Wilbur, is timeless. This classic children's story is wonderful as a read-aloud book for this age and later can be read by the child around third grade.

girls, each of whom lived at a different time in American history. Each book has about 50 pages divided into four or five chapters and contains some illustrations. Read one of the number one books about a girl first; try *Meet Samantha* by Susan Adler or *Meet Molly* and *Meet Felicity,* both by Valerie Tripp. (*Meet Addy,* another Tripp book, may not be as good a choice for this age, because the story is about a mother who is trying to escape from slavery in the 1860s. This mother decides to leave her baby behind and escape the South with an older child—a difficult concept to understand at this age.)

A series we read aloud to my son when he was six years old was *The Boxcar Children,* a series of books about four siblings, ages 5 to about 12, who solve mysteries. The beginning is a little sad in that the children are orphans, but their enterprising nature leads them to create a comfortable home in an abandoned boxcar and earn money in creative ways. They eventually are reunited with a grandfather whom they grow to love. If your child likes the first book, there are over 60 to choose from about lots of different places and topics. During third grade my son reread some books we had read aloud to him.

Once your child is accustomed to creating mental images while listening and has the attention span to remember the plot for several days, then try reading longer children's stories. My children's favorite book at this stage was *Charlotte's Web.* You will enjoy this stage because you can now read excellent literature that is captivating for both you and your child.

My Child Is Taking a Long Time to Read a Story. Does That Mean It's Too Difficult for Him?

Most children take a long time to read a story at this stage. Once your child is a more skilled reader, the length of time to read will be a criterion used to determine if a book is too difficult. At this stage, there are three things to watch:

- number of reading errors
- child's level of frustration
- how well the child comprehends the story

Don't worry about the length of time it is taking, as long as your child is not frustrated with the task. However, if he is making errors on more than half the words on each page or can't tell you anything about the story when finished, consider dropping back to an easier level for a while. Make sure that your child feels success. Nothing discourages an interested reader more than trying to read a book that is too hard for him.

Should I Dissuade My Child from Rereading Books That Are Too Easy for Him?

Children just learning to read frequently choose to read books that are easy for them, or below their reading level. This is quite normal, and it is best to allow your child to enjoy these books. From time to time your child needs to experience the joy of reading fluently—that is, without making any errors or stumbling on unknown words. It is great for a child to read books that are so easy for him that he can simply enjoy the story and not have to spend a lot of energy figuring out any new words. Repeated readings of easy books builds reading fluency. As long as your child doesn't appear "stuck" in this stage, or intimidated from trying more challenging books again, this is perfectly normal.

How to Coach Your Beginning Reader

Does an Emergent Reader Sound Out Each Word, or Recognize Some Whole Words by Sight?

A child generally recognizes by sight a certain quantity of words before he is able to read with enough fluency to feel successful. If all words must be sounded out, reading is too laborious.

Dr. Bill Honig, former State Superintendent of Public Instruction for California, explains in his book, *Teaching Our Children to Read:*

> Reading more text of increasing complexity depends on two elements—becoming automatic with more words and increasing decoding skills. The reason automaticity is so important is that if students are to read for meaning, they can attempt to stop to figure out only about 1 word in 20; they must be automatically recognizing about 95% of the words.[4]

Because some of the most common words in the English language are nonphonetic words and must be memorized and recognized by sight, the child needs to learn some of these words first. These nonphonetic words include words that are some of the oldest in our language, such as *the, was,* and *said.*

How Does a Child Automatically Recognize a Word?

A word will become part of the child's list of automatically recognized words after he has successfully figured it out several times. Research shows that it takes between 4 and 15 successful attempts to read a word before it becomes automatic.[5] For children with reading problems, it may take up to 40 exposures to a word; this is one of the signs of a serious reading problem.

A child who doesn't yet know how to read will recognize a few distinctive words in familiar contexts. He will know the name on a cereal box or the word on a street sign by its shape and color; however, if you show him the words out of context he will not know them. At this stage, known as visual cue reading, he is not really reading. But he is beginning to build up a small sight vocabulary. A child doesn't learn to read by memorizing sight words. However, the acquisition of 50–100 sight words closely correlates with learning to sound out letters. Most children learn to sound out beginning consonants, then ending consonants, and eventually the vowels. Learning to sound out words is a gradual process; it typically occurs at the same time that he is memorizing a small quantity of sight words. It's not an either/or process—they occur together.

There are a few words that constitute a high proportion of all words in print, especially in beginning books. (See the list of the 150 most frequent words in English schoolbooks in Chapter 5.) Some of these words are nonphonetic Anglo-Saxon words with odd spellings, which have remained from the oldest layers of our langauge. Sometimes a child benefits from a little coaching to master these words. Once when my daughter was just on the verge of reading, I bought a set of flash cards of high-frequency words and brought them along on a vacation. While we were on the plane we worked with flash cards, sorting the words into piles of those she knew and didn't know, and playing games with the cards. This was the only time I used flash cards, but it was just enough to help her master these words. Although we don't endorse drilling your child with flash cards because it can discourage his desire to want to read, this is one time when playing a game with high-frequency words—especially those that are nonphonetic—may give your child a boost in reading.

If My Child Doesn't Know a Word, Do I Tell Him What It Is, or Ask Him to Figure It Out?

If the unknown word can be sounded out phonetically, and your child has adequate knowledge of the sounds of letters, then it is best to ask him to figure it out. However, if the unknown word is one that cannot be sounded out phonetically (i.e., *knob,* where the *k* is silent), then it is best to supply the word.

If the unknown word is one you believe that your child can figure out, then try to suggest a strategy and work it through with him. For example, if the word he doesn't know is *cookie,* then let's work it through. You may want to supply the beginning sound to get him started and let him try to finish the second half of the word. You might try asking "What sound does a *c* make?" and so on. Although the goal is for your child to recognize words by grouping letters into chunks such as syllables, at the beginning he may need help letter by letter. Eventually he will know the sounds of letter combinations so that he will be able to sound out *coo* followed by *kie.*

If the unknown word is a compound word such as *anyone,* try covering the second syllable and ask him if he knows the first syllable. Then cover the first syllable so he can read the second syllable. Then ask him to put the two words together. This will help him develop the strategy of studying unknown words to see whether they contain words he already knows.

Regardless of whether you supply the unknown word or your child figures it out, encourage him to repeat the word. If he rereads the sentence including the word just learned, it helps him recall the word the next time he encounters it.

My Child Has a Habit of Guessing When He Encounters a Word He Doesn't Recognize. Should I Discourage Guessing?

Experts explain that an overemphasis on guessing new words, either from context or pictures, doesn't help in learning to read independently. First, guessing instead of reading through the word doesn't help the child learn the letter patterns. Furthermore, even if the child guesses correctly, because the letter patterns weren't studied, the word will be no easier to recognize later. In addition to diverting attention from the details of the word, guessing does not produce the correct word often enough to be an effective strategy. Based on research by Dr. David Share and Dr. Keith E.

Stanovich, guessing an unrecognized word from context clues is successful only 10 percent of the time.[6]

My Child Likes to Skip Words He Can't Figure Out. Should I Encourage My Child to Try to Figure Out Each Unknown Word Rather than Skipping Them?

Some skipping of words is acceptable in the very beginning stages of reading if the student is reading for meaning. He should be successful in reading 90–95 percent of the words to be considered to be reading fluently. It is important that reading is enjoyable for your child. Therefore, if he skips a few words, it's fine.

The instructional approach of skipping unknown words was widely encouraged with the whole language approach, because comprehending the meaning of the sentence was considered more important than stopping to decipher each word. Habitual skipping of unknown words and guessing from context in lieu of sounding out words is not endorsed by most reading experts today. As described in Chapter 1, California is restructuring its reading curriculum guidelines in response to their precipitous decline in reading achievement. In 1996 the California Department of Education released a publication called *Teaching Reading: A Balanced, Comprehensive Approach to Teaching Reading in Prekindergarten Through Grade Three.* This research advises:

> To become skillful readers, children must learn how to decode words instantly and effortlessly. It is for this reason that children must be taught initially to examine the letters and letter pattern of every new word while reading. Similarly, while practicing phonetic decoding, children must not be taught to skip new words or guess their meaning.[7]

My Child Studies the Pictures for Clues to Help Figure Out Unknown Words. Is This a Good Strategy?

All children use pictures as clues. Since early reader books contain pictures on each page, it's natural for your child to use the pictures.

The pictures help keep kids engaged in the story and enjoying reading. One of the most important attributes of pictures is that they help a student anticipate what will happen, develop visual images, and connect the text with his own experiences. All of these things help with comprehension.

Pictures and context clues can be especially helpful when the reader sounds the word out and then wants to verify it. Sometimes a child will pronounce something that sounds close to the word, and then by looking at the pictures confirm what the word is and realize that he needs to pronounce it differently to be correct.

As your child gains word attack skills, encourage him to study the words and not rely too heavily on the pictures for determining unknown words. Only through lots of practice looking carefully at letter combinations in words will the process of word recognition become automatic. Then there is no substitute for lots of reading, both oral and silent.

Do I Correct All Errors My Child Makes While Reading Aloud?

Deciding which errors to correct is tricky. While it is important to help your child learn new words, you want to achieve a balance between making sure he is distinguishing the letters in a word and discouraging him by correcting too often. If your child seems frustrated or discouraged, ease off in your corrections. Maintain the flow of the story. If he gets bogged down with a passage, read it for him. If possible wait until your child finishes the sentence to correct a word he has read incorrectly. This allows him to read to the end and hear whether the sentence makes sense. Hopefully he will hear his error and correct the word himself. If he does not, then either ask your child if the sentence he just read makes sense, or offer the correction. You can also point to the missed word and ask him to reread it. The important thing here is to not overdo it; reading should be enjoyable, so excessive error correction may inhibit a child's reading.

If My Child Wants to Read Silently at This Stage, Is This OK?

Yes, encourage silent reading. Reading aloud and silent reading are both helpful at this early stage of learning to read. When your child reads aloud you can make sure he is reading words correctly. If he only reads silently he may substitute words or skip over unknown words. Reading aloud daily also allows mutual enjoyment of reading. Plan some time for him to read aloud and some silent reading time, too.

Should I Encourage My Child to Point to the Words as He Reads?

If your child is losing his place frequently, then following along with his finger is an excellent way to keep his place in the text. Losing the place on the page is frustrating and detracts from comprehending what has been read. He needs to have all his attention focused on figuring out unknown words, remembering the words he has already read, and comprehending the sentence.

If your child needs help in keeping his place, but dislikes using his finger, try laying a bookmark sideways and sliding it down the page. It may be hard for your child to hold the book and coordinate the bookmark if you are reading in bed. Try moving the bookmark for your child, or holding the book so the child can move the bookmark himself.

Don't worry about whether pointing to hold his place will become a habit that is hard to break later. Most children go through this finger-pointing stage and most will simply drop it when they don't need it.

Is It a Good Idea for My Child to Look Ahead at the Pictures?

As adults we don't want to know the end of a movie or a good book someone is recommending because we want to be surprised. For emergent readers, however, looking ahead at the pictures is useful because it helps the child make predictions about where the story is going. If your child wants to look ahead at the pictures, encourage him to do so. Talk about the pictures and what he predicts is going to happen.

Elsewhere in this book we have discouraged the whole language practice of using pictures to guess unknown words. The use of pictures to help activate comprehension strategies is not to be confused with being overly dependent upon pictures for guessing unknown vocabulary words. Predicting, talking about the meaning, and retelling the story all support comprehension—habits that are good to start early.

Is It Important to Read at a Regular Time Daily?

Good reading habits established early are easier to maintain. For many families, it is most convenient to establish a scheduled time of the day when your child can count on reading. For our family, this was at bedtime. Other families may prefer another time during the day. When my children were at the very beginning stages of reading we also read earlier in the day, because it sometimes took longer to finish a book than expected.

Continue reading aloud to your child daily, even after your child begins reading to you. When your child begins to read, try changing your bedtime reading routine so that your child reads to you for 15 minutes, followed by you reading aloud to him.

Establishing good reading habits is a theme mentioned several places in this book. Most people don't get around to reading with their children each and every day; our lives are subject to lots of interruptions and scheduling changes. If you don't get around to reading one day, you're not a bad parent. Begin fresh the next day. Just remember to begin reading with your child early, and read together as often as possible.

Benchmarks to Assess Reading Progress

If My Child Isn't Reading as Early as His Friends, Should I Be Concerned?

Reading is like so many other things with children—an early advantage doesn't *always* last over time. Some recent research does indicate that children who begin reading early are the best readers in high school. Although reading earliest is not the key to being a good reader, there is one reliable guideline about achieving proficiency—the more the child reads, the better he gets at it.

If your child isn't reading regularly by the end of first grade, he may begin to fall behind. Children who do not read well and often throughout second and third grades miss learning content that their peers are picking up through their reading. Therefore, rather than worrying about whether your child reads before entering first grade, parents should focus on whether their children are reading often enough once they begin reading.

How Do I Know Whether My Child Is on Track in Reading Progress?

Recently a very frustrated mother confided her concerns about whether her daughter was reading as well as she should be for a mid–first-grader. The mother related her conversations with her child's teacher. During the fall conference the mother had asked how her daughter was reading. The teacher replied "Don't worry, her skills are developing." After another month the mother had again approached the teacher to express her concern, but was reassured that the child's reading was "progressing." During a third conversation with the teacher, this mother pointed out explicit details about how long the child spent trying to determine unknown words, the child's frustration and reluctance to read at home, and her observations that her child was reading at a level considerably below her peers. The mother asked the teacher if the child should be tested to determine if there was a problem. It was during this third conversation that the teacher finally said that the girl was in one of the lower reading groups and, in fact, was trailing her peers. The teacher suggested that the family purchase a computer and try using some educational software.

This mother was frustrated with the lack of definitive information from the teacher. While sharing her frustration with me, she said:

How do I know if my child's reading is on track for her grade level? This is my only child, and I have no idea what she is supposed to be doing by January of first grade. I'd really like to trust this teacher, but somehow I just can't. This is too important to just let it go.

This mother was losing confidence in the teacher. The teacher's "wait-and-see" attitude and approach of providing little information to the parent, alarmed the mother, who was now networking to get help from other sources. The mother was trying to figure out whether her daughter was experiencing a reading problem and if they should take more proactive steps.

Many parents have described a similar experience of not feeling that the school was monitoring their child's reading progress well enough. In general, a child should be reading simple early reading books by the middle of first grade. These books might only contain from 15 to 20 words per page and from 15 to 20 pages, but the child should be reading at this level by January of first grade. Although knowing this guideline is helpful, we believe parents are looking for more precise information than the general guideline given here. In order to provide more specific information, we have included a benchmark chart on the following pages to outline levels of achievement in specific reading skills. This chart describes the reading achievement of the average child, described with examples parents can understand. The caveat for any such chart is that children all develop at different rates; concluding that there is a problem based solely on seeing a lag between where your child is and what the chart says would not be prudent. If you believe your child's development lags, ask a professional.

The reading benchmark chart is from the following source:

- *Preventing Reading Difficulties in Young Children,* report of the National Research Council, Table 2.2—Accomplishments in Reading.

Benchmarks for Reading[8]

Kindergarten Accomplishments

- Knows the parts of a book and their functions.
- Begins to track print when listening to a familiar text being read or when rereading own writing.
- "Reads" familiar texts emergently (i.e., not necessarily verbatim from the print alone).
- Recognizes and can name all uppercase and lowercase letters.
- Understands that the sequence of letters in a written word represents the sequence of sounds (phonemes) in a spoken word (alphabetic principle).
- Learns many, though not all, one-to-one letter-sound correspondences.
- Recognizes some words by sight, including a few very common ones (*a*, *the*, *I*, *my*, *you*, *is*, *are*).
- Uses new vocabulary and grammatical constructions in own speech.
- Makes appropriate switches from oral to written language situations.
- Notices when simple sentences fail to make sense.
- Connects information and events in texts to life and life to text experiences.
- Retells, reenacts, or dramatizes stories or parts of stories.
- Listens attentively to books teacher reads to class.
- Can name some book titles and authors.
- Demonstrates familiarity with a number of types or genres of text (e.g., storybooks, expository texts, poems, newspapers, and everyday print, such as signs, notices, labels).
- Correctly answers questions about stories read aloud.
- Makes predictions based on illustrations or portions of stories.
- Demonstrates understanding that spoken words consist of a sequence of phonemes.
- Given spoken sets, such as *dan*, *dan*, *den*, can identify the first two as the same and the third as different.
- Given spoken sets, such as *dak*, *pat*, *zen*, can identify the first two as sharing a same sound.
- Given spoken segments, can merge them into a meaningful target word.
- Given a spoken word, can produce another word that rhymes with it.
- Independently writes many uppercase and lowercase letters.
- Uses phonemic awareness and letter knowledge to spell independently (invented or creative spelling).
- Writes (unconventionally) to express own meaning.
- Builds a repertoire of some conventionally spelled words.

- Shows awareness of distinction between "kid writing" and conventional orthography.
- Writes own name (first and last) and the first names of some friends or classmates.
- Can write most letters and some words when they are dictated.

First-Grade Accomplishments

- Makes a transition from emergent to "real" reading.
- Reads aloud with accuracy and comprehension any text that is appropriately designed for the first half of grade one.
- Accurately decodes orthographically regular, one-syllable words and nonsense words (e.g., *sit*, *zot*), using print-sound mappings to sound out unknown words.
- Uses letter-sound correspondence knowledge to sound out unknown words when reading text.
- Recognizes common, irregularly spelled words by sight (*have*, *said*, *where*, *two*).
- Has a reading vocabulary of 300 to 500 words—sight words and easily sounded-out words.
- Monitors own reading and self-corrects when an incorrectly identified word does not fit with cues provided by the letters in the word or the context surrounding the word.
- Reads and comprehends both fiction and nonfiction that is appropriately designed for grade level.
- Shows evidence of expanding language repertory, including increasing appropriate use of standard more formal language registers.
- Creates own written texts for others to read.
- Notices when difficulties are encountered in understanding text.
- Reads and understands simple written instructions.
- Predicts and justifies what will happen next in stories.
- Discusses prior knowledge of topics in expository texts.
- Discusses how, why, and what-if questions in sharing nonfiction texts.
- Describes new information gained from texts in own words.
- Distinguishes whether simple sentences are incomplete or fail to make sense; notices when simple texts fail to make sense.
- Can answer simple written comprehension questions based on material read.
- Can count the number of syllables in a word.
- Can blend or segment the phonemes of most one-syllable words.
- Spells correctly three- and four-letter short vowel words.
- Composes fairly readable first drafts using appropriate parts of the writing process (some attention to planning, drafting, rereading for meaning, and some self-correction).

(continued)

- Uses invented spelling/phonics-based knowledge to spell independently, when necessary.
- Shows spelling consciousness, or sensitivity, to conventional spelling.
- Uses basic punctuation and capitalization.
- Produces a variety of types of compositions (e.g., stories, descriptions, journal entries), showing appropriate relationships between printed text, illustrations, and other graphics.
- Engages in a variety of literary activities voluntarily (e.g., choosing books and stories to read, writing a note to a friend).

Second-Grade Accomplishments

- Reads and comprehends both fiction and nonfiction that is appropriately designed for grade level.
- Accurately decodes orthographically regular, multisyllable words and nonsense words (e.g., *capital*, *Kalamazoo*).
- Uses knowledge of print-sound mappings to sound out unknown words.
- Accurately reads many irregularly spelled words and such spelling patterns as diphthongs, special vowel spellings, and common word endings.
- Reads and comprehends both fiction and nonfiction that is appropriately designed for the grade.
- Shows evidence of expanding language repertory, including increasing use of more formal language registers.
- Reads voluntarily for interest and own purposes.
- Rereads sentences when meaning is not clear.
- Interprets information from diagrams,charts, and graphs.
- Recalls facts and details of texts.
- Reads nonfiction materials for answers to specific questions or for specific purposes.
- Takes part in creative responses to texts, such as dramatizations, oral presentations, fantasy play, etc.
- Discusses similarities in characters and events across stories.
- Connects and compares information across nonfiction selections.
- Poses possible answers to how, why, and what-if questions.
- Correctly spells previously studied words and spelling patterns in own writing.
- Represents the complete sound of a word when spelling independently.
- Shows sensitivity to using formal language patterns in place of oral language patterns at appropriate spots in own writing (e.g., decontextualizing sentences, conventions for quoted speech, literary language forms, proper verb forms).
- Makes reasonable judgments about what to include in written products.

- Productively discusses ways to clarify and refine writing of own and others.
- With assistance, adds use of conferencing, revision, and editing processes to clarify and refine own writing to the steps of the expected parts of the writing process.
- Given organizational help, writes informative, well-structured reports.
- Attends to spelling, mechanics, and presentation for final products.
- Produces a variety of types of compositions (e.g., stories, reports, correspondence).

Third-Grade Accomplishments

- Reads aloud with fluency and comprehension any text that is appropriately designed for grade level.
- Uses letter-sound correspondence knowledge and structural analysis to decode words.
- Reads and comprehends both fiction and nonfiction that is appropriately designed for grade level.
- Reads longer fictional selections and chapter books independently.
- Takes part in creative responses to texts, such as dramatizations, oral presentations, fantasy play, etc.
- Can point to or clearly identify specific words or wordings that are causing comprehension difficulties.
- Summarizes major points from fiction and nonfiction texts.
- In interpreting fiction, discusses underlying theme or message.
- Asks how, why, and what-if questions in interpreting nonfiction texts.
- In interpreting nonfiction, distinguishes cause and effect, fact and opinion, main idea and supporting details.
- Uses information and reasoning to examine bases of hypotheses and opinions.
- Infers word meaning from taught roots, prefixes, and suffixes.
- Correctly spells previously studied words and spelling patterns in own writing.
- Begins to incorporate literacy words and language patterns in own writing (e.g., elaborates descriptions; uses figurative wording).
- With some guidance, uses all aspects of the writing process in producing own compositions and reports.
- Combines information from multiple sources in writing reports.
- With assistance, suggests and implements editing and revision to clarify and refine own writing.
- Presents and discusses own writing with other students and responds helpfully to other students' compositions.
- Independently reviews work for spelling, mechanics, and presentation.
- Produces a variety of written work (e.g., literature response, reports, "published" books, semantic maps) in a variety of formats, including multimedia forms.

My Child's First-Grade Teacher Mentioned Some Reading Terms. What Do the Terms Decoding, Word Attack Skills, *and* Reading Strategies *Mean?*

During your conference with your child's first-grade teacher, you may hear a few reading terms. The most commonly used reading terms for this stage of reading are:

- *decoding*
  The process of analyzing spoken or graphic symbols of a familiar language to ascertain their intended meaning. Note: to learn to read, one must learn the conventional code in which something is written in order to decode the written message. In reading practice, the term is used primarily to refer to word identification rather than to identification of higher units of meaning.[9]
- *word attack skills*
  When a reader is learning how to read an unknown word, he employs "word attack" skills. These skills include all the things a child does to try to figure out an unknown word, which includes breaking the word into syllables, looking for letter patterns, or identifying the vowel.
- *reading strategies*
  Every reader, beginning or advanced, possesses a set of approaches for how to read. A typical set of strategies for a new reader includes looking at the pictures, using context to understand the meaning, and sounding out unknown words. A more advanced reader has additional strategies, such as knowing how to adjust the reading rate to fit the task (i.e., skimming vs. studying).

A complete list of reading terms, plus definitions, appears in Appendix 2.

Should I Push My Child to Read If He Is Reluctant?

This is one of the questions that parents ask most frequently. If your child doesn't seem interested in reading to you, it is best to continue reading to him as often as you can. It *will* pay off—he will enjoy listening to stories so much that it will eventually give him the motivation to want to read himself.

If your child is halfway through first grade and is reluctant to begin reading to you, it's time to make some more observations about why he is reluctant. Children who have had plenty of exposure to reading as a preschooler and who know the alphabet generally do not resist learning to read; because it is something they observe older children and adults doing, they typically are anxious to learn how to read. A child who is having difficulty may express it in one of the following ways:

- reading is hard
- reading is harder for him than math
- he can't read as well as the other children

If your child expresses any of these frustrations, it's time to ask more questions. You need to determine if

- your child is missing some key skills, such as the ability to sound out;
- he is not getting reading instruction at school that is appropriate for him; or
- he may have a learning disability that is impairing his ability to learn to read easily.

See Chapter 10 for more information on reading difficulties.

Word Games and Activities to Develop Early Reading Skills

Are There Any Activities I Can Do with My Child at This Stage?

There are some great activities you can do to help your child build skills to support his reading. The activities included in this chapter develop your child's skill in looking for letter patterns in words—a skill we know helps make him a better reader. The first couple of activities help your child associate letters with the sounds in words. Since children usually know the consonant sounds first, and the vowels come later, we have placed the vowel activities at the end of the chapter.

Word sorting is a popular technique used by many educators to develop early reading skills. Because it is excellent for building skills in a game-like format, we have included a description of it in this book for you to do at home with your child. One word sort was included in the preschool chapter. Activity 6.9 is a picture sort emphasizing the initial consonant sound of the word. Picture sorts are good for children in the pre-reading stage, when your goal is to draw attention to the sounds in words, not the letters.

We have included a variety of word sorts in this chapter. A word sort is an activity where the child is asked to sort printed word cards into appropriate columns, distinguishing for a characteristic of the word. It might be by letter sound, letter pattern, rhyming families, or by meaning. When all the cards fit into a column, the sort is a closed sort. An open sort, one that includes a miscellaneous column for all words that don't fit into a labeled column, is more difficult than a closed sort.

The activities included in this chapter are just the beginning of what you can do. Develop your own sorts for more variety.

Activity 7.1—Matching Letters to Pictures[10]

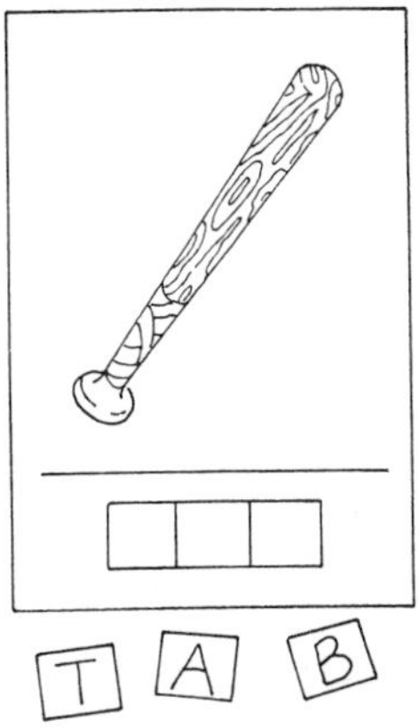

In this activity you will show your child a picture, and he will write the word from the letter cards you provide. All pictures are of three-letter simple consonant-vowel-consonant words. You will provide the correct letters, which your child will relate to the sounds in the word and place in the proper order.

Note: Some children may be ready for this activity during kindergarten. We placed this activity in the first-grade chapter because your child needs to know the sounds of letters before playing this game, and some schools don't teach this until the beginning of first grade.

What You Need

- Picture cards with three boxes—you can cut pictures out of magazines, or draw a simple sketch of the objects listed below. Paste the pictures on a sheet of paper or cardboard and draw three boxes below that are the size of the letter cards.
- Letter cards—you can make these on 3" x 5" index cards cut in half—use all lowercase letters.

What You Do

- Put one picture card down in front of your child.
- Ask your child to name the picture.
- Lay out the three letter cards that spell the word.
- Ask your child to move the letters up into the correct places in the three boxes on the picture card.
- Ask your child to read the word he just wrote (it helps to have him slide his finger under each letter as he reads it to reinforce the blending of sounds).

If this activity is difficult for your child, help him separate the three sounds in the words before he looks at the letters. Then ask him to tell you the sound of each letter before positioning the letters above. If he can't tell you the letter sound easily, he is not ready for this activity.

Some easy three-letter words you can use for this activity are listed below. You need pictures of each word, and then make the appropriate letter cards.

lad	man	cat	kid	sap	pal
leg	fan	hat	bag	top	rat
net	peg	pot	mat	dot	lap
rag	cup	hen	dog	bat	lip

Activity 7.2—Choosing Letters[11]

This activity is an extension of Activity 7.1. It is a little more difficult because the child needs to choose the appropriate three letters. In Activity 7.1 you provided the three letters in the word, and your child needed to position them in the right order. Here he needs to select the correct three letters from a selection of six to eight letters.

What You Need

- Picture cards with three boxes—these are described in Activity 7.1.
- Letter cards—you can make on 3" x 5" index cards cut in half—use all lowercase letters.

What You Do

- Put one picture card down in front of your child.
- Ask your child to name the picture.
- Lay out six to eight letter cards, including the three that spell the word.
- Ask your child to move the letters up into the correct places in the three boxes on the picture card.
- Ask your child to read the word he just wrote (it helps to have him slide his finger under each letter as he reads it to reinforce the blending of sounds).

When you first present this activity to your child, make sure your child knows the sound of each of the letters offered. You can move each letter into a line, giving the sound and asking your child to echo it. Move the first letter into the correct place on the picture card and say its sound, then the second, and finally the third. Blend the sounds into a word while sliding your finger under the letters as you say them.

Activity 7.3—Sound Board[12]

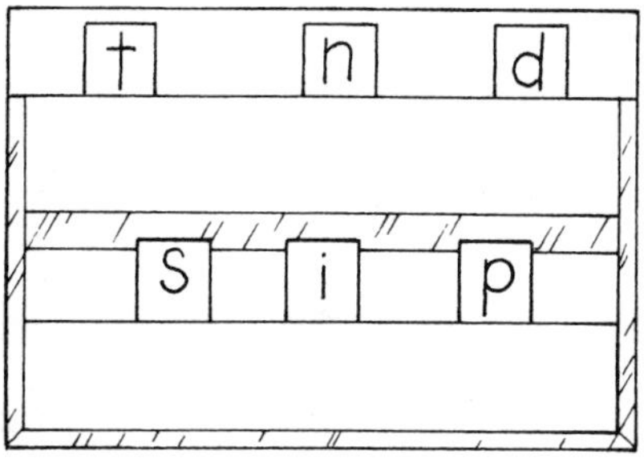

Educators refer to this activity as a sound board because they use a board with pockets to hold the letters. The child is asked to select letters from the top pocket and move them to the bottom pocket to write a word.

This activity is included in a Reading Readiness workshop taught by Suzanne Carreker of the Neuhaus Education Center. Her sound board is a piece of cardboard 8½" high by 11" wide, with two horizontal pockets to hold the letters.

What You Need

- Sound board—you can make it with two 8½" x 11" pieces of cardboard. Use one as the back and cut the other to make the pocket strips. Tape the bottom and sides of two 2" strips horizontally across the 11" width.
- Letter cards—you can make these with 3" x 5" index cards cut in half—use all lowercase letters—write the letters on the top of the card so they can be read when stuck in the pockets.

What You Do

- Put the sound board in front of your child.
- Position six letters in the top pocket.
- Say the word you want your child to write.
- Ask your child to echo the word and move the appropriate letters down to the lower pocket.
- Ask your child to read the word.
- Then ask him to change one letter to spell a different word.

Variations:

After your child can do this easily, try several variations. Increasing the number of letter choices makes the task more difficult. Changing the middle vowel is more difficult than changing the beginning or ending consonants.

Letters Displayed:	
i p n s t d	sip Change sip to tip Change tip to dip Change dip to nip Change nip to sip
i t p n s d f l	pit Change pit to sit Change sit to fit Change fit to lit Change lit to pit
a t p l f d h	hat Change hat to fat Change fat to fad Change fad to lad Change lad to had
a t n l i p	lip Change lip to lap Change lap to tap Change tap to tip Change tip to nip Change nip to nap

Activity 7.4—Blend Bingo Game[13]

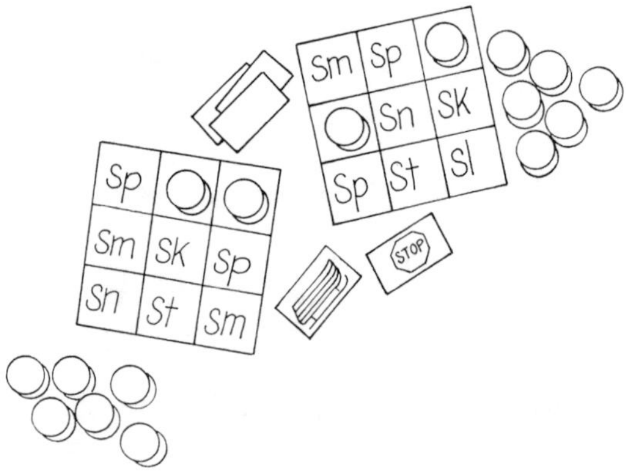

This is a great game to help your child learn to distinguish the consonant blends in words.

What You Need

- A couple of bingo cards—make these by starting with firm paper or cardboard and dividing the page into nine squares. Then write one consonant blend on each square so that the cards are different.
- Picture bingo cards—cut out pictures from a magazine to glue on cards or draw sketches so that each card has a picture of an object that starts with one of the consonant sounds.
- Markers (such as pennies, buttons, or plastic colored disks)

What You Do

- Each player selects a bingo card and some markers.
- Review the pictures to make sure your child recognizes them and associates the appropriate word with the picture.
- Players take turns drawing a card from the stack and calling out the picture name.
- Players place a marker on the corresponding square of their bingo card if they have the consonant blend that begins the word on the picture card—only one square is covered for each word, even if their card contains the same consonant blend more than once.
- The first player to cover all nine squares says "bingo" to win.

An example of six blends and some words is given below. You can easily create these lists of words by using a child's dictionary.

sl	***sn***	***st***	***sp***	***sk***	***sm***
slug	snake	stop	spot	skate	smile
slipper	snorkel	stick	space	skin	small
slogan	snow	stilts	spaghetti	ski	smelt
sled	snowball	step	spaniel	sketch	smock
slope	snout	stencil	spade	skillet	smog
slide	snuggle	stethoscope	sparrow	skip	smoke
sleet		stew	spatula	skirt	smooth
slacks		stereo	speck	skunk	smudge
		sticker	spectrum	skull	
		stingray	spice		
		stirrup	spider		
		stitch	spinach		
		stocking			

Activity 7.5—Word Sort by Long and Short Vowel Sound[14]

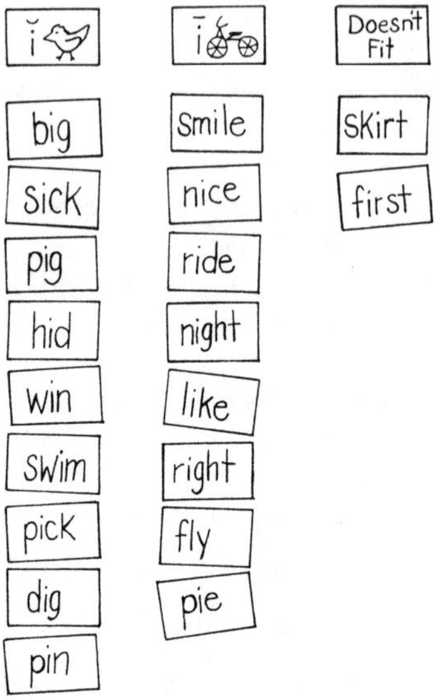

This activity helps your child differentiate between long and short vowel sounds. You will provide two columns, one showing a picture of a word with a long vowel sound and the other showing a picture of a word with the short sound of the same vowel. Your child will place words below the appropriate column, depending upon whether it has the short or long sound of the vowel. This activity can be adjusted to the appropriate level of difficulty for your child, depending on which words you use and whether you add a third column.

What You Need

- Picture cards for the column heading
- Word cards to be sorted

What You Do

- Place a picture card at the top of two columns. One should have the long sound and the other the short sound for a given vowel. For example, place a picture of a bike for the long *i* and a chick for the short *i* sound.
- Give your child a card, one at a time.
- Ask him to tell you what that word is.

- Ask him to place it in the appropriate column based on the sound of the vowel.
- If he makes a mistake or is uncertain, ask him to read down the whole column starting with the heading.

Variations:

1. Use words for column headings instead of a picture card.
2. Add a "Doesn't Fit" column header and include cards that don't fit into either the short or long vowel column; this changes the activity from a closed to an open sort. You can then include words where the vowel sound is controlled by an *r.*
3. Make cards for your child's spelling list for this week and include them in a sort.

See the sketch for an example of an open *short and long i vowel sort* with a "Doesn't Fit" column.

Activity 7.6—Word Sort by Vowels[15]

This is a word sort that asks your child to distinguish between two different vowels. First, play this as a closed word sort so that the words you give him belong in one column or the other. A variation that makes it more challenging is to introduce a "Doesn't Fit" column and include words that don't fit in either of the two designated columns.

What You Need

- Word cards—you can make these on 3" x 5" index cards.

What You Do

- Place the two words that head the columns.
- Give your child one card at a time.
- Ask him to say the word.
- Have him place the word under the appropriate column, depending on which vowel sound the word has.
- Ask him to read down the column of words to self-correct any mistakes at the end.

Variations:

1. Add a "Doesn't Fit" column and include some words which don't fit either category.
2. Ask your child to make his own word cards by selecting words from a book he is reading.

Three sample lists are provided below. The words used for column headings appear in bold italics, followed by words for the sort.

bad	***bell***						
tan	rag	fan	let	bell	said	bag	rat
lap	tall	net	yet	back	clan	sack	den
sell	Ned	bad	Dan	ran	pen	send	pet

pit	***pot***						
tin	pig	trick	drop	cot	rock	pit	win
wig	sick	hop	dot	chin	dig	brick	pot
shop	got	pin	fig	stick	chop	stop	not

wag	***wave***						
pat	clam	bag	strange	wave	gnat	mat	jacks
glad	plate	date	slam	pat	sad	race	paste
stand	sat	wag	bat	ape	tape	pale	

Can You Recommend Any Commercially Available Products for This Stage?

There are some good products available to develop reading skills. Among all the commercially available computer software claiming to offer reading instruction, we like *Read, Write, and Type* best. Another product worth exploring is the new *Hooked on Phonics Learn to Read* kit. The original product has been completely redesigned and improved. The kit includes a parent tool kit and five sequenced minikits that contain an audiocassette tape, letter cards for word building, a workbook, and 10–15 decodable books. Although it is not intended to be a comprehensive reading curriculum, and it does not contain enough practice for children with reading disabilities, *Hooked on Phonics Learn to Read* should be a useful supplement for home instruction by parents. This product contains well-designed phonics lessons, engaging activities that should be easy for parents to do, and books that give children practice reading words they have learned to sound out. The 30 children's books included in the kit were written especially for *Hooked on Phonics Learn to Read* by recognized authors such as David McPhail, and field tested on children prior to publication. The books alone make this kit worthwhile.

Commercially Available Products

Name of Product	*Company*	*Description of Products*
Audiocassette tape of Early Reader books	various publishing companies	Audiotape with voice reading a book, such as *Frog and Toad*—copy of book included for child to follow along while listening.
Electronic Storybooks—books on CD-ROM	various publishing companies	Popular children's stories, such as *Arthur's Teacher Trouble*, on computer—child can hear story read, highlight unknown words for pronunciation, and activate animated skits by clicking on background objects.
Read, Write, and Type computer software	The Learning Company	Based on research over many years, then licensed by The Learning Company—child must defeat "Vexor the Virus" by learning the name, sound, and keyboard location of letters. Sequential building of pre-reading skills.
Hooked on Phonics Learn to Read	Gateway Learning Corporation 1-800-ABCDEFG www.hookedonphonics.com	This is a new version of *Hooked on Phonics.* It has been completely redesigned. To supplement audiotapes and letter cards, the new product includes decodable books, workbooks, and word-building activities (ages 4–8).
Boggle Junior	Parker Brothers	In the box of this game are several letter cubes, cards with pictures and words, and a plastic container with a timer. It's a great game to promote spelling and word recognition of three-letter words.

Chapter Eight

Second Grade

What to Expect, Now That Your Child Has Begun Reading

Second grade is a year when your child has already begun reading, but is still learning many important new skills—some of which may be less obvious to you. Probably the key skill for this year is to develop fluency. Returning to our bike analogy, this is the stage when your child goes from riding cautiously down the sidewalk to cruising. She gets so comfortable on that bike that she picks up speed little by little, swerves easily to miss a rut in the pavement, and can handle abrupt changes in speed and direction without losing control and falling off. Similarly with reading she begins to read faster and faster, growing in her ability to decipher unknown words and handle text of increasing difficulty. She can add more inflection in her voice while reading aloud because she recognizes more words instantly and has more attention available to think about how to let her voice communicate the story.

The development of fluency is an extremely important step in your child's reading development. During third grade, the difficulty of the reading increases dramatically. Teachers expect children to be able to learn more from their independent reading; less time is taken in class to make sure that your child decoded the material properly. She needs to be ready. To be a really good reader and to get ready for third grade, the most important thing is for her to read frequently this year.

Try different genres this year. Don't forget about nonfiction, because many children really love to read children's nonfiction books about famous people, countries, electricity, animals, and so on.

How You Can Help Your Child's Progress

What Can I Do to Help My Child Develop Fluency?

There are some things you can do to help your child become a more fluent reader. Here are some ideas:

IDEAS TO INCREASE YOUR CHILD'S READING FLUENCY

- Reread books that are at an easy level for your child. This helps develop fluency. Encourage your child to go back a step from time to time and reread a book that she read three months ago.
- Try alternating reading with her—first you read a page and then she reads a page through a story. Then switch pages and reread it again.
- Read aloud simultaneously, which is sometimes called choral reading.
- Get two copies of the same book, and you read aloud while she follows along in the text. This should be a book at her reading level.

- Perform a play. Have her reread the story several times to practice her lines.
- Have her follow along in the text while she listens to a book on tape.

All of these suggestions are ways to get your child to reread the same text more than once. This technique is helpful for developing fluency. But probably the most critical guideline to remember for developing fluency is that your child needs to read lots of text.

For most families the greatest challenge in motivating their child to read frequently is the number of other distractions. Many parents express concerns about how to get kids to want to read instead of watching TV, playing video games, or spending hours glued to noneducational computer games. I decided that even though my children like TV and videos better than reading, it is my responsibility to decide how much is enough and to place limits. No child likes to brush her teeth, but the consequences of not brushing are serious. No child likes to get a shot at the doctor's office, but it's something we know is for her own good. We have to watch her suffer a little pain and stay committed to what we're doing. I know when I make my children turn off the TV and insist that we will all spend some time reading, it is also for their long-term benefit. And I know that my children are going to resist sometimes and give me an argument about the TV. We have rules in our family about how much TV the children can watch, when they can watch it (after completing homework), and what programs are acceptable. We also have expectations (I'm careful not to call them "rules") about reading—everyone reads at bedtime. It's a habit we started very early, so my children really don't question it. It's part of the bedtime routine. In order to feel good about insisting that each child reads, I view it as my job to make sure there are good books available. Going to the library or bookstore is part of my household role, just like going to the grocery store. I want to feed their minds, not just their bodies.

Discover Nonfiction Books

Can You Recommend Any Good Nonfiction Books?

For some children nonfiction books are a key to getting them to read more frequently at this stage. When my son was in second grade he desperately needed to read often, but wasn't naturally inclined to choose to read when he had free time. He was late in learning to decode and had been tutored in phonics. Now he was catching up and could decode pretty well, but his speed was slow and he stopped frequently to sound out words. We knew that all that tutoring would be less productive if we couldn't get him to read. We tried lots of fiction books with varying success. During one conference with his second-grade teacher, she suggested that we try some nonfiction books. He loved history and science, so we checked out library books on the Declaration of Independence, Abraham Lincoln, and electricity. This was just the hook we needed to get him reading. Eventually we used these same interests to get him to cross over to fiction. He eventually read *Ben and Me*,[1] a story about Ben Franklin's mouse, and *Johnny Tremain*,[2] a story about a young boy who lived in Boston just at the time of the Boston Tea Party and the start of the Revolutionary War.

There are several wonderful series of children's nonfiction books. Many of these series cover a wide variety of topics. For example, the "If you Lived . . ." series covers life at a time in history, including:

- life in colonial times
- life with the Sioux Indians
- life at the time of the Civil War
- life at the time of the great San Francisco earthquake
- life on the Mayflower
- life with Abraham Lincoln

What makes this series of books special is that a child can feel what it was like to live during a time in history. In the book about living during the colonial times the author describes what clothes were like then, what it was like to go to church and school, and what games the children played.

Some examples from some of our favorite nonfiction series are listed in the table on page 248.

Encourage Your Child to Write

Should I Encourage My Child to Write?

It's helpful for your child to continue writing as much as possible throughout these early reading years. Writing helps reinforce reading and vice versa. Each time your child writes a word, she either automatically knows how to spell the word, or she has to figure out how it might be spelled. When she writes an unknown word, she must first think about the speech sounds she hears in the word, then choose which letters represent those speech sounds, and then write those letters. This beneficial process forces her to focus on how a word in her oral vocabulary is spelled. After she writes it, then she examines it to see if it looks right. Even if an adult doesn't look at her writing to offer a correct spelling, she may pay more attention the next time she sees that word in writing. This process of approximating the spelling and then confirming it is a great way to learn to spell words; being able to write words makes it easier to read them. This reading-writing connection reinforces critical skills.

Is There Any Good Writing Software for Children?

There are a number of excellent computer software programs for writing. In selecting which one to buy, it's mostly a matter of choosing one with the features you prefer. This is not like choosing a phonics program, where the quality of the educational content is critical. With writing programs, just choose what you like. Some have extensive libraries of clip art to use like stickers in illustrating pictures for the story. If you want this feature, look at the Imagination Express series by Edmark, which includes a neighborhood, rain forest, and castle themes. The

Series and Sample Title	*Description*
History	
A New True Book *The Declaration of Independence* by Dennis Fradin (Children's Press Chicago, copyright by Regensteiner Publishing Co.,1988)	45-page overview of what it is, what events in history led to its creation, and how it was written—type is large and pictures appear on each page
Childhood of Famous Americans *Abraham Lincoln: The Great Emancipator* by Augusta Stevenson (Aladdin Paperbacks, copyright 1932 by Bobbs-Merrill)	192-page book that tells the story of Abraham Lincoln's life
. . . If You Lived in . . . *. . . If You Lived in Colonial Times* by Ann McGovern (Scholastic, 1992)	80-page book that answers questions about what life was like for a child during this time
David A. Adler's Picture Book Biography series *A Picture Book of George Washington* by David A. Adler (Holiday House, 1989)	picture book describing the life of George Washington
Science and Social Science	
Eyewitness Books *Pyramid* by James Putnam (Dorling Kindersley, 1994)	each page is filled with pictures and captions describing famous pyramids
Eyewitness Science *Electricity* by Steve Parker (Dorling Kindersley, 1992)	covers the history of how electricity was discovered and how it is used
Seymour Simon's Books About the Solar System *Our Solar System* by Seymour Simon (Morrow Junior Books, 1992)	series of books about individual planets, the sun, the earth's moon, and the solar system; each has magnificent pictures and text

Amazing Writing Machine by Broderbund makes it easy to make a picture book. After you have typed your child's story, the software inserts picture boxes throughout the text, which your child can illustrate. After my children finished drawing pictures to accompany their story, we took it to a nearby copy shop and had it bound with a spiral binder and plastic cover.

How Will I Know If My Child Is Reading Text That Is Too Difficult for Her?

A child is reading at a comfortable reading level when she reads 95 percent of the words correctly and can demonstrate good comprehension of the material. That means that she misses only 1 word out of every 20 words in the text. This is a good level for your child for everyday reading; she will learn new vocabulary but shouldn't feel frustrated at this level. For developing fluency, it's helpful to read some material that is even a little easier than this. That would mean your child misses only 1 word out of every page if there are 30 or 40 words per page.

Determining an appropriate reading level depends upon what goal you want the child to achieve. For fluency, it's helpful to read easy text. For learning new vocabulary, it's best to stretch and read text that is a little harder. A child is reading material that is too hard if she is missing about 1 word out of every 10, or reading at or below a 90 percent level. Even if she is not initially frustrated, there is a risk that she will become so if she reads at this level for long. Drop back and try easier text for a while.

Word Games and Activities

Are There Any Activities I Can Do with My Child to Help Develop Word Skills at This Point?

Even though we have emphasized that developing fluency is the key reading goal for second grade, it is still important to keep building word study skills. The better your child is at reading words, the more fluently she will read. We have included a few examples of the kinds of word study activities you can do with your child. These are only examples—you will be able to think of variations on these activities and others. In first grade our activities emphasized initial consonant sounds. Here we assume your child has mastered the initial consonant sounds and the long vowels. We are now focusing on short vowels and more difficult word beginnings, such as consonant blends (e.g., *bl, fl,* and *st*) and digraphs, where the two letters make a single unique sound (e.g., *sh, ch, th, wh,* and *ph*).

We have included below a word list of sample words with long vowel sounds to help you in making the activities. You will notice that these long vowel words contain more difficult spelling patterns than words used in games in first grade. There are some words with the consonant-vowel-consonant-silent-*e* pattern and vowel teams (*ai* in *paint*).

Suggested Long Vowel Words for Word Sort Activity[3]

Long a (ā)	*Long* e (ē)	*Long* i (ī)	*Long* o (ō)
gate	deer	nine	boat
game	jeep	dice	goat
nail	key	smile	rope
paint	leaf	prize	hose
rake	seal	drive	nose
vase	sheep	fire	comb
shave	dream	tie	ghost
chair	wheel	tire	toes
blade	sleeve	price	float
plane	sleep	cry	globe
plate	sweep	fly	yo-yo
scale	queen		snow
skate	tree		
train			
grapes			

Activity 8.1—Hopping Frog Game[4]

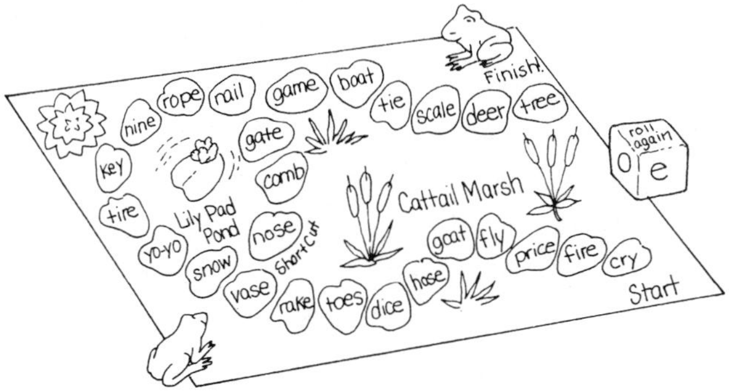

This game will reinforce your child's understanding of short vowel sounds. Create the game board in the style of the game Candy Land but with words used for the path instead of colors. Players roll a die labeled with vowels and move to the next word on the course with that short vowel sound. Use plastic frog markers and place the words in circles to create a game of frogs hopping across lily pads to the end of the course.

See the word list provided in this chapter for ideas of words to use in making your game board. You can also play this game with easier vowel-consonant-vowel words when your child is younger—ages 4–6.

What You Need

- A game board you make—start with a piece of cardboard, draw circles or squares that connect to form a course shaped like an *S*. For the frog theme, glue green circles on the board to represent lily pads. You can add a shortcut path so that a player landing on one spot gets to take a shorter path to the end.
- Vowel die—tape the sides of a die and write the vowels (*a, e, i, o, u*) on five sides, plus "roll again" or "lose a turn" on the sixth side.
- Markers—use plastic frog markers. Some other theme ideas include plastic dinosaurs and a rock course, or plastic farm animals and barns.

What You Do

- Each player selects a marker; decide who will go first.
- The first player rolls the die and looks for the first word on the board with that vowel sound.
- Tell your child it is the vowel sound that matters and that sometimes the vowel sound is spelled without the letter in the word (i.e., *fly*—long *i*).
- She pronounces the word and moves her marker to this word.
- The second player proceeds.
- The first player to finish the course wins.

Activity 8.2—Word Maker Game with Blends and Digraphs[5]

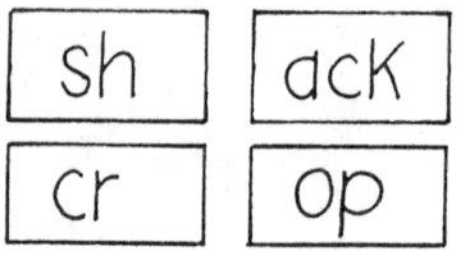

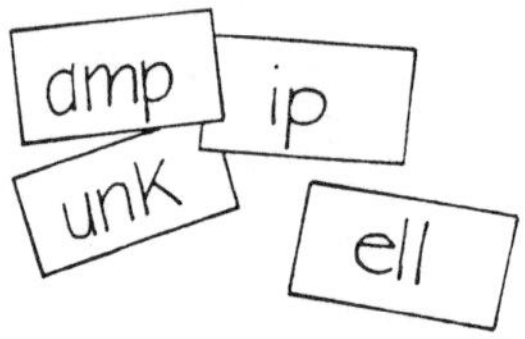

Your child will work with two different decks of cards, one with word beginnings and the other with endings, combining the cards to see how many words she can create. This activity is a little more difficult than working with consonant-vowel-consonant words because the word beginnings are blends of two sounds (i.e., *st, wh*).

What You Need

- A set of cards with word beginnings and endings
- Pencil and paper to record words

What You Do

- Divide the cards into two piles—one for the beginning of the words (consonant blends and digraphs) and the other for the ending (word family endings).
- Ask your child to pick four endings and lay them on the table.
- Next she picks two beginnings.
- From these six cards she tries to create as many words as possible—she can reuse any card after recording a word.
- Ask her to record the words she makes on a sheet of paper—prepare this paper by drawing vertical lines to make multiple columns, one for each turn.
- Pick a different beginning card and try to create other words with the same endings.
- Compare how many words were created with different word beginnings.
- To make it more challenging, increase the number of cards from each deck.

A list of word beginnings and endings is provided below. The consonant blends and digraphs for the word beginning cards are listed on the first four lines. The 10 lines below those are the word endings. (V = vowel and C = consonant)

Word Beginnings—Consonant Blends and Digraphs

s-blends	*sc*	*sk*	*sm*	*sn*	*sp*	*st*	*sw*
r-blends	*br*	*cr*	*dr*	*fr*	*gr*	*pr*	*tr*
l-blends	*bl*	*cl*	*fl*	*gl*	*pl*	*sl*	
digraphs	*sh*	*ch*	*th*	*wh*	*ph*		

Endings

a-C	*at*	*an*	*ag*	*ap*	*ad*
i-C	*it*	*ip*	*in*	*ig*	*ill*
o-C	*ot*	*og*	*op*		
e-C	*et*	*en*	*ed*	*ell*	
u-C	*ut*	*ug*	*un*		
V-*sh*	*ash*	*ish*	*ush*		
V-*ck*	*ack*	*ick*	*ock*	*uck*	
V-*nk*	*ank*	*ink*	*unk*		
V-*ng*	*ing*	*ang*	*ung*		
V-*mp*	*amp*	*imp*	*ump*		

Activity 8.3—Letter Cube Word Maker[6]

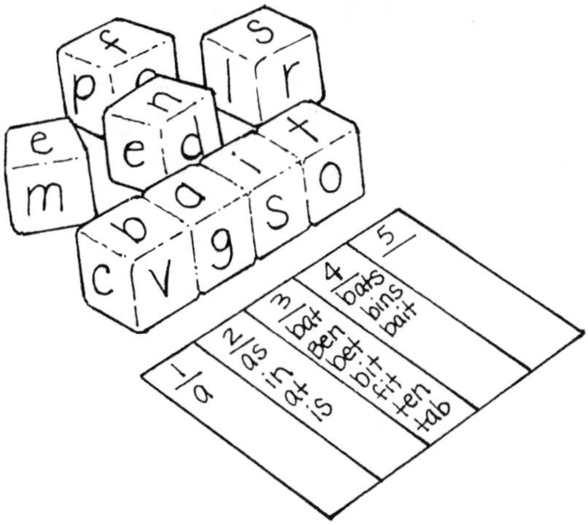

This is a variation of Scrabble that is faster and involves changing the letters around to continue making as many words as possible. Ask your child to roll dice or cubes with letters on them and then try to make as many words as possible before her time runs out. Letters can be reused in words over and over. The winner is the player who uses the most letters in words.

What You Need

- 5–8 dice with letters (letter cubes can be found in commercial games such as Boggle and Scattergories—you can also make them by covering the sides of dice with masking or first aid tape and writing letters on the tape)
- Timer—sand clock timer or clock timer
- Piece of paper and pencil to record words

What You Do

- Take turns being the recorder and the player. The recorder writes the words the other player makes.
- The player rolls the dice, turns the letters to face her, and lines them up.
- The timer is started and she has until the end of the time to create as many words as possible.
- The player may not turn the cube over to use a letter from another side.
- The player gets credit for a word by arranging the letter dice, saying the word, and spelling it to you. Then she can reuse those letters in other words. (For example, after saying *a* and *at* she can then add *c* to spell *cat* by reusing the *at.*)
- To record the words make a tally sheet with five columns labeled 1 through 5. It is easiest to record the words under columns labeled for the number of letters in the word. This facilitates tallying the score at the end of play. To score a player, count the number of words in each column and multiply by the number of letters in that column of words. For example, this player created 1 one-letter word, 3 two-letter words, 4 three-letter words, and 2 four-letter words. Her score for this turn would be 27.

# words created		***# letters/word***		
1	×	1	=	1
3	×	2	=	6
4	×	3	=	12
2	×	4	=	8
				Total 27

Chapter Nine

Third Grade

What's Important for Your Child This Year

We discussed the importance of developing fluency in the last chapter. Fluency is something that continues to develop over this year, and many more years beyond second and third grades. In third grade the emphasis is on developing comprehension skills. Children need to be working on comprehension throughout the learning-to-read years, but your child is uniquely positioned to concentrate on this critical skill during third grade. He has mastered basic decoding and can read fairly fluently. Word study takes less effort because he's learned strategies that work efficiently. Now he is learning about words with several syllables.

To develop good comprehension skills, your child should be questioning while he is reading. He needs to be thinking about what he just read, and what's coming next. Did it make sense? What did the author mean by that word? Why did the author use that word? What's going to happen next? Why did this character say that? How is that character ever going to get out of this situation? Does he realize the implication of what he just did? Why did the author write a scene that way?

Your child needs to be able to summarize and retell in his own words what happened in the story. Now is the time for him to realize that bringing his own experiences to the text will help him interpret what the author means beyond the exact literal words on the page.

Some good comprehension skills to develop at this stage are to sequence, summarize, and articulate the main idea. After reading a story, a child needs to be able to recall what the events were in order. He also needs to know the main idea of the story, or even of a given paragraph. He needs to know how to summarize what occurred in either the entire story or a paragraph. In learning to summarize, it is critical that your child learn to use his own words, not go back and repeat the text as written. Later he will be asked to go beyond just being able to summarize and tell the main idea; he will have to compare and contrast, evaluate and make judgments, and draw conclusions.

Your child will need these excellent comprehension skills for the stage in reading beyond this one. He will be using these comprehension skills to read strategically—that is, to know when to skim and when to study thoroughly, and which words are the most important for understanding the meaning. He will also learn how to read strategically in another sense. Your child will learn when it is important to stop and figure out the meaning of a word he doesn't know, and what clues about its meaning lie within the surrounding text.

What Approaches Should I Expect the Classroom Teacher to Use to Teach Comprehension?

Comprehension skills can be developed deliberately. There are a number of approaches your child's teacher might use to teach comprehension skills. We will discuss three of the most popular. It is helpful for you to know what these approaches are, not only to monitor whether your child's teacher is teaching them, but also to understand how you can help develop your child's skills while reading together.

The first of these comprehension techniques is called Directed Reading-Thinking Activity, also known as the DR-TA[1] approach. The purpose of this approach is to teach children how to make predictions throughout their reading. The teacher stops at several points throughout the text and asks the child to predict what will happen next. After reading some portion of the text, she stops and asks questions such as this:

- What will ______ do about ___________?
- What makes you think so?
- What clues has the author given you to predict that?
- What did the author say that supports (or refutes) that?
- Can you show me where in the text it gives you a clue?
- Why do you think the author said that?

Then reading proceeds to another point and stops again for more predictions. Often the children are asked to write about their predictions.

A second comprehension technique that teachers often use in the classroom is called the K-W-L approach.[2] This is used before reading to help the student activate prior knowledge about a topic and to establish a purpose or goal for reading the text. It is usually initiated by the teacher drawing three columns on the blackboard and labeling them as follows:

- K—What I Know
- W—What I Want to Know
- L—What I Learned

An example is given on page 258. This is an example of how the K-W-L approach might be used before reading a story about an emperor penguin. The first two columns would be completed as a class before reading the book. The third column would be filled in with the class after reading the book.

Example of the K-W-L Approach for a Book on an Emperor Penguin

K *What I Know*	*W* *What I Want to Know*	*L* *What I Learned*
• Emperor penguins are bigger than most penguins. • They have a nice tuxedo. • They live at the South Pole. • They have bright orange and yellow around their faces. • They can live in the water.	• How big are they? • Do they only live at the South Pole? • How long do they hold their breath underwater? • What do they eat? • Do they live in groups?	• They eat fish. • The males are responsible for taking care of the egg. • They can toboggan on their stomachs. • They have nurseries where all the babies go. • They have their babies during the winter months. • They migrate on ice rafts.

Although at home you would not need to formally fill out columns, you can see that this technique can be applied in your reading with your child. Before reading a book, you can discuss what you already know about the topic. Then get your child to think about what his questions are. What would he like to know about this topic? Then you can reflect together on what you each learned that you didn't know before reading the book. Try it some time. It's fun.

The third approach is called visual imagery. This approach is used to help children use their imaginations to construct a visual representation of what they are reading. You can do this with your child by stopping after reading a descriptive passage. Ask your child to close his eyes and tell you what the character is wearing, what color his clothes are, what the expression on his face is like, where he is standing, what is behind him, and so on. It is fun to stop and get out the crayons and each draw what we imagine. After comparing drawings it's great to go back and reread the passage and see what details you each missed. Visual imagery is extremely helpful in capturing your child's attention and bringing more focus to his listening. He needs to develop these visual images to better remember what he's reading. It's one more way to help increase his comprehension, whether he is listening or reading himself.

Activities You Can Do with Your Child

We talked earlier in this chapter about how important it is that the child ask questions while reading. Questioning word meanings is one of those skills. This is why we have included an activity to focus your child's attention on the alternative meanings of two words that sound alike (see Activity 9.4, p. 264). Another important word study skill is to analyze words for their roots, prefixes, and suffixes. Expert readers are able to pick these out quickly while studying an unknown word. Activities 9.1 and 9.2 will help develop your child's skill at observing the root word and the prefixes and suffixes surrounding it.

Recommended Reading

Are There Any Books You Can Recommend for This Stage?

In the third grade, your child may enjoy some of the series of books, such as *The Black Stallion* or *Boxcar Children* series. Many third-graders get so interested in one writer's work that they stick with that one author until they exhaust every title. Don't worry if this happens. They will read something else eventually. Many parents express this concern about the *Goosebumps* series. If your child really loves one author, encourage your child to write a letter to the author and send it to the publisher along with a self-addressed, stamped envelope. Sometimes your child will receive a response.

In Appendix 3 you will find a list of our suggested books for the third grade.

Activity 9.1—Prefix and Suffix Card Game

This is a very simple game to help you draw your child's attention to prefixes and suffixes. This should help him more readily see them in words he reads. The research shows that good readers can quickly see prefixes, suffixes, and root words as chunks of letters.

What You Need

- Word cards—you can make these with index cards using the list on page 262.
- Paper and pencil to record words

What You Do

- Separate the words into three decks—one for prefixes, one for root words, and one for suffixes.
- Ask your child to pick two cards from the prefix column and two from the suffix column.
- Lay them down on the table with the prefixes on the left, a blank column in the middle, and the suffixes on the right.
- He next picks five cards from the root word pile.
- Ask your child to create as many words as possible with these nine cards and record them on the paper (they have to be real words).
- Tally his score for each combination of five cards. Words with either a suffix or prefix get two points, and words with both receive a bonus score of five points each.
- Continue by choosing five root words for each combination. Then choose new prefix and suffix cards and begin again.

Activity 9.2—Word Tree[3]

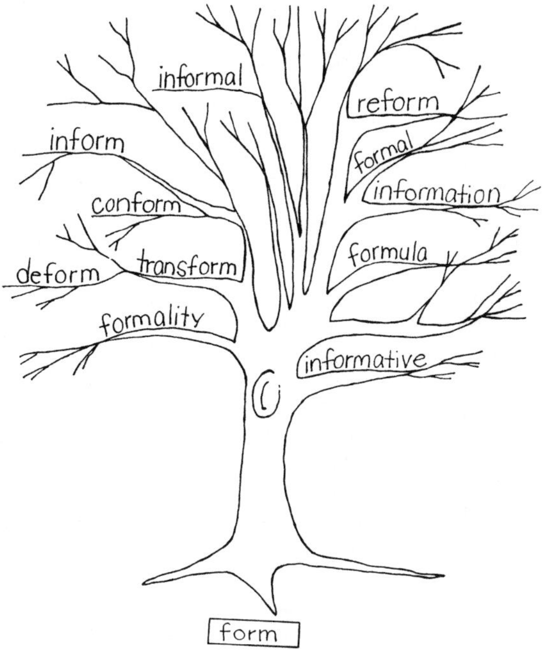

In this activity you and your child write the root word at the bottom of a tree and then write as many different forms of the word on the branches as you can recall (see the sample list on p. 262 for ideas). This is a great activity for looking at how the root word is part of so many different words.

What You Need

- A sheet with a tree—you can draw this once and then make copies
- Root word cards
- A pencil to record words on the word tree

What You Do

- Select a root word card.
- Write the root word in the box under the tree.
- Think of as many forms of the root word as possible and write them on the branches.

Variation:

You can draw the root word on a piece of paper and then laminate it. Use a grease pencil to write in the other words.

Sample List of Words for Activities 9.1 and 9.2[4]

Prefix	*Suffix*	*Root Word*	*Words for Activity 9.1*	*Additional Words for Activity 9.2*
re-	-s	port	portable, porter,	import, export,
in-	-ed		deport, report, portal	transport, support,
a-	-ing			important,
con-	-er			importantly,
de-	-y			unimportant
dis-	-ly	form	reform, deform,	transform, formula,
com-	-tion		inform, information,	formality,
un-	-ful		conform, formal,	informative
ex-	-ness		informal	
en-	-est	tract	contract, retract,	tractor, attract,
be-	-ment		detract, distract,	abstract,
pre-	-ic		extract, subtract,	protractor
per-	-ous		tractable, intractable,	
pro-	-able		traction, protract	
e-	-al	like	likes, liked, likable,	
sub-	-ive		likeness, liking, alike,	
over-	-ish		dislike	

Activity 9.3—Apple and Bushel Game[5]

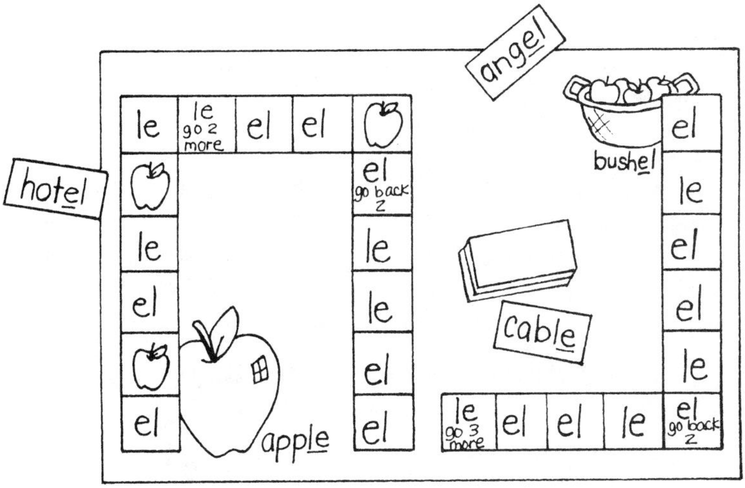

This game is an example of an activity you can create to focus your child's attention on spelling patterns.

What You Need

- Apple and Bushel game board—you can make this by taking a piece of firm paper (such as a file folder opened) and drawing the boxes and writing the word endings.
- Word cards (you can make two sets—one with the *-el* and *-le* word endings left off the words, and the other with the complete words; see the list of sample words on p. 264)
- Game markers

What You Do

- Decide the order in which players will take turns.
- Ask your child to draw a card and read the word out loud.
- Player moves his marker to the nearest *-le* or *-el* ending that correctly completes his word.
- The game continues until one player reaches the bushel at the end of the game course. To get into the bushel, he has to draw an *-el* word. For each *-le* word he draws, he must move backward to the closest *-le* square and try again on the next turn.

Sample Words with *-le* and *-el* Endings				
-le			*-el*	
apple	little	rattle	angel	model
settle	meddle	cattle	gravel	travel
nibble	pebble	maple	camel	motel
cable	table	fable	level	hotel
handle	gentle	candle	excel	pretzel
curdle	turtle	peddle	bushel	damsel
angle			compel	

Activity 9.4—Homophone Book[6]

Homophones are two words that sound the same, but are spelled differently and have different meanings. This is an activity in which you glue pictures or draw sketches in a spiral notebook to illustrate the different meanings of homophones.

What You Need

- A spiral notebook, or small three-ring notebook
- Glue, pencil, crayons, or markers

What You Do

- Using the list of homophones on the next page, select some word pairs.
- Cut out pictures from magazines and glue or tape two pictures on each page to communicate the meaning of each word in the homophone pair.

List of Homophones[7]

ant, aunt
ate, eight
bale, bail
bare, bear
base, bass
bell, belle
break, brake
cell, sell
cent, scent
creek, creak
deer, dear
died, dyed
due, do, dew
fair, fare
fir, fur
flair, flare
flee, flea
flour, flower
gate, gait
hair, hare
haul, hall
heard, herd
led, lead
main, mane
male, mail
maze, maize
meet, meat
mist, missed
need, knead
pale, pail
past, passed
peak, peek
pear, pair
piece, peace
plane, plain
pole, poll
poor, pour
rain, reign
rap, wrap
red, read
rough, ruff
sail, sale
sea, see
shoe, shoo
son, sun
sore, soar
sow, sew
stair, stare
stake, steak
strait, straight
sweet, suite
symbol, cymbal
tale, tail
threw, through
wait, weight
waist, waste
week, weak

Part Three

What to Do When Reading Is Difficult for Your Child

Chapter Ten

Reading Difficulties and Disabilities

> The psychological, social, and economic consequences of reading failure are legion. It is for this reason that the NICHD considers reading failure to reflect not only an educational problem, but a significant public health problem as well. . . . Mr. Chairman, some children learn to read and write with ease . . . unfortunately, it appears that for about half of our nation's children, learning to read is a much more formidable challenge, and for at least 20 to 30 percent of those youngsters, reading is one of the most difficult tasks that they will have to master throughout their life. As you know, this is very unfortunate because if you do not learn to read and you live in America, you are not likely to make it in life.[1]
>
> *Dr. G. Reid Lyon Testimony to a committee of the U.S. House of Representatives, July 10, 1997*

Definitions of Learning Disabilities and Dyslexia

What Is a Learning Disability?

A learning disability, informally defined, is an unexpected and unusual difficulty learning an academic skill. From the child's perspective, it's as if something is standing in the way of learning with the same ease as other children. The term "learning disability" is a relatively new one. Its formal definition has changed several times since it was first mentioned in state and federal laws in the early 1970s, and it continues to evolve. The term was suggested by Dr.

Samuel Kirk, "to describe individuals of at least average intelligence who seem capable of school success, but who have unexplained difficulty in acquiring basic academic skills."[2] The definition approved by the National Joint Committee on Learning Disabilities, an interagency group, has been refined periodically to accommodate the results of research. The legal definitions used to determine if children have handicapping conditions and qualify for special education services differ quite widely from one state to another. It is generally agreed, however, that most individuals with a learning disability experience difficulty in ways that stand out in relation to their other abilities, and in relation to what non-disabled children experience. For example, an individual who has difficulty learning to read may learn math as easily as his peers. An individual with a learning disability usually needs expert instruction, and she almost always has to expend more effort than other children do in that particular domain of learning.

Learning disabilities exist in individuals at all levels of intellectual ability—slow, average, bright, and brilliant. Highly gifted people with learning disabilities often suffer damage to self-esteem because of the extreme asymmetry they experience between learning ease in one domain and learning difficulty in another. Although most people with learning disabilities are able to learn with expert instruction and dedicated work, some individuals become emotionally overwhelmed and give up before they are able to successfully learn how to read, write, or spell well.

Many different terms are used to describe these conditions. Some of the terms that occur most frequently include:

- developmental learning disorder
- neuropsychological dysfunction
- perceptual handicap
- specific language disability

The terms "learning difference," "different learning style," or "learning difficulty" refer to conditions that are less extreme or debilitating than a learning disability, and are found in individuals who are generally in the "normal" range of individual variation. In other words, differences in learning ability are very common. The question is, how different must someone be in order to justify using the term "learning disability"? How debilitating must a problem be before we call it a "handicapping condition"? Sometimes these issues are contentious, and they are often at the heart of legal debates about children's rights.

For this book we have chosen to use the term *learning disabilities* because we believe that these are intrinsic conditions that can affect an individual's life just as profoundly as many kinds of physical disabilities. We assume that more children have genuine learning disabilities than those who are actually categorized by special education services in the schools. Using a euphemism does not serve the needs of many people affected by these very real disorders.

There are many kinds of learning disabilities, and several ways of classifying and describing them. There is no widely accepted system consistent across disciplines or across federal and state laws. Neuropsychologists, educators, psychologists, and researchers in reading tend to use different systems for labeling and describing learning difficulties. The categories used by psychologists and educators in the field are not always in agreement with the categories in our laws. For example, in New Jersey, there is no such thing as dyslexia, and to qualify for special services, the individual has to be labeled "perceptually handicapped." In Texas, there is a category for the diagnosis of dyslexia in the public school system, but the category and the regulations governing it are separate from those in special education. One can be "learning disabled" in Vermont, but not in New York, because of differences in the eligibility criteria for access to special services. Nevertheless, in the research literature on learning disabilities, commonly recognized subtypes include:

- disorders of spoken language (language comprehension and language production)
- reading (decoding and comprehension)

- written language (composition, spelling, and handwriting)
- math calculation and problem solving
- nonverbal abilities (sense of time, space, motion, and pattern)

Disorders of attention (with or without hyperactivity) are classified separately. Sometimes an individual can be affected by several learning disabilities. Difficulty in learning to read is the most common issue for more than 80% of people with learning disabilities.[3] Difficulty with reading and related language skills is often referred to as "dyslexia."

What Is Dyslexia?

As stated in a brochure published by the International Dyslexia Association entitled, *Basic Facts About Dyslexia: What Everyone Ought to Know,* the response to the question "What is dyslexia?" is as follows:

> Dyslexia is difficulty with language. For people with dyslexia, intelligence is not the problem. The problem is language. They may have difficulty with reading, spelling, understanding language they hear, or expressing themselves clearly in speaking or in writing. An unexpected gap exists between their potential for learning and their school achievement.[4]

If we surveyed people on the street to see what they know about dyslexia, most people would describe it as that condition where people reverse letters, such as *b* and *d.* This superficial understanding of dyslexia is very common but not grounded in science. Reversals are not the hallmark of dyslexia. Sylvia O. Richardson, M.D., author of another brochure published by the International Dyslexia Association entitled, *Doctors Ask Questions About Dyslexia: A Review of Medical Research,* addresses the letter reversal issue:

> Five- and six-year-old dyslexics may reverse letters or numbers, but this is also true of non-dyslexic children. The difference is that non-dyslexic children begin to correct their errors, while the dyslexics are delayed in establishing directionality. However, *reversal is not the major criterion in identification of dyslexia.* The major defining characteristic of dyslexia is specific deficit in the processing of phonological information. In other words, the dyslexic has particular difficulty in breaking the symbol-sound code of the language—in understanding the alphabetic principle.[5]

Sally Shaywitz, codirector of the Yale Center for the Study of Learning and Attention and professor of pediatrics at the Yale University School of Medicine, defines dyslexia as "an unexpected difficulty learning to read despite intelligence, motivation, and education."[6] Dyslexics have trouble recognizing, manipulating, and learning the speech sounds (phonemes) that correspond to the letters in our writing—a skill called phonological processing. As a consequence, they have trouble learning to sound out words. It is this core difficulty that makes learning to read a challenging process. Making rapid and accurate associations between speech sounds and letters, both for reading and spelling, is the core difficulty for most dyslexic people. They need more explicit and systematic training to master these associations. It's not that they *can't* learn the code, it's that they will learn it through special techniques, slowly, and with a great deal of practice. Later in life, they usually have trouble with spelling and may not enjoy reading because it is slow and requires effort.

Dyslexia is a broad category; individuals with dyslexia may have difficulty with a variety of related language tasks. The core problem in the beginning stages is with reading and spelling. However, dyslexic people may also have trouble speaking clearly, pronouncing long or new words, or learning a foreign language. They may also be affected by problems in other areas, such as telling left from right, paying attention, or coordinating their fingers for typing or writing. Some of the symptoms are shown on page 274.

COMMON SYMPTOMS OF DYSLEXIA

- difficulty learning the sounds that go with letters
- belabored reading of words in isolation or in context
- difficulty recalling words or names that are known (word retrieval problems)
- pronouncing sounds or syllables incorrectly ("basghetti" for spaghetti, or "aminal" for animal)
- difficulty spelling and/or forming letters
- trouble memorizing math facts and calendar concepts
- difficulty managing sentence structure, word choice, and organization in writing
- difficulty organizing in space and time

The term "developmental dyslexia" is used to differentiate a condition that was not acquired through a brain injury (acquired dyslexia). In most cases, dyslexia is developmental; there is no known cause other than differences in the way the brain developed prior to birth and shortly after birth. Most of the time, science suggests, those differences in brain development were influenced by the genetic code or conditions over which a mother has no control.

Do All People Who Have Trouble Learning to Read Have Dyslexia?

The simplest answer to this question is no. Imagine analyzing a classroom of children based on their ease in learning to read. We could plot a distribution of reading ability on a chart that would extend from extreme difficulty on the left, to the larger group of average children clustering in the middle, to the few on the right who learned to read easily before they even came to school. This curve would most likely be shaped like a bell curve, similar to the distribution of people's height, weight, or ability to run. Where we draw the line on our continuum to delineate how many children would be called dyslexic is a point of disagreement and debate. Is it just the 5 to 6 percent who are identified for special education services? Would the entire 20 percent who experience significant difficulty learning to read be considered dyslexic? Should the line extend up to the 40th percentile, a point at which people still do not read with ease or pleasure? Probably not. But we believe the term is appropriate for somewhere between 5 and 20 percent of the population, with varying levels of severity. Parents should know, however, that scientists are not yet in agreement about a specific point on the curve at which we should draw the line between "dyslexic" and "non-dyslexic."

Scientists are also still working on discovering and understanding other kinds of reading problems that are not like the typical person we describe here. For example, some people just seem to be very slow at reading, but can easily sound out words. Are they dyslexic? Some people claim to fall asleep the minute they look at print. Are they dyslexic? Some children seem to read words without much understanding. Are they dyslexic? And some complain about having to read from left to right, preferring to read from right to left. What is going on with them? There is much yet to discover about reading differences.

How Many Children Experience Reading Difficulties?

Historically, dyslexia was a term that was reserved only for those who had an *extremely* difficult time learning to read. Psychologists who completed diagnostic evaluations of children almost never used the "d" word (dyslexia) in the diagnosis section of their report. They believed that parents would be devastated by this label, so they selected terms like "specific language disability" or "auditory processing difficulty" instead. Recent studies, however, have shown that one out of five show unexpected difficulty with reading that requires special instruction, and that those children score low on tests of speech sound awareness, individual word reading, reading fluency, and reading comprehension.

In order to determine how many children have difficulty, researchers at Yale University selected over 400 kindergarten children and followed them for their entire school career (the

Connecticut Longitudinal Study). The children were not those who were receiving services at reading clinics, but instead were entire classes who were selected well before it was clear which children would later develop difficulties learning to read. On the basis of these longitudinal studies of children before they failed at anything, researchers arrived at the conclusion that nearly 20 percent experienced difficulty learning to read—a much greater number than had been previously believed. This is far greater than the number identified by the schools for special education services. According to a recent story in *Newsweek* (October 27, 1997), entitled, "Kids Who Can't Learn," in 1996 approximately 2.6 million children, or 4.36 percent of the nation's students, were in publicly funded learning disabilities programs, at a cost of $8.12 billion.[7]

How do we account for the enormous difference between 5 and 20 percent? Is it that many more students have special needs than are actually identified? Does this mean that they need special education testing and teaching, or does it mean that something different needs to happen in our regular classrooms that would prevent reading failure from occurring in the first place?

Some critics argue that the increase in the number of students being diagnosed with learning disabilities (LD) is actually due to overly critical parents who are unwilling to accept their children's normal limitations. There have been a number of articles in the popular press recently accusing high school and college students of seeking an LD diagnosis in order to get special academic accommodations, including access to taking the SAT test on an untimed basis. In a recent article in *The New Republic* (August 25, 1997), the author writes:

> In prosperous, sun-dappled school districts around the country, exotic new learning disabilities are popping up, each requiring its own costly cure. In Orange County, where "executive function disorder" (difficulty initiating, organizing, and planning behavior) reigns, parents have begun demanding that schools foot the bill for horseback riding lessons.[8]

While there may be a few cases of abuse of the laws that were designed to provide necessary supports for students with learning disabilities, most parents have reasonable concerns about their children's well-being when they ask for testing or services. Public hostility to the plight of students with learning disabilities represents ignorance about the biological, behavioral, and genetic evidence for their existence, as well as the very real educational challenges these children experience.

Faced with conflicting and unreliable data on the prevalence and nature of learning disorders and the appropriate means for treating them, Congress mandated in 1985 an increase in funding for research. At the time of this mandate in 1985, the term "learning disability" had been in use for nearly 20 years and a federal law had been in place since 1975 that protected the rights of such students.

Congress's Rationale for Funding Research to Study Reading Difficulties

Concern	*Description*
reading difficulties are unexpected	they occur in children who have the mental ability, motivation, and frequently the support of parents and teachers to be able to learn to read
the difficulty is persistent	it stays with the child unless there is informed early identification and appropriate intervention takes place
this disability has a debilitating impact	the child's ability to learn and function in school and in the workplace is affected

Congress was particularly interested in learning answers to these questions:

- How many children are affected?
- What are the causes of reading difficulties?
- Which treatment methods are most effective?

Reading disorders were explored in depth before other types of learning disorders were, because reading problems are so common. A well-designed and adequately funded program of research was initiated and carried out at a number of sites. This program is ongoing and should continue for at least another decade. To date researchers have published the following findings about reading acquisition and reading disabilities:[9]

- The ability to read and comprehend depends upon rapid and automatic recognition and decoding of single words. Slow and inaccurate word decoding are the best predictors of reading difficulty.
- Longitudinal studies confirm that 10 million, or 17.6 percent, of children are affected.
- Girls are nearly just as likely to have reading difficulties as boys, but are not recognized as often.
- The deficit is persistent, enduring, and not a developmental lag—74 percent of children who are reading disabled in the third grade are still disabled in the 10th grade.
- Over 200 studies converge on phonological awareness as the key weakness in children with reading disabilities.

These children are slow, labored, word-by-word readers. They are poor at decoding but may have a variety of other strengths, which may include:

- wonderful oral vocabulary
- robust critical thinking, excellent problem solving, and vast general knowledge
- good comprehension if listening to stories read aloud
- sound conceptual formulation and reasoning capabilities

Despite these other strengths, when it comes to the printed word, they get bogged down. Their strengths do not necessarily help

Major Conclusions of Research Studies

Number of Children Affected	• ten million children, or 17.6 percent, have reading difficulties
Who Is Affected	• girls are just as likely to have reading difficulties as boys, but are not recognized as often • reading difficulties are not dependent on intelligence, socio-economic status, or parent's education
Duration of Difficulty	• reading difficulties are enduring and persistent • difficulties are not developmental lags
Causes	• word recognition difficulties are the most reliable indicators of reading disability • inability to read words quickly and accurately precludes reading fluency and comprehension • inability to easily read words is caused by phonological deficits—child can't break words down into the phonemes, or speech sounds • there may be some genetic basis
Identification	• early identification is critical because the earlier the intervention, the easier it is to remediate • inexpensive screening measures identify "at-risk" children in mid-kindergarten with 85 percent accuracy
Treatment	• effective intervention depends upon the proper instructional approach at an appropriate level of intensity and duration • most effective strategies for teaching these children to read have explicit and systematic instruction in knowledge of the letters, awareness of speech sounds, and letter-sound correspondences (phonics) with supported practice in reading and writing

them through the special task of learning to read the printed word.

In the Connecticut Longitudinal Study and at other sites, researchers also found that if intervention is not provided before the age of eight, the probability of reading difficulties continuing into high school is 75 percent. It could be that neurological difficulties make it difficult for children of this age to catch up. Or it could be that children by this time have experienced several years of failure and won't respond well to intervention. Or, as some recent studies suggest, the kind of intensive instruction children need is hard to obtain in public school after third grade.

List of Early Warning Signs

What Are the "Red Flag" Warning Signs of a Reading Difficulty?

It is difficult to provide parents with a precise list of the surefire signs of a learning disability because each individual will have some of these, but not all. If your child has several of the warning signs listed on page 281, you may want to research further.

In the publication by the International Dyslexia Association entitled, *Basic Facts About Dyslexia: What Everyone Ought to Know,*[10] the following list of warning signs is provided:

SOME EARLY SIGNS OF
A LEARNING DISABILITY

- difficulty learning to talk
- difficulty listening and following directions
- difficulty remembering
- difficulty pronouncing words correctly or expressing ideas clearly

---

Most of the time it is the parent—rather than the school—who first recognizes a potential problem. We interviewed parents of

Early Warning Signs of a Learning Disability

From the Coordinated Campaign for Learning Disabilities[11]

Preschool

- late talking, compared to other children
- pronunciation problems
- slow vocabulary growth, often unable to find the right word
- difficulty learning numbers, the alphabet, days of the week
- extremely restless and easily distracted
- trouble interacting with peers
- poor ability to follow directions or routines

Kindergarten–Fourth Grade

- slow to learn the connection between letters and sounds
- confuses basic words (*run, eat, want*)
- makes multiple reading and spelling errors including letter reversal (*b/d*), inversions (*m/w*), transpositions (*felt/left*), and substitutions (*house/home*)
- transposes number sequences and confuses arithmetic signs (+, −, ×, /, =)
- slow recall of facts
- slow to learn new skills, relies heavily on memorization
- impulsiveness, lack of planning
- unstable pencil grip
- trouble learning about time
- poor coordination, unaware of physical surroundings, prone to accidents

children who have learning disabilities to study what they first observed that set off the warning signal for them. One parent whose daughter has a learning disability describes what she saw first. She knew her daughter couldn't recognize symbols when her child was three years old. This mother would show her an *A* and say "This is an A." Then she'd take it away. Fifteen seconds later she would put the block out again and ask, "What is this?" Her daughter would say, "I don't know," or "It's a 3." She couldn't retain it. Yet the girl knew every character on every TV show she watched. She was obviously bright. Her issue was strictly related to symbols. Now this child is entering kindergarten and she only knows about 2 out of 26 letters of the alphabet. The mother says, "It's not like we haven't tried."

Another mother said she knew something wasn't right when her daughter was four years old. Her daughter would be trying to ask for something in the file cabinet but she couldn't remember the word for it. She would say, "You know—the box where you put all the papers in it." It was like a guessing game. She just couldn't remember the words for things, a disability known as a word retrieval problem.

Another mother, whose son has reading difficulties and attention problems, described how she talked and talked to the pediatrician about her son's speech problems. The pediatrician would only ask him questions and listen to a few responses. Then he would always say, "Let's wait. I think he's in the normal range." She said that when he started at Montessori preschool at age two years and nine months, he wasn't speaking at the level of the other kids. His speech improved when he was around other children, but he was still way behind where he should be. It was the preschool teacher in her son's Montessori school who finally suggested that she might want to have her child tested.

This mother expressed frustration that her son's pediatrician had been little help, not only about the speech problems, but that he had also disregarded her worries about her son's hearing. She repeatedly had mentioned to the pediatrician that he might be having a hard time hearing. After an in-office hearing test, the

---

OTHER SIGNS ONCE A CHILD STARTS FIRST OR SECOND GRADE

- difficulty learning the alphabet
- difficulty sequencing letters or numbers
- difficulty rhyming
- difficulty with sequence and memory for words
- difficulty learning to read, write, and spell

---

pediatrician told her not to worry. They later discovered that the child did have hearing problems, possibly related to repeated ear infections when he was young. After having tubes put in his ears, things improved. Her frustration is that she had been in the pediatrician's office every six months saying that she really didn't think her son could hear. This mother wishes she had trusted her instincts and taken her son for a more extensive audiology exam earlier. She also said that, after she began reading books on learning disabilities, they all said that a child who begins talking and then abruptly stops for a while is a red flag. Her son did that. But of course she wasn't reading books on learning disabilities back then because she didn't know he had one. This mother remarked, "It almost seems as if a lot more information about warning signs should be in those books we all read about the first years of life."

Another mother of a 10-year-old girl with learning disabilities said that when her daughter was three or four years old she avoided the drawing table at preschool. This mother said that when she observed this class of 20 preschoolers, it seemed like the most natural thing for children to want to learn about the alphabet. Not so for her daughter. It was the least natural thing for her child, who preferred gross motor activities. Her daughter was the one who didn't want to stop her other activities to join the circle for story time. She also observed that her daughter didn't like to be read to

---

ADDITIONAL CHARACTERISTICS THAT MAY ACCOMPANY DYSLEXIA

- poor ability to finish work on time
- poor pencil grip and messy handwriting
- poor attention and poor ability to stick with a task
- poor sense of time or space
- poor concept of before and after, right and left
- poor organization and inability to keep track of possessions
- difficulties with arithmetic and mathematics
- poor study habits and inability to complete homework
- may be literal, concrete, or inflexible

---

at home. She didn't want to go to the library and pick out books. This mother describes reading to her daughter as a most frustrating experience. She believed that she was doing the right thing by reading to her child, but it was almost as if this language stimulation was too much for her child.

Another mother whose son had trouble learning to read commented that she noticed that her preschool son hated it when she read rhyming stories to him. She said that while reading a nursery rhyme, she would leave off the last word to see if he could fill it in. He couldn't. While he was in a Montessori preschool, he always gravitated toward the maps and math activities and never chose anything to do with letters. It was also clear what his strengths were. He could build with his Legos better than the other children. Before discovering his reading problems, the first-grade teacher called this mother into the classroom one afternoon to show her what he had built in the block corner. She said that she used to teach third grade, and even her third-graders couldn't construct buildings quite like this. This boy had to be tutored in reading with a systematic multisensory phonics approach, but he is certainly exceptional in the visual-spatial area.

The main message from these parents' stories is to *trust your instincts.* If you think there may be a problem, keep asking questions and researching for more information until you are satisfied.

What Causes Dyslexia? Are Reading Problems Hereditary?

Researchers do not know the exact causes of dyslexia. However, they do know that the brain of a dyslexic individual is organized differently from the brain of a non-dyslexic individual, and they have demonstrated that in many cases the condition is hereditary. They know that it appears in families; recent research suggests particular chromosomes upon which the inherited trait is carried. Genetic research has shown the presence of dyslexia in families, especially in twin studies.[12]

Although for nearly a century scientists have understood that the brains of dyslexic individuals are different, it was the pioneering work during the 1960s and 1970s by Dr. Norman Geschwind and Dr. Albert Galaburda that drew the medical community's interest to this field. Current findings from the brain research laboratory at Harvard Medical School indicate that the anatomy and functioning of the brain appear to be different for individuals who are affected by this disability. The brains of dyslexic subjects have left hemispheres that are equal in size to that of the right. In normal brains, the left side is usually larger than the right. In most people, the left half supports language comprehension and expression more than the right. In the brains of dyslexic subjects, neurons have migrated in clusters to the outer layer of brain, where they should not be located. The neurons are believed to have escaped through a lesion in a membrane and then migrated too far to the outer cortex to form what are called "ectopias." Ectopias—clusters of cells that are out of place—form during the second trimester of gestation. Scientists hypothesize that these misplaced neurons may impede the development of neural pathways and networks necessary for reading.

In addition to being structured differently, the brain of the dyslexic may actually function differently while performing language tasks. Through functional neuro-imaging of dyslexic people, a technique by which levels of brain activity in specific regions of the brain are measured, researchers have observed unexpectedly low levels of activity in those areas responsible for reading. In other words, the dyslexic person may be hampered by underactive circuits in the language centers. Experiments are now under way to determine if intensive, appropriate instruction can change those brain activitation patterns.

What to Expect If Your Child Is Tested for Dyslexia

How Do Specialists Determine If a Child Has a Learning Disability?

Most regulations about the diagnosis of learning disabilities require measurement of a child's intelligence and achievement levels and demonstration that there is a discrepancy between intellectual ability and academic performance. Intelligence tests are supposed to measure a person's problem-solving and reasoning abilities (IQ or intelligence quotient), whereas achievement tests are supposed to measure what has been learned in school. A child receives a diagnosis of a learning disability if her IQ predicts a much higher level of achievement than she demonstrates on tests of reading, writing, or math. In addition, most states require documentation of a "processing deficit" to verify that the lack of achievement is not due to motivational issues, lack of school attendance, or poor teaching. A good assessment, however, does more.

The International Dyslexia Association distributes a booklet that provides an overview of the testing process. In this booklet, *Testing: Critical Components in the Clinical Identification of Dyslexia,* the authors explain that the diagnostic process should include a variety of assessments. See the table on pages 288–289 for an overview of the testing components. Evaluation of dyslexia, if properly done, involves a review of a person's school history, response to instruction, and day-to-day behavior. It cannot be done simply on the basis of a battery of tests. There is no "dyslexia test battery" that will answer by numbers alone whether a student is dyslexic or not. Neither is there such a test battery for Attention Deficit Disorder (ADD). Tests are tools in the hands of a knowledgeable evaluator, who must know what to look for. The examiner must have enough background in language and reading to interpret the errors and response patterns of the student.

If I Suspect Reading Difficulties, How Do I Get My Child Tested? What Can We Expect from the Testing Process?

There are two approaches to getting your child tested. One is to get the school to do the testing and the other is to have your child privately tested. There are advantages and disadvantages to each decision. Although parents have a right to have their child tested if the child is having difficulty in school, many schools have long waiting lists of referred children. When the school does the testing, they generally pull the child out of classes and test him during the school day using school personnel or consultants. These people may be more or less qualified, but it is sometimes difficult to assess their qualifications. Parents should know that licensed psychologists and school psychologists do not, as a matter of routine, have any training in language or reading disabilities and may know very little about what tests to use, what to look for, or how to interpret information. If you find a qualified expert in private practice, you may have more control over the circumstances and nature of testing. But finding a qualified person takes time, effort, and money, and even then the person may be booked for many months. The full psychoeducational testing process now costs on average between $1,000 to $1,800 in major metropolitan areas. Sometimes, if parents can show that school-based testing would be inappropriate and an outside evaluation is necessary, the school system will pay for testing by an outside expert. However, schools are not obligated to foot the bill unless they have already done their own in-house evaluation and there are still legitimate disagreements about the child's needs. This whole process can take months; meanwhile, the child is without help.

An individual who is qualified to test a child with reading difficulty must have a strong background in language, reading, writing, and psychological evaluation. Their training is usually in psychology, reading and language education, or speech/language pathology; typically a lead evaluator will hold a doctorate in her field, and frequently an interdisciplinary team will be involved. Don't hesitate to ask about credentials and whether he/she has diagnosed dyslexia in other individuals.

If you decide to privately test your child, there are some steps you can take to help you identify a good evaluator. Several recommendations follow.

Components of Testing to Assess Dyslexia[13]

Category	*Includes:*
Family and Individual History	• other family members who had difficulty learning to read, write, and spell • health or medical impairments to learning • any delays in speaking • parents' concerns about speech, language, motor skills, or attention span
Cognitive Ability, or Intellectual Aptitude (IQ)	• either a Weschsler or Stanford-Binet IQ test • test should measure individual's aptitude for learning in verbal, logical, mathematical, visual-motor, visual-spatial, symbolic, memory, and attentional domains
Specific Language Skills	• speech sound and syllable awareness • word pronunciation • word retrieval • rapid naming • knowledge of word meanings • comprehension and production of sentence structure (syntax) • expressive verbal ability, including organization of ideas, elaboration, and clarity of expression • comprehension of what is heard and read
Single-Word Decoding	• the ability to read single words out of context • apply phonic word attack to reading nonsense words • oral paragraph reading fluency and accuracy

Components of Testing to Assess Dyslexia[13]

Category	*Includes:*
Reading Comprehension	• timed readings of longer passages • evaluation of whether individual appears to use context and good reasoning skills to guess at meanings when reading silently
Spelling	• dictated spelling test (not multiple choice) • analysis of errors for speech sound omission, letter sequence confusion, and poor memory for common words
Written Composition	• composition of a story or essay for students capable of writing more than sentences • analysis of word choice, conceptual organization, sentence quality, elaboration of ideas, grammar, and use of punctuation and capitalization • informal tasks such as writing a paraphrase, combining simple sentences into compound and complex sentences, writing an outline and summary of a passage, or writing part of a structured paragraph
Handwriting	• ability to form letters, both alone and in words • analysis of writing to see if it sits consistently on the baseline • consistency and slant of letters • right- or left-handed • appropriate pencil grip • appropriate rotation of paper • visibility to review work previously written (especially for left-handed)

SOURCES OF INFORMATION ON PROFESSIONALS TO TEST YOUR CHILD

- Ask friends and acquaintances for recommendations of professionals they know.
- Ask your pediatrician for referrals.
- Call your local office of the International Dyslexia Association or the Learning Disabilities of America for a list of referrals.
- Look for LD clinics associated with hospitals or universities nearby.

Once you get a couple of names, then continue researching to see if anyone you know can tell you about personal experiences using any of these diagnosticians. Although you should certainly ask your pediatrician for a referral, don't be surprised if you don't get many answers there. Many parents relate stories of discussing concerns about learning disabilities with their pediatricians and getting nowhere. Pediatricians see children with learning problems frequently, but get very little training in medical school on learning disorders. Those who have an interest often educate themselves by working closely with other clinicians on interdisciplinary teams. Most parents experienced in LD will tell you that their best source of information is actually other parents.

When you are scheduling testing for your child, be sure to describe to the diagnostician what you observe. It is critical to be as specific as you can about what your child does easily and the areas where you are concerned. Give examples, where possible. Bring examples of the child's writing or schoolwork. Provide any feedback, or concerns, of others who have worked with your child, such as former teachers. Examples from everyday life help the psychologist assess what tests may be needed. Most of the time you will request "psychoeducational testing," which means that it will be a thorough battery of tests. On average, your child will spend three to five hours being tested, sometimes divided into several sessions. Expect to get a thorough written report somewhere in the range of 6 to 10 pages, which includes the evaluator's observations and recommendations, not just the test scores.

The evaluator should give you a thorough questionnaire to explore the child's history and developmental patterns. Intelligence testing using either the Weschsler or Stanford-Binet IQ test is a normal part of the testing routine. These tests, if used well, also provide a basis for interpreting the child's characteristics as a learner. In addition to intelligence testing, achievement tests will be administered. Beyond this the psychologist will determine which tests to include based on the identified concerns. This is why your input up front is important. The chart on pages 292–293 summarizes functional areas often assessed and some tests that are commonly used. Keep in mind, however, that new tests are issued every year, so a chart such as this becomes obsolete every two or three years.

Are There Any Laws to Provide Me Leverage in Getting the School to Test My Child or Deliver Special Services?

Yes, there are some laws that were designed to assure that all children are entitled to a free public education that is appropriate to their individual needs. It is these laws that provide some help in leveraging the school to assess your child if a problem is suspected. The critical federal laws are:

1. IDEA—Individuals with Disabilities Act, Public Law 101-476
    - Part B, ages 3 through 21
    - Part H, early intervention services, birth through age two
2. Section 504 of the Rehabilitation Act of 1973
3. The Americans with Disabilities Act (ADA) of 1990

Under some laws, the school must assess your child within 30 days of determining that assessment is needed. If you believe your child should be tested, document your request in writing. Because this

Assessment of Reading Difficulty

Area of Functioning	*Specific Skills to Test*	*Commonly Used Tests*
Reading Words	*Letter and Word Decoding* • real words in lists • nonsense words in lists • knowledge of phonic patterns • decoding new words in context *Reading Whole Words* • high-frequency sight words	Woodcock Reading Mastery Test Woodcock-Johnson Psychoeducational Battery Weschsler Individual Achievement Test The Decoding Skills Test The Kaufman Test of Educational Achievement
Pre-Reading Skills	*Phoneme Awareness* • rhyming, blending, segmenting, identifying syllables and speech sounds	Lindamood Auditory Conceptualization Test Rosner Test of Auditory Analysis Skills Torgesen-Bryant Test of Phonological Awareness (TOPA) Test of Phonological Skills (Linguisystems) Yopp-Singer Sound Blending Test
	Alphabet Knowledge	Slingerland Screening Test Emergent Literacy Survey Woodcock Reading Mastery Test
Reading Fluency and Comprehension	*Oral Reading*	Gray Oral Reading Test Informal Reading Inventory
	Silent Reading Comprehension	Woodcock Johnson Nelson-Denny Weschsler Individual Achievement Test Kaufman Test of Educational Achievement

Assessment of Reading Difficulty

Area of Functioning	*Specific Skills to Test*	*Commonly Used Tests*
Spelling	*Writing Words to Dictation*	Test of Written Spelling Wide Range Achievement Test Qualitative Inventory of Spelling Development
	Spelling Words in Writing	Analysis of written compositions
Oral Language Skills	*Listening Comprehension* • word knowledge • understanding sentence structure • passage or paragraph understanding	Test of Language Development Test of Adolescent Language Clinical Evaluation of Language Fundamentals
	Expressive Language • speed of naming • sentence production • describing summarizing	Test of Word Knowledge Rapid Automatic Naming Weschsler Individual Achievement Test
Writing	*Composing a Story or Narrative*	Test of Written Language Weschsler Individual Achievement Test
	Knowledge of Symbolic Conventions	Test of Written Language Test of Written Expression Woodcock-Johnson
Intellectual Ability	*Verbal Reasoning*	Weschsler Intelligence Scale for Children—III
	Nonverbal Reasoning	Test of Nonverbal Intelligence Woodcock-Johnson Test of Cognitive Abilities
Visual-Motor Skills	*Form Copying*	Bender Gestalt Test Visual Motor Integration Test
	Writing	Rey Complex Figure Drawing Slingerland Screening Test

area of the law is so extensive and varies to some degree by state, contact your school and local school district office. In addition to requesting information from the school system, call the Learning Disabilities of America branch office to see if they can provide any other guidance. Parents can hire attorneys or legal advocates to assist them in their efforts to seek services for their child.

For further information, obtain a copy of a brochure entitled, "Legal Rights," which is part of an information kit on learning disabilities distributed by the Coordinated Campaign for Learning Disabilities. Contact your public library for a copy. According to this brochure, parents have the right to have their child tested in all areas related to the suspected disability. This assessment is to be made by a multidisciplinary team charged with the responsibility to assess your child and determine his eligibility for special education services. You have the right to attend the eligibility committee meeting.

If My Child Is Tested, Will I Get a Definite Diagnosis?

Testing is absolutely the first step before proceeding with any other steps. It is the only way to identify what the child's strengths and weaknesses are and to quantify how far below her potential the child is working. Testing should provide information about whether the child has strengths or weaknesses in language functioning or visual-spatial, nonverbal functioning. Observations made by the evaluator are as valuable as the scores themselves. Problems with pacing, strategy use, paying attention, or expressing ideas can be noted in this way.

Although testing is a critical first step in planning how to help your child, we also caution parents to be realistic about how helpful the exercise might be. Parents can feel very frustrated if, at the end of psychoeducational testing, they still do not have definitive answers to many of their questions. Imagine paying $1,800 or more, putting your child through a couple of testing sessions, and still not knowing if your child has a learning disability! Although parents almost always feel as if they learned some valuable things, many are disappointed that testing can yield ambiguous results or fail to provide clear solutions. With our current state of knowledge, diagnosis is complex, imprecise, and sometimes unreliable. There are no medical tests like blood or urine tests that give you the definitive "yes" or "no" you are seeking. Learning disabilities are not diseases; they are more akin to a condition like obesity. Where do we draw the line? Aren't there a number of concerns that would determine whether we would call someone "obese"? One criterion may not apply to everyone.

Parents seeking a black-and-white set of answers could be disappointed in testing even if they find a qualified examiner. One parent told us that when her child was tested, the psychiatrist ended his review session by asking the parents whether they needed an LD diagnosis to seek services from school. He explained that their child did have a significant discrepancy between IQ and achievement, so according to state definitions he could say the child was learning disabled in his report. However, the psychiatrist continued by saying that whether the child is called "LD" or not is irrelevant. Of course, these parents believed that the determination of whether their child has a learning disability would hardly be considered "irrelevant."

Another parent of three girls, two of whom have learning disabilities, expressed her frustration about trying to get an early diagnosis. When her second child wasn't learning things that her first child had mastered easily, she began to suspect problems. So in the spring of her kindergarten year the mother took her daughter to an extremely reputable LD center affiliated with a nearby hospital for testing. After spending $1,700 for testing, she still did not have a diagnosis. She was told of a possibility that her daughter had a problem, but that she should bring her back in a year to be retested. They said that she was a little behind and might benefit from some tutoring. The mother took her back one year later (in April of first grade) and she was told that her daughter definitely did have some LD problems. They also said that she probably needed a different tutor. However, the clinic did not help the mother find either the original tutor or a replacement. When the third daughter exhibited some warning signs as a preschooler, this mother was sure that daughter number three was

LD, but decided to take a different approach to testing. She took this child to her second daughter's tutor for some informal screening. This highly competent tutor did a quick evaluation and gave her some concrete recommendations for less than $100 ($1,600 less than the cost of full testing). The mother is reluctant to have the third child evaluated, doubting the tests would be useful.

Another parent of a six-year-old boy who attends a private school for students with learning disabilities in the Chicago area, expressed her frustration with the way the diagnostician delivered his report. Prior to enrolling her child, the mother had him tested for delayed speech and language. She and her husband walked out of the testing meeting with a psychologist at a major university clinic in a state of shock: the psychologist told them that their son had learning disabilities and that it was questionable whether he would make it through high school. The psychologist had little else hopeful or useful to offer the family. Nevertheless, now the mother has been reassured by her son's progress in his school program and she is more optimistic about his future.

These three stories demonstrate several things:

- testing involves both clinical science and professional judgment
- choosing a good evaluator involves asking specific questions about qualifications of the person to evaluate dyslexia
- you can ask the evaluator in advance if he/she will be able to refer you to tutors in your area if tutoring is recommended
- although sometimes you will receive a specific diagnosis, you may get information about your child's strengths and weaknesses without a definitive diagnosis
- a good evaluator will stress your child's strengths and weaknesses
- ask who actually does the testing—graduate students or the expert
- ask if the evaluator provides counseling to parents after testing

There are other uses for testing besides seeking a diagnosis. A parent whose child receives special education services at school uses testing as a way of getting concrete information. If a teacher tells her how much they believe the child has improved throughout the year and the mother doesn't see the progress, she can have her child retested on the achievement tests outside of school. This strategy provides independent evidence of how much improvement has really occurred.

If My Child Has a Learning Disability Does It Mean She Will Never Be Successful in School or Work?

Probably one of the most overwhelming emotions felt by parents upon learning that their child has a learning disability is the fear that their child will never be successful in school. For parents who were successful in school and believe that education is the key to future opportunities in life, the prospect of school failure in their child is terrifying. Many of these parents have spent hours reading to their child, providing her with enriching experiences and educating her at home. Parents who have made this kind of an investment wonder what good it will do.

Most children with learning disabilities can manage to cope with school and are able to achieve their potential. Many find ways of coping with their problems. Although it may take longer, students with learning disabilities eventually find their niche, just as other students do. To be successful, however, children may need special accommodations, expert teaching, and a lot of hard work. Most students need extra tutoring in reading with a multisensory structured language approach. Others need more extensive accommodations at school, such as books on tape, depending upon the severity and type of the learning disability.

The most important message for parents is to continue to hold high aspirations for your child's achievement, but realize that you may be involved in helping to solve problems, monitor, and advocate for this child more than another. You may have to accept that some things will always be difficult for your child. For example, a dyslexic child may learn to read with special tutoring, but spelling may continue to be difficult for years beyond when she fully catches up in reading.

How to Find a Good Reading Tutor

How Do I Find a Reading Tutor for My Child?

Finding a good tutor is one of the most important things you will do. Most parents cannot directly teach their child to read, so they must find the right person to do this. Not only must the tutor be well trained and experienced in a particular approach, but he or she must also be good at working with children—especially your child. The "chemistry" must be right. You want your child to *want* to go to the tutor.

The first step is to understand what your child needs and be sure that you know what instructional approach will be best for her. If you are lucky, at the end of testing you will get helpful advice about the teaching approach that would be most beneficial for your child. Some testing reports contain a recommendation that the child be tutored using a multisensory structured approach to teaching phonics. Sometimes the report will advise that the child be tutored using the Orton-Gillingham approach. If the recommendations section of the testing report is not specific, you will have to do your own research on the alternative approaches and determine which makes the most sense for your child.

Next, you will need to develop a list of possible tutors who know how to teach reading using a designated approach. The psychologist who tested your child may recommend some tutors. There are several national and local organizations that provide tutor referrals. The two national organizations most widely known for this are the International Dyslexia Association (IDA) and Learning Disabilities of America (LDA). Both have an extensive network of state branches. Call their national 800 numbers, ask for the telephone of their local branch for your state, and then call them to request a list of tutors in your area. Expect them to provide you with a list of at least three tutors. Most likely they will not give you referrals so you will need to do your own research. Sometimes the best source of information is to check with your friends to see if anyone knows anything about the tutors on the list. It is important to interview several tutors and establish some criteria for what type of experience and background is the minimum acceptable level to you.

Many times, at the conclusion of the diagnostic evaluation, the psychiatrist conducting the tests will give the parents the name of at least one tutor. However, this does not always happen. One parent shared with us her experience about seeking a tutor. When the psychologist met with her to discuss his conclusions after delivering a complete battery of psychoeducational tests to determine if her child had a learning disability, the psychologist recommended that her seven-year-old son be tutored in phonics. When she asked him for a referral, he gave her the name of a tutoring center in a nearby community. The mother called them to discover that they only serve high school students. When she called the psychologist back, he said he really didn't know any private tutors. Still confused about the test results, the mother then paid an educator, who tutors a friend's child, a consultation fee to determine what the next step should be. This educator advised that a few more tests were needed to further understand what kind of tutoring approach would be most effective. The educator introduced her to a professor in the special education department of a prestigious university, who completed a few additional tests. At the end of this, when the parent asked the professor for a tutor referral, he recommended that his wife would be a good tutor.

This mother asked the wife about her credentials and what approaches she used to teach reading. Luckily this parent was knowledgeable and savvy enough to be uncomfortable with this blatant conflict of interest. When this mother asked the professor's wife if she was trained in any of the multisensory phonics approaches, the wife responded that she had copied notes from a friend who attended a training course. When the mother again asked her what approach she used, the wife said that she used an "eclectic approach." The mother decided not to hire the professor's wife because she was not able to explain her approach. It just seemed like her son would be getting more of the same type of instruction he got in school. The professor's wife also charged the highest per-hour rate in the area.

In utter frustration, this mother enrolled in two graduate courses in reading at a local teacher training college and luckily met the president of the local branch of the IDA, who taught one of the courses. This course validated her instincts that the tutoring approach mattered. The mother discovered that her son needed a multisensory, systematic, structured, intensive phonics approach. The president of the local branch of the IDA gave her a list of six tutors in her community who were trained and experienced in the Orton-Gillingham approach. The mother interviewed these tutors and hired one who eventually taught her child to read.

A move to establish uniform training criteria for professional tutors is just getting under way. An organization called the International Multisensory Structured Language Education Council (IMSLEC) is serving as an umbrella for all approaches that value and implement valid teaching principles for teaching dyslexic students to read. The organization is committed to assuring standards of excellence in the professional preparation of Multisensory Structured Language Education specialists. Members train teachers in many approaches, including Orton-Gillingham, Lindamood-Bell, Alphabetic Phonics, Spalding, Herman, Slingerland, Wilson Language, and Jane Greene's *Language!* approach.

Before hiring a tutor, we recommend that you make sure you know what kind of instructional approach your child needs. Then interview at least three tutors. A list of key questions to ask in a telephone interview is provided.

TWELVE KEY QUESTIONS TO ASK A POTENTIAL READING TUTOR

1. Please describe your background and training (i.e., degrees, teaching experience, state certifications).
2. Do you use a systematic multisensory structured approach to teach reading? Have you completed special training in any of the multisensory structured phonics approaches? When did you complete this training?
3. How long have you been tutoring children in reading?

4. Approximately how many students have you tutored over the past five years?
5. Do you spend any of the session helping the student with homework or do you concentrate only on remediation?
6. Will I be expected to work with my child at home between sessions?
7. How do you interact with the student's school?
8. How often will you provide feedback to me regarding my child's progress, and in what format?
9. What is your hourly fee?
10. How many sessions per week do you recommend?
11. Would you give me the name and telephone number of several parents of students you are currently tutoring or have tutored?
12. Could we schedule a free consultation so that I can meet you and see your office?

How Important Is the Approach the Tutor Uses?

This is probably one of the most important things to consider, and in some ways the hardest for parents to assess. Consider the personal story of a family who has children in our neighborhood school. My son was in the same kindergarten class as a little girl whom we shall call "Alice." Alice was clearly bright and was one of the most eager and enthusiastic children in kindergarten. She was very verbally confident and volunteered answers in class readily, always having some background in every topic, which she was eager to share with her classmates. She comes from a good family, with two dedicated and caring parents. Alice began to have problems learning to read in first grade. Her mother and I would exchange stories from time to time. At the end of first grade we had our son tested and during August, just before the beginning of second grade, he started tutoring twice a week with a tutor who was very experienced in multisensory structured phonics approaches. He received intensive Orton-Gillingham tutoring twice a week throughout all of second grade. Alice received tutoring after school once a week from her current second-grade teacher.

During the fall of third grade I got a call from the mother of one of Alice's best friends. She was looking for a reading tutor. After a month in tutoring, this little girl made dramatic improvement. This mother talked to Alice's mother about the incredible breakthroughs her daughter was making with systematic phonics tutoring. Alice's mother then decided to have her daughter tutored by the same Orton-Gillingham (O-G) tutor once a week, along with an additional time each week with her second-grade teacher. After about a month, Alice finally commented to her mother one day, "Gee, Mom, Mrs. D. [the O-G tutor] could sure teach Mrs. G. [the second-grade teacher] a lot about how to teach reading!" It's amazing that this eight-year-old girl could tell the difference between tutoring that was just more of what did not help, and tutoring that exactly met her needs.

The Eight Most Common Multisensory Structured Phonics Approaches to Teaching Reading

Are All Phonics Approaches the Same?

Phonics and whole language are known by the public as two alternative approaches to teaching children to read. However, these are both general terms distinguishing whether the approach is code-based or meaning-based. If you determine that your child needs a more structured phonics-emphasis approach, there is still more to know before you can decide which approach would be best for her.

The basic multisensory structured language technique known as the Orton-Gillingham approach was developed in the 1930s and 1940s. During the 1920s a neurologist named Samuel Orton began an intensive study of the people he called "word blind," who subsequently became identified as dyslexic. He was not only interested in studying what they could and couldn't do, but also became intrigued with whether it was possible to teach these children to read. For many years he worked with Anna Gillingham, a linguist, who also was experimenting with methods to teach the most seriously dyslexic people to read. Together, and with a handful of colleagues, they developed an approach for teaching the structure of sound-symbol relationships, using all the senses to reinforce associations. Since then, the Orton-Gillingham approach has been adapted, developed, modified, and updated by a number of institutes, agencies, and private practitioners.

Clinicians who work with students who have experienced reading failure generally subscribe to one of these approaches. The approaches vary according to whether they are designed for whole groups or single individuals, and whether the students are in the early or middle grades (or beyond). Multisensory learning can be invoked with any level of language organization. Students might learn the sound-symbol relationships through drawing letters in sand trays while saying the letter sound. They might learn about paragraph structure by building a three-dimensional structure that shows the connection among ideas. They might write letters on a piece of masonite while simultaneously saying their sounds. By bringing the other senses into play, the learner can bolster a weak sense of language structure.

There are a variety of structured multisensory phonics approaches. Some of the most widely known are listed on pages 304–305. All of these programs teach language structure in a systematic and cumulative manner. Sounds, syllables, sentences, meaningful word parts, paragraphs and themes are taught and practiced in reading and writing. Constant review and repetition are part of each of these approaches.

Is the Reading Recovery Program Effective?

Reading Recovery, a different kind of tutorial approach, was developed from the work of Marie Clay for use in New Zealand

Structured Multisensory Phonic Approaches[14]

Description	*Unique Characteristics*
Alphabetic Phonics	
• considered an "organization and expansion" of the Orton-Gillingham (O-G) approach	• structured daily lessons with 11 activities • students taught how to code words using diacritical marks
Auditory Discrimination in Depth (ADD)—Lindamood-Bell	
• teaches auditory conceptualization skills basic to reading, spelling, and speech • emphasizes the ability to remember and compare phonological structures	• uses colored blocks to train children to be sensitive to different speech sounds in words and nonsense words • identifies each speech sound (phoneme) according to the position of the lips, teeth, and tongue in making the sound [i.e., lip poppers (p & b), tip tappers (t & d)]
Jane Greene's *Language!* Program	
• for middle grade and adolescent poor readers	• teaches language structure at all levels; integrated lessons on sounds, words, sentences, and text
Orton-Gillingham (O-G)	
• multisensory, structured, sequential teaching of the letter-sound correspondences	• structured, multisensory teaching of sounds, syllables, morphenes, and spelling patterns linked to reading and writing
Project Read	
• considered to be an adaptation of the O-G approach to the classroom	• uses many novel cues such as puppets and gestures

Structured Multisensory Phonic Approaches[14]

Description	*Unique Characteristics*
Slingerland	
• designed as an O-G adaptation for the classroom	• teaches handwriting • introduces blending of phonemes through placing letters in pocket charts
Spalding	
• has many similarities to Orton-Gillingham, but incorporates a stronger writing component	• emphasizes proper handwriting along with learning the letters
Wilson Reading System	
• considered to be an O-G application for adolescent and adult students	• designed for students in grades 5–12, but can be used with younger students • program sequenced in 12 steps that are based on 6 syllable types, each with codes • finger-to-thumb tapping of phonemes • offers a program for use in schools • teaches student to draw scooping underlines to divide syllables

during the mid-1970s. Reading Recovery is intended to prevent serious reading failure in first-graders. The program is implemented by trained tutors, who provide special instruction to first-grade children who are behind in reading. Instruction lasts only for first grade. Reading Recovery, which offers a complete package to school districts looking for a solution for the bottom readers, has gained in popularity and claims to have served approximately 60,000 children in North America during the 1993–1994 school year. The intervention for struggling readers is intense and one-to-one, with highly trained tutors delivering 30-minute daily sessions to the lowest 10 to 20 percent of the class, who meet entry criteria. Advocates claim a high rate of success in bringing tutored children up to the average reading level of the class within 60 lessons, or 12 weeks.

Because of the increasing popularity of the program and its high per-pupil cost, researchers have independently investigated its claims of effectiveness. To date, independent researchers have been unable to replicate or verify some of the company's claims. New Zealand researchers have shown that the lessons, which do not include systematic teaching of phonics, are more effective for children if the decoding instruction is explicit, sequential, and organized. One school system calculated that the cost of Reading Recovery was $9,211 per child tutored successfully, a cost that seems difficult to justify because the effects do not last without additional intervention.[15] Many children do not qualify for the program and many more start but drop out if they do not make sufficient progress. Those children may well be the ones with more serious dyslexia or phonological learning problems, although insufficient research has been done to identify the characteristics of students who succeed and fail. A recent critical review of Reading Recovery research quoted correspondence between legislators in California, who were members of a committee conducting an audit of the Reading Recovery program:

> We found that Reading Recovery works, but not as well as its proponents claim; that its effects largely dissipate over time; and that it costs about the equivalent of an additional year of schooling for the children who participate—even accounting for savings in other expenditures.[16]

Additional studies suggest that what goes on in the regular classroom is most important in reading success or failure. If more money were spent training, supervising, and supporting classroom reading teachers, less money might be needed for costly remedial instruction. Those children who need special instruction, moreover, usually need it for several years, not just first grade.

What About FastForward?

Another approach to treatment of language learning disorders, which parents may have read about in the popular press is called FastForward. It is an approach that uses computer-generated speech sounds to train a child to improve her ability to hear phonemes at increasingly faster speeds. This training was developed to benefit children who had one specific type of learning disability—early and severe language delay—which some studies suggest may affect as many as 8 percent of all children.[17] The designers of FastForward claim that language-impaired children may process speech too slowly and that they have a "timing" deficit underlying their delayed language learning. The theory proposes that slowing down the speech sounds on the computer allows the child to distinguish them. At the beginning of training the child hears speech sounds that are artificially slowed down; words are literally stretched out so that the sound segments are easier to perceive. The objective is to train the child to gradually increase the speed at which she can distinguish phonemes in words. The computer program is designed to incrementally speed up the presentation of speech sounds over an eight-week training at an intense level of use, about four hours per day.

When this product was first announced in January of 1995, the press touted it as a possible cure for dyslexia. However, at the time of its release, there were no controlled studies available that showed its effectiveness with dyslexic or school-aged children. At the time of the media hype, other scientists questioned the claims of its promoters, pointing out that the claims of its authors had not been independently verified.[18]

Now two years after the article announcing the approach, the software is available from a private company established by the original researchers called Scientific Learning Company. Speech and language pathologists can now enroll in courses offered across the country to learn how to use the approach and accompanying computer software with their students. Even if this approach may eventually be proven effective for helping language learning–

impaired children, we believe it is premature to recommend it as a treatment for developmental reading disabilities.

The Importance of Early Identification and Intervention

Can Reading Failure Be Prevented?

Recent, well-designed studies have shown clearly that early intervention prevents reading disabilities in all but the most severely disabled children. We know that children at risk for reading problems can be brought up to the average range or better if kindergarten and first-grade programs teach critical language and reading skills effectively. If kindergarten children are helped to discover the individual sounds in words, and if they leave kindergarten knowing their letter names and sounds, they are likely to succeed at reading. If first-grade children are taught how to decode words and given enough practice applying their decoding skills to meaningful reading and writing, they are likely to succeed. One study in Houston, Texas—which is now being repeated—examined inner-city children who traditionally score low on achievement tests. Four different classroom teaching programs were compared—direct and systematic phonics, embedded or less direct phonics, and whole language. The approach that used direct and systematic phonics, phoneme awareness, practice with decodable text, and instruction in comprehension, was clearly superior in bringing children up to grade level.

Another major project led by Dr. Joseph Torgesen of Florida State University studied how to help children in the bottom 10 percent on tests of reading aptitude in kindergarten. The study analyzed the effectiveness of alternative approaches to teaching basic reading skills. The program (Lindamood-Bell, or Auditory Discrimination in Depth) that was most helpful with students who have low phonological skill emphasizes awareness of speech sound segments and their representation in print. Major gains in reading single words and comprehending were achieved in 80 hours of tutorial intervention with first- and second-graders. In addition, major gains were achieved with third-, fourth-, and fifth-graders after 80 hours of instruction using the same approach. The older children required two hours of intensive teaching per day, however, to bring their achievement scores up to grade level. They remained slow at reading and needed much more work on reading fluently for understanding.

Children who do not read well begin to suffer the consequences in other academic learning. Over time their IQ scores may drop because they are not exposed to the vocabulary, the background information, and the complex ideas found in books. Because children who can't read aren't able to access all the information taught during the school day, they may miss out on important content. So a reading problem, allowed to go on untreated, has a cumulative debilitating effect.

In Dr. Reid Lyon's testimony before the Committee on Education and the Workforce, a committee of the U.S. House of Representatives, on July 10, 1997, he offered this summary about how critical it is to identify these children early:

> We have learned that for 85 to 90 percent of poor readers, prevention and early intervention programs that combine instruction in phoneme awareness, phonics, spelling, reading fluency, and reading comprehension strategies provided by well-trained teachers can increase reading skills to average reading levels. However, we have also learned that if we delay early intervention until nine years of age (the time that most children with reading difficulties first receive services), approximately 75 percent of these children will continue to have difficulties learning to read throughout high school and their adult years. To be clear, while older children and adults can be taught to read, the time and expense of doing so is enormous compared to what is required to teach them when they are five or six years old.[19]

What Do I Do If My Child's School Says It's Just a "Developmental Lag"?

Beware of the "developmental lag" diagnosis. Although some children do develop slowly and will benefit from extra time to grow up, "developmental lag" has been used too often to allay parents' concerns. Research done at Yale and elsewhere strongly suggests that most cases of reading failure do not spontaneously get better, and children generally do not catch up once they fall behind, unless they receive intensive assistance. Many parents of children who have experienced reading problems regret waiting too long to find help.

Most children are ready to learn letters, letter sounds, simple word recognition, and spelling by sounds (inventive spelling) by the age of five. Therefore, we strongly recommend that parents look at the benchmark chart in Chapter 7. If your child is not demonstrating the skills listed on this chart, then we advise you to begin to ask whether the skills are taught in the school program. If they are, ask whether your child is having trouble learning basic reading and language when the instruction has been adequate. Refuse to accept the "developmental lag" excuse; ask the school to teach your child what he or she needs to know.

The ease of identifying children at risk for reading problems can best be summarized by this quote from Dr. Reid Lyon's additional testimony. Dr. Lyon explained to our legislators:

> Phonemic awareness skills assessed in kindergarten and first grade serve as potent predictors of difficulties learning to read. With a test that takes only 15 minutes to administer, we have learned how to measure phonemic awareness skills as early as the beginning of kindergarten, and over the past decade we have refined these tasks so that we can predict with approximately 92% accuracy who will have difficulty learning to read. We have learned that the average cost of assessing each child during kindergarten or first grade with the predictive measures is approximately $10 to $15. This cost estimate includes the costs of the assessment materials.[20]

Given the low cost of identifying children at risk for reading failure, there is no excuse for any school in this country not to screen all kindergarten children using these measures.

Isn't It Harmful to Label a Child as Learning Disabled?

For the most part, no. Children with learning disorders or dyslexia are different and most likely they are aware of it from an early age. They are often relieved when they know that adults can identify what is going on with them. Informed parents are better advocates for their children; with a diagnosis they can gain access to information, resources, and services. It is a relief for parents to have some way to understand what they have been observing about their child, possibly since infancy.

Priscilla L. Vail, in her book, *About Dyslexia: Unraveling the Myth,* explains how a diagnosis can be positive:

> Medical research now shows that the combination of emotional peace and psychological energy opens extra pathways to thinking and learning. Children expand their abilities (and use their strengths to support their weaknesses) when they are in joyful, secure environments. Oddly, the more secure the child feels, the greater his willingness to risk. And without risk, there is no real learning.[21]

A classroom where the other children can do things the dyslexic child cannot easily do doesn't feel like a safe learning environment.

Whether you want to have your child identified as learning disabled within the school system depends on one criterion—if it is beneficial to your child, it's all worth it.

APPENDIX 1

Resource Lists for Parents

Suggested Books, Videos, and Web Sites for More Information on Reading

Books

Beginning to Read: Thinking and Learning about Print—A Summary by Marilyn Jager Adams (summary prepared by Stahl, Osborn, & Lehr) [Center for the Study of Reading, 1990, University of Illinois (217) 244-4083]
This summary of Marilyn Adams's book is written in a less technical manner than its original source.

Help Me to Help My Child: A Sourcebook for Parents of Learning Disabled Children by Jill Bloom
(Little, Brown and Company, 1990)
Book written by the mother of an LD child. Gives lots of information and her story.

Your Child's Growing Mind: A Practical Guide to Brain Development and Learning From Birth to Adolescence by Jane M. Healy, Ph.D.
(Doubleday, 1987, 1994)
Describes how important the environment is to a child's developing brain.

The Schools We Need and Why We Don't Have Them by E. D. Hirsch, Jr.
(Doubleday, 1996)
A broad overview of why Hirsch believes that schools fail children today.

(continued)

Suggested Books, Videos, and Web Sites for More Information on Reading *(continued)*

Teaching Our Children to Read: The Role of Skills in a Comprehensive Reading Program by Bill Honig
[Corwin Press, 1996, Thousand Oaks, CA (805) 499-9734]
Explains why direct instruction in skills is critical in teaching reading. Written for educators, but parents who are not intimidated by educator's terminology can read it, too.

Keeping a Head in School: A Student's Book about Learning Abilities and Learning Disorders by Dr. Mel Levine
[Educator's Publishing Service, 1990, (800) 225-5750]
Can be used to read and discuss with a child what his/her learning disability is and how to make accommodations.

About Dyslexia: Unraveling the Myth by Priscilla L. Vail
(Modern Learning Press, 1990)
Short (50-page) book that provides an overview of dyslexia in nontechnical language.

Research Reports and Literature from Organizations

The Orton Emeritus Series
[The International Dyslexia Association, (410) 296-0232]
Series of pamphlets written in language ideal for parents. Topics include an overview about dyslexia, testing, and social problems.

Every Child a Reader: The Report of the California Reading Task Force
[California Department of Education, 1995, (800) 995-4099, 26 pages]
Contains 10 recommendations to improve reading instruction and a reading curriculum timetable.

Teaching Reading: A Balanced, Comprehensive Approach to Teaching Reading in Prekindergarten Through Grade Three
[California Department of Education, 1996, (800) 995-4099, 34 pages]
Describes instructional components of recommended reading program and grade-level expectations. Prepared for educators.

Becoming a Nation of Readers
[Center for the Study of Reading, 1984, University of Illinois, (217) 244-4083]
Report of the Commission on Reading, written in parent-friendly language.

Suggested Books, Videos, and Web Sites for More Information on Reading

Web Sites

http://www.ldonline.org
[LD Project at WETA, in association with Parents and Educators Resource Center (PERC), National Center for Learning Disabilities (NCLD), and the Coordinated Campaign]
Best Web site available on LD. Contains information, articles, and even a store for ordering tapes and books.

http://interdys.org
[Web site of the International Dyslexia Association (IDA)]
Contains information on IDA branches, publications, conferences, research, and other pertinent information for parents and educators.

http://cde.ca.gov
(Web site of the California Department of Education)
Contains information about the California Reading Initiative.

http://proactiveparent.com
(Web site created by one of the authors of this book)
Contains additional information for parents, including new recommended books, links to other reading Web sites, and more activities.

Other Resources

Bridges to Reading
[Parents and Educators Resource Center (PERC), (800) 471-9545]
Kit for parents who suspect their child has a reading problem.

Learning Disabilities—Learning Abilities
[Vineyard Video Productions, (800) 664-6119]
Series of six videotapes on learning disabilities.

Organizations to Contact for More Information

Center for Development and Learning (CDL)
208 S. Tyler St., Suite A
Covington, LA 70433
(504) 893-7777

Children and Adults with Attention Deficit Disorder (CHADD)
499 NW 70th Ave., #308
Plantation, FL 33317
(954) 587-3700
http://www.chadd.org
A parent-based organization that offers local support groups, conferences, and information to the public.

Council for Exceptional Children (CEC) and the Division for Learning Disabilities (DLD)
1920 Association Drive
Reston, VA 22091-1589
(703) 620-3660 or
(800) 328-0272
http://www.cec.sped.org
http://curry.edschool.virginia.edu/~sjs5d/dld/

Council for Learning Disabilities (CLD)
P.O. Box 40303
Overland Park, KS 66204
(913) 492-8755

Educational Resources Information Center (ERIC)
ERIC Clearinghouse on Disabilities and Gifted Education
1920 Association Drive
Reston, VA 22091
(800) 382-0272
http://www.indiana.edu/~eric_rec

International Dyslexia Association (IDA)
8600 LaSalle Road, Chester Building, Suite 382
Baltimore, MD 21286
(410) 296-0232
(800) ABC-D123 (222-3123)
http://www.interdys.org
Provides information about reading difficulties. Tutor referral lists also available.

Organizations to Contact for More Information

Learning Disabilities Association of America (LDA)
4156 Library Rd.
Pittsburgh, PA 15234
(412) 341-1515
http://www.ldanatl.org
Provides information to the public about learning disabilities.

National Center for Law and Learning Disabilities (NCLLD)
P.O. Box 368
Cabin John, MD 20818
(301) 469-8308

The National Center for Learning Disabilities (NCLD)
381 Park Ave., Suite 1420
New York, NY 10016
(212) 545-7510
http://www.ncld.org
Publishes annual journal, *Their World*, and offers information and publications for parents.

National Information Center for Children & Youth with Disabilities (NICHCY)
P.O. Box 1492
Washington, DC 20013-1492
(800) 695-0285
http://www.nichcy.org

The National Right to Read Foundation
Box 490
The Plains, VA 20198
(800) 468-8911
Foundation has a newsletter and an extensive resource list of publications.

Parents' Educational Resource Center (PERC)
1660 S. Amphlett Blvd., Suite 200
San Mateo, CA 94402-2508
(415) 655-2410
http://www.perc-schwabfdn.org
Foundation started by Charles Schwab to promote awareness of learning disabilities, especially dyslexia.

Note: This is a partial list of resources we believe are particularly useful to parents. There are many other resources available.

Appendix 2

Glossary of Terms

Balanced approach An approach to teaching reading that uses a combination of explicit skill instruction and literature study. In the media this term is often used to refer to an approach that combines both whole language and phonics principles.

Basal reading program A set of materials used to teach reading to whole classes. Typically these are sold by major educational publishing companies and include a collection of student texts, a teacher's manual, and sometimes, supplemental materials for teaching or practicing skills.

Blend 1. To combine sounds to make a whole word. This term can be used to denote the process of combining sounds. 2. It can also refer to two or three consonant sounds spoken in sequence before or after a vowel, as in *st*, *cr*, or *pl*.

Code-emphasis Reading approaches that emphasize the decoding of words by their distinct letter-sound correspondences. These approaches generally provide more explicit sequential instruction in the component skills of reading.

Comprehension The extraction of meaning from written words.

Context clues Information that is helpful in decoding a word or comprehending the meaning of the words. This information comes from the surrounding words, phrases, pictures, placement on the page, type, and so forth.

Controlled vocabulary Words a child should be able to read. Some series of early readers closely tie the literature to the letter sounds previously taught in order to assure the child sees only words he should be able to read successfully.

Curriculum guidelines Written documents that provide information about the curriculum to be taught in the classroom.

Decoding The reader's ability to translate print into speech (identify the word) without respect to whether the word's meaning is understood. A child who has trouble looking at printed letters in text and pronouncing a word is said to have trouble decoding.

Developmental lag When a child's development in a particular area is behind either his peers or some benchmark standard. This term does not, however, mean that the child will outgrow the problem.

Digraph Two letters that represent one speech sound. Examples are the letters *th* for the sound */th/* in *thing*, *ch* for */ch/* in *chick*, and *wh* for */wh/* in *which*.

Dyslexia Difficulty with reading that is related to difficulty with language. It is generally assumed to be due to neurological differences in brain function and may vary in degree from mild to severe.

Encode The process of translating sound into symbols. Encoding is the opposite of decoding. Spelling requires encoding, whereas reading requires decoding.

Fluency When a reader is able to read at a fast pace, generally without stopping much to identify words. Researchers believe that in order to gain fluency, a reader has to develop rapid and perhaps automatic word identification processes.

Inventive spelling A child's attempt to map the sounds from speech to print. When a child writes the letters to represent the sounds he hears in words without worrying about book (or proper) spelling, it is known as inventive spelling because the child invents the spelling of the words as he hears them.

Learning disability Informally defined, an unexpected and unusual difficulty learning an academic skill. This difficulty in learning a skill stands out in relation to the individual's other abilities and is unrelated to level of intelligence. It may affect one area (such as reading or math), or it may be broader (such as a problem with attention).

Letter recognition The ability to name a letter when shown the symbol or to find the symbol that goes with the letter name.

Letter-sound correspondence The association of a letter with a speech sound. A child who can say or write the correct letter(s) for a speech sound is said to understand letter-sound correspondence.

Meaning-emphasis An approach to teaching reading that organizes the program to stress comprehension, or reading for meaning, rather than deciphering each word in the text.

Multisensory systematic phonics Some approaches to teaching reading are known as structured multisensory systematic phonics. All of these terms are important in this description. These approaches teach the child the letter-sound relationships in a structured and systematic manner, often with a prescribed sequence. They are multisensory by using tactile and large motor skills in activities, such as skywriting, sand trays, sandpaper letters, or rough carpet samples to imprint the letter shape with its corresponding sound.

Nonphonetic word A word that is not spelled as it sounds. Examples of nonphonetic words are *the*, *said*, and *was*.

Phoneme The smallest unit of speech that can be combined with others to make words.

Phonemic awareness The conscious awareness that words are composed of separate sounds and the ability to identify and manipulate those sounds. As described in the National Research Council's report, *Preventing Reading Difficulties in Young Children* (pg. 53), "A child with phonemic awareness is able to discern that *camp* and *soap* end with the same sound, that *blood* and *brown* begin with the same sound or, more advanced still, that removing the /*m*/ from *smell* leaves *sell*."

Phonics Instruction in how the sounds of speech are represented by letters and spellings. The media has used this term to refer more broadly to approaches that include explicit instruction in the component skills in reading, which is in contrast to approaches that emphasize reading for meaning and de-emphasize teaching the explicit skills. Instruction in phonics is actually only one part, albeit a key component, of a balanced approach to teaching reading.

Phonological awareness The ability to attend to the sounds of speech in language. Phonological awareness is a more inclusive term than phonemic awareness. Indications of this awareness include noticing similar sounds in words, appreciating rhymes, and counting syllables.

Print awareness The awareness of the conventions and characteristics of written language. This includes awareness of ideas, such as a book is read from left to right, front to back, and that there are spaces between words.

Reading strategies Approaches for how to read. A typical set of strategies for a new reader includes looking at the pictures, using context to understand the meaning, and sounding out unknown words. A more advanced reader has additional strategies, such as knowing how to adjust the reading rate to fit the task (i.e., skimming vs. studying).

Sight word A word that can be immediately recognized as a whole and does not require word analysis for identification. Sometimes the term is used to refer to words that have unusual spellings, cannot be sounded out but must be recognized by sight, and must be taught as a whole.

Sounding out The strategy of pronouncing a word by trying to retrieve the sound for each letter in the word. It is a practice that is encouraged for emerging readers rather than skipping an unknown word or guessing from context or picture clues.

Vowel patterns A pattern whereby a vowel is pronounced with its long or short sound based on what other letters surround it.

For example, the first vowels in *wave* and *stove* are long vowels because of the silent *e* at the end of the word.

Whole language The name of an approach to teaching reading that emphasizes teaching reading through literature without explicit instruction in how the alphabetic letters represent sounds.

Word attack strategies Strategies a reader uses to identify an unknown word. These strategies include all the things a child does to try to figure out an unknown word, which include breaking the word into syllables, looking for letter patterns, or identifying the vowel.

Word identification The ability to pronounce a word. Word identification doesn't mean that the reader knows what the word means, just that he can look at the printed word and pronounce it.

Appendix 3

Lists of Recommended Books for Your Child

Picture Books to Read Aloud to an Infant or Toddler Child

Author	*Title*	*Publisher and Copyright Date*
Ahlberg, Janet and Allen	*Each Peach Pear Plum*	Viking, Scholastic, 1978
Arnold, Tedd	*No Jumping on the Bed*	Dial, 1987
Barton, Byron	*Trucks*	HarperCollins, 1986
Brown, Margaret Wise	*Goodnight Moon*	HarperCollins, 1947
Bruna, Dick	*Miffy*	Methuen, 1964
Carlstrom, Nancy White	*Jesse Bear, What Will You Wear?*	Simon & Schuster, 1963
Gibbons, Gail	*Trains*	Holiday House, 1987
Hill, Eric	*Where's Spot?*	Putnam, 1980
Martin, Bill, Jr., and Eric Carle	*Brown Bear, Brown Bear, What Do You See?*	Holt, 1967, 1983
Martin, Bill, Jr., and John Archambault	*Chicka Chicka Boom Boom*	Simon & Schuster, 1989
Numeroff, Laura Joffe	*If You Give a Mouse a Cookie*	HarperCollins, 1985
Oxenbury, Helen	*Tom and Pippo Make a Friend*	Simon & Schuster, 1989

Picture Books to Read Aloud to a Preschool or Kindergarten Child

Author	*Title*	*Publisher and Copyright Date*
Allard, Harry	*Miss Nelson Is Missing*	Houghton Mifflin, 1977
Barrett, Judith	*Cloudy With a Chance of Meatballs*	Macmillan, 1978
Bartone, Elisa	*Peppe the Lamplighter*	Lothrop, Lee & Shepard, 1983
Bemelmans, Ludwig	*Madeline*	Viking, 1939, 1967
Brett, Jan	*The Mitten*	G. P. Putnam, 1989
Brown, Marc	*Arthur's Teacher Trouble*	Little, Brown, 1986
Burton, Virginia Lee	*Mike Mulligan and His Steam Shovel*	Houghton Mifflin, 1939, 1967
	The Little House	Houghton Mifflin, 1942, 1969
	Katy and the Big Snow	Philomel, 1969
Cooney, Barbara	*Miss Rumphius*	Viking Penguin, 1982
DeBrunoff, Jean	*The Story of Babar*	Random House, 1933, 1961
dePaola, Tomie	*The Legend of the Indian Paintbrush*	Putnam & Grosset, 1988
Freeman, Donald	*Corduroy*	Viking Penguin, 1968
Gag, Wanda	*Millions of Cats*	Coward McCann, 1928
Hall, Donald	*Ox-Cart Man*	Viking Penguin, 1979
Hoban, Russell	*A Baby Sister for Frances*	Harper Trophy, 1964, 1992
Holabird, Katharine	*Angelina Ballerina*	Random House, 1983
Hughes, Shirley	*An Evening at Alfie's*	Morrow, 1985
Hutchins, Pat	*The Doorbell Rang*	William Morrow/ Scholastic, 1986
Lionni, Leo	*Frederick*	Random House, Alfred Knopf, 1967

Picture Books to Read Aloud to a Preschool or Kindergarten Child

Author	*Title*	*Publisher and Copyright Date*
McCloskey, Robert	*Make Way for Ducklings*	Viking Press, Penguin, 1941, 1969
McCully, Emily Arnold	*Mirette on the High Wire*	Putnam & Grosset, 1992
Marshall, James	*George and Matilda*	Houghton Mifflin, 1972
Polacco, Patricia	*Babushka's Doll*	Simon & Schuster, 1990
Rathmann, Peggy	*Good Night, Gorilla*	Putnam & Grosset, 1994
Rey, H. A.	*Curious George*	Houghton Mifflin, 1941, 1969
Seuss, Dr.	*The Cat in the Hat*	Houghton Mifflin, 1957
	Green Eggs and Ham	Random House, 1960
Steig, William	*Doctor DeSoto*	Farrar Straus & Giroux, 1982
Steptoe, John	*Mufaro's Beautiful Daughters*	William Morrow, 1987
Van Allsburg, Chris	*The Wreck of the Zephyr*	Houghton Mifflin, 1983
Viorst, Judith	*Alexander and the Terrible, Horrible, No Good, Very Bad Day*	Atheneum, 1972
Waber, Bernard	*Lyle, Lyle, Crocodile*	Houghton Mifflin, 1965
	Ira Sleeps Over	Houghton Mifflin, 1972
Williams, Vera B.	*A Chair for My Mother*	Greenwillow, 1982
Yolen, Jane	*Owl Moon*	Putnam & Grosset, 1987

Books for a First-Grade Student
Beginning Reader—First Stage

Author	*Title and Publisher*	*Lexile Score*
Brown, Laura Krasny	*Rex and Lilly: Playtime* (Little, Brown, 1995)	30
	Rex and Lilly: Family Time (Little, Brown, 1995)	40
Eastman, P. D.	*Go, Dog Go!* (Random House, 1961, 1989)	<10
Seuss, Dr.	*Hop on Pop* (Random House, 1963)	157
Ziefert, Harriet	*Cat Games* (Penguin, 1988)	124
	Harry Goes to Fun Land (Penguin, 1989)	182
	A New House for Mole and Mouse (Penguin, 1987)	163

Books for a First-Grade Student Beginning Reader—Second Stage

Author	*Title and Publisher*	*Lexile Score*
Bonsall, Crosby	*Who's Afraid of the Dark?* (HarperCollins, 1980)	90
Cocca-Leffler, Maryann	*Ice-Cold Birthday* (Putnam & Grosset, 1992)	140
Edwards, Roberta	*Five Silly Fishermen* (Random House, 1989)	57
Herman, Gail	*What a Hungry Puppy!* (Putnam & Grossett, 1993)	66
Hoff, Syd	*Danny and the Dinosaur* (HarperCollins, 1986)	100
	Sammy the Seal (HarperCollins, 1959)	40
Parish, Peggy	*Be Ready at Eight* (Simon & Schuster, 1979)	140
Seuss, Dr.	*The Cat in the Hat* (Houghton Mifflin, 1957) (Random House, 1985)	150
	Green Eggs and Ham (Random House, 1960)	10
	One Fish, Two Fish, Red Fish, Blue Fish (Random House, 1960, 1988)	260
Smith, Laura	*The Sunset Pond* (Flyleaf Publishing, 1997)	N/A
	Frank the Fish Gets His Wish (Flyleaf Publishing, 1997)	N/A

(continued)

Books for a First-Grade Student
Beginning Reader—Second Stage *(continued)*

Author	*Title and Publisher*	*Lexile Score*
Picture Books		
Bridwell, Norman	*Clifford the Big Red Dog* (Scholastic, 1963, 1985)	260
Brown, Margaret Wise	*Goodnight Moon* (Harper & Row, 1947, 1975)	250
Bourgeois, Paulette	*Franklin is Bossy* (Scholastic, 1993)	220
	Franklin is Messy (Scholastic, 1994)	350
Carle, Eric	*The Very Hungry Caterpillar* (Putnam & Grosset, 1969)	200
	The Very Busy Spider (Putnam & Grosset, 1989)	230
	Do You Want to Be My Friend? (HarperCollins, 1976)	N/A
Crews, Donald	*Freight Train* (Scholastic, 1978) (William Morrow)	220
Martin, Bill, Jr., and Eric Carle	*Brown Bear, Brown Bear, What Do You See?* (Henry Holt, 1967, 1983)	N/A

Books for a First-Grade Student
Beginning Reader—Third Stage

Author	*Title and Publisher*	*Lexile Score*
Series Books		
Christian, Mary Blount	*Penrod's Pictures* (Macmillan, 1991)	N/A
Cosby, Bill	*The Meanest Thing to Say* (Scholastic, 1997)	350
Lobel, Arnold	*Frog and Toad All Year* (HarperCollins, 1976)	210
	Frog and Toad Together (HarperCollins, 1970)	330
Marshall, James	*Fox on the Job* (Penguin, 1988)	140
	Fox in Love (Penguin, 1982)	220
	Fox on Wheels (Penguin Books, 1983)	170
Minarik, Else Holmelund	*Little Bear* (HarperCollins, 1957, 1985)	370
Parish, Peggy	*Amelia Bedelia* (HarperCollins, 1963, 1991)	120
	Play Ball, Amelia Bedelia (HarperCollins, 1972)	230
Rylant, Cynthia	*Mr. Putter and Tabby Pour the Tea* (Harcourt Brace, 1994)	270
	Henry and Mudge in the Family Trees (Simon & Schuster, 1997)	400
Van Leeuwen, Jean	*Oliver Pig at School* (Penguin, 1990)	340

(continued)

Books for a First-Grade Student
Beginning Reader—Third Stage *(continued)*

Author	*Title and Publisher*	*Lexile Score*
Other Books		
Bonsall, Crosby	*The Case of the Hungry Stranger* (HarperCollins, 1992)	240
Christian, Mary Blount	*The Toady and Dr. Miracle* (Simon & Schuster, 1985)	290
Hoban, Russell	*Bedtime for Frances* (HarperCollins, 1960, 1988)	360
King, P. E.	*Down on the Funny Farm* (Random House, 1986)	212
Sharmat, Marjorie	*Nate the Great* (Putnam, 1986)	130
Zion, Gene	*Harry and the Lady Next Door* (HarperCollins, 1960)	350
Picture Books		
Allard, Harry, and James Marshall	*Miss Nelson Is Missing* (Houghton Mifflin, 1977)	340
Hutchins, Pat	*The Doorbell Rang* (Scholastic, 1986)	310
Rey, H. A.	*Curious George* (Houghton Mifflin, 1941)	400
Shaw, Nancy	*Sheep in a Jeep* (Houghton Mifflin, 1986)	N/A
Waber, Bernard	*Ira Sleeps Over* (Houghton Mifflin, 1972)	310

Books to Read Aloud to a First-Grade Student

Author	*Title*	*Publisher and Copyright Date*
Each Chapter Is a Different Story		
Bennett, William J.	*The Children's Book of Virtues*	Simon & Schuster, 1995
Milne, A. A.	*The World of Pooh*	Penguin, 1926, 1954
Short Chapter Books		
various authors	*The American Girls Collection,* series	Pleasant Company, various dates
Longer Chapter Books		
Atwater, Richard and Florence	*Mr. Popper's Penguins*	Little, Brown, Scholastic, 1938, 1966
Lindgren, Astrid	*Pippi Longstocking*	Viking Press, Viking Penguin, 1950, 1978
Warner, Gertrude Chandler	*The Boxcar Children*	Alfred Whitman, 1942, 1950, 1969, 1977
White, E. B.	*Charlotte's Web*	Harper & Row, 1952, 1980

Books for a Second-Grade Student

Author	*Title and Publisher*	*Lexile Score*
Easiest		
Brenner, Barbara	*Wagon Wheels* (HarperCollins, 1984)	400
Brenner, Martha	*Abe Lincoln's Hat* (Random House, 1994)	340
Byars, Betsy	*The Golly Sisters Go West* (HarperCollins, 1985)	N/A
Coerr, Eleanor	*The Josephina Story Quilt* (HarperCollins, 1986)	380
	The Big Balloon Race (HarperCollins, 1984)	440
Average		
Adler, David	*Cam Jansen and the Mystery of the Stolen Diamonds* (Puffin Books, Viking Press, 1980)	420
Park, Barbara	*Junie B. Jones Is a Party Animal* (Random House, 1977)	N/A
Sachar, Louis	*Marvin Redpost: Is He a Girl?* (Random House, 1993)	N/A
Spinelli, Jerry	*Fourth Grade Rats* (Scholastic, 1991)	340
Harder		
Blume, Judy	*Freckle Juice* (Macmillan, Bantam Doubleday Dell, 1971)	490
	Superfudge (E. P. Dutton, 1980)	490
	Are You There God? It's Me Margaret (Macmillan, 1970)	490

Books for a Second-Grade Student

Author	Title and Publisher	Lexile Score
Cameron, Ann	*The Stories Julian Tells* (Alfred Knopf, Random House, 1981)	520
Christopher, Matt	*The Lucky Baseball Bat* (Little, Brown, 1991)	450
Dadey, Debbie, and M. Thornton Jones	*Triplet Trouble and the Talent Show Mess* (Scholastic, 1995)	500
Danzinger, Paula	*Amber Brown Is Not a Crayon* (Putnam & Grosset, 1994)	740
	The Cat Ate My Gymsuit (Delacorte, 1974, 1984)	580
Haywood, Carolyn	*Eddie's Menagerie* (Morrow, 1978)	530
Kline, Suzy	*Horrible Harry and the Ant Invasion* (Viking Penguin, Scholastic, 1989)	490
	Horrible Harry in Room 2B (Viking Penguin, 1988)	480
Peterson, John	*The Littles* (Scholastic, 1967)	460
Sachar, Louis	*Sixth Grade Secrets* (Scholastic, 1967)	450
	Sideways Stories From Wayside School (Follett, 1978)	N/A
Sobol, Donald	*Encyclopedia Brown, Boy Detective* (E. P. Dutton, Bantam, 1963)	590
Taylor, Sydney	*All-of-a-Kind Family* (Follett, Bantam Doubleday Dell, 1951, 1979)	750

Books to Read Aloud to a Second-Grade Student

Author	*Title*	*Publisher and Copyright Date*
Banks, Lynne Reid	*The Indian in the Cupboard*	Doubleday, Avon, 1980
	The Return of the Indian	Doubleday, Avon, 1986
Carlson, Natalie Savage	*The Family Under the Bridge*	Harper & Row, Scholastic, 1958, 1986
King-Smith, Dick	*The School Mouse*	Hyperion, 1995
Lisle, Janet Taylor	*Afternoon of the Elves*	Franklin Watts, Scholastic, 1989
Winthrop, Elizabeth	*The Castle in the Attic*	Holiday House, Bantam Doubleday Dell, 1985
White, E. B.	*The Trumpet of the Swan*	Harper & Row, Scholastic, 1970

Books for a Third-Grade Student

Author	*Title and Publisher*	*Lexile Score*
Average		
Avi	*Who Stole the Wizard of Oz?* (Alfred A. Knopf, 1981)	510
Byars, Betsy	*The Computer Nut* (Viking Penguin, 1984)	510
Cleary, Beverly	*Henry Huggins* (William Morrow & Co., 1950)	650
Dadey, Debbie	*Cupid Doesn't Flip Hamburgers* (Scholastic, 1995)	570
Dixon, Franklin	*The Case of the Cosmic Kidnapping* (Hardy Boys) (Pocket, 1993)	655
Duffy, Betsy	*How to Be Cool in Third Grade* (Penguin Group, 1993)	N/A
	A Boy in the Doghouse (Simon & Schuster, 1991)	N/A
MacLachlan, Patricia	*Sarah, Plain and Tall* (HarperCollins, 1985)	540
McKenna, Colleen O'Shaughnessy	*Good Grief . . . Third Grade* (Scholastic, 1993)	570
Sachar, Louis	*There's a Boy in the Girl's Bathroom* (Alfred Knopf, Inc. 1987)	530
Tripp, Valerie	*Meet Molly: An American Girl* (Pleasant Company, 1986)	630
Warner, Gertrude	*The Boxcar Children* (Albert Whitman, 1942)	500

Books for a Third-Grade Student

Author	*Title and Publisher*	*Lexile Score*
Harder		
Avi	*Poppy* (Avon, 1995)	670
Babbitt, Natalie	*Tuck Everlasting* (Farrar Straus & Giroux, 1975)	700
Banks, Lynne Reid	*The Return of the Indian* (Doubleday, 1986)	710
Butterworth, Oliver	*The Enormous Egg* (Little, Brown, 1956)	840
Dahl, Roald	*James and the Giant Peach* (Alfred A. Knopf, 1961)	870
	Charlie and Chocolate Factory (Puffin Books, 1964)	890
Hurwitz, Johanna	*Aldo Applesauce* (William Morrow & Co., 1979)	730
L'Engle, Madeleine	*A Wrinkle in Time* (Farrar Straus & Giroux, 1962)	750
Lindgren, Astrid	*Pippi Longstocking* (Penguin, 1950)	890
McKenna, Colleen O'Shaughnessy	*Fourth Grade Is a Jinx* (Scholastic, 1989)	780
	Fifth Grade: Here Comes Trouble (Scholastic, 1989)	740
Selden, George	*The Cricket in Times Square* (Bantam Doubleday Dell, 1960)	770
Silverstein, Shel	*A Light in the Attic* (HarperCollins, 1991)	(poetry)

Books for a Third-Grade Student

Author	*Title and Publisher*	*Lexile Score*
Speare, Elizabeth	*The Sign of the Beaver* (Bantam Doubleday Dell, 1983)	790
Steig, William	*Dominic* (Farrar Straus & Giroux, 1972)	910
	Abel's Island (Farrar Straus & Girous, 1976)	890
White, E. B.	*Charlotte's Web* (Harper & Row, 1952)	700
	The Trumpet of the Swan (Harper & Row, 1970)	730
Wilder, Laura Ingalls	*Little House on the Prairie* (HarperCollins, 1935)	780

Recommended Books to Read Aloud to a Third-Grade Student

Author	*Title*	*Publisher and Copyright Date*
DeJong, Meindert	*The Wheel on the School*	Harper Trophy, 1954
Forber, Esther	*Johnny Tremain*	Houghtton Mifflin, 1943
Gipson, Fred	*Old Yeller*	Harper & Row, 1956
Lawson, Robert	*Ben and Me: A New and Astonishing Life of Benjamin Franklin as Written by His Good Mouse Amos*	Little, Brown, 1939
Lewis, C. S.	*The Chronicles of Narnia,* a series of seven books	HarperCollins, 1950s
Slepian, Jan	*The Broccoli Tapes*	Putnam & Grosset, 1988

Notes

Chapter 1

1. Collins, James. "How Johnny Should Read," *Time* 150, no. 17 (Oct. 27, 1997), 78.
2. Shaywitz, Sally. "Dyslexia," *Scientific American* 275, no. 5 (Nov. 1996), 98–104.
3. Adams, Marilyn Jager. *Beginning to Read: Thinking and Learning About Print* (Boston: MIT Press, 1990), 26.
4. Ibid., 27.
5. McPike, Elizabeth. "Learning to Read: Schooling's First Mission," *American Educator* 19, no. 2 (summer 1995), 3.
6. Rubin, Bonnie Miller. "Reading Wars: Endless Squabbles Keep Kids from Getting the Help They Need," *Chicago Tribune* (March 2, 1997), Perspective section, p. 1.
7. See the comprehensive review of research in Snow, Catherine E., Burns, M. Susan, and Griffin, Peg. *Preventing Reading Difficulties in Young Children* (Washington, DC: National Academy Press, 1998), 7.
8. For support of this statement, see the following sources:

- Brown, I. S. and Felton, R. H. "Effects of Instruction on Beginning Reading Skills in Children at Risk for Reading Disabilities," *Reading and Writing: An Interdisciplinary Journal* 2, (1990), 223–241.
- Foorman, Barbara R., et al. "The Role of Instruction in Learning to Read: Preventing Reading Failure in At-Risk Children," *Journal of Educational Psychology* 90, (1998), 1–15.

9. Duff, Christina. "How Whole Language Became a Hot Potato In and Out of Academia," *Wall Street Journal* (Oct. 30, 1996), 1.
10. Adams, op. cit., 26, 27.
11. Haynes, V. Dion. "In Blast From Past, California Schools Plan to Re-Embrace Phonics," *Chicago Tribune* (May 10, 1996), sect. 1, 8.
12. Honig, Bill. *Teaching Our Children To Read: The Role of Skills in a Comprehensive Reading Program* (Thousand Oaks, CA: Corwin Press, 1996).
13. Rossi, Rosalind. "Reading Scores Tumble: Steep Decline in Test Results Reported in Schools Statewide," *Chicago Sun-Times* (Sept. 8, 1997), 1.
14. "Results of the Illinois Reading Summit," (August 1996), Illinois State Board of Education.
15. Stanovich, Keith E. "Romance and Reality," *The Reading Teacher* 47, no. 4, (December 1993/January 1994), 285, 286.
16. Moats, Louisa C. "The Missing Foundation in Teacher Education," *American Educator* 19, no. 2 (Summer 1995), 9.
17. For many examples of the consequences of poor instruction, see McGuinness, Diane. *Why Our Children Can't Read and What We Can Do About It: A Scientific Revolution in Reading* (New York: The Free Press, 1997), 15–31.
18. Lyon, G. Reid and Chhabra, Vinita. "The Current State of Science and the Future of Specific Reading Disability," *Mental Retardation and Developmental Disabilities Research Review* 2 (1996), 2–9. Also see: Fletcher, J. M. and Lyon, G. R. "Reading: A Research-Based Approach," in *What's Gone Wrong in America's Classroom?*, ed. W. Evers (Palo Alto, CA: Stanford University, Hoover Institution, 1998), 49–90.
19. Rubin, op. cit.
20. See the summary of studies in the introduction to Adams, M. J., et al., *Phonemic Awareness in Young Children: A Classroom Curriculum* (Baltimore: Paul Brookes, 1998).
21. See the *Guide to the California Reading Initiative*, Sacramento County Office of Education, Comprehensive Reading Leadership Program (916-228-2635).

Chapter 2

1. Adams, Marilyn Jager. *Beginning to Read: Thinking and Learning About Print* (Boston: MIT Press, 1990), 8.
2. Ibid., 7–8.
3. "Your Home Is Your Child's First School," International Reading Association, Newark, DE.
4. Adams, op. cit., 85.
5. Kropp, Paul. *Raising a Reader: Make Your Child a Reader for Life* (New York: Doubleday, 1993), 30.
6. Adams, op. cit., 91.

Chapter 3

1. Andersen, Richard C., et al. *Becoming a Nation of Readers: The Report of the Commission on Reading* (Champaign, IL: Center for the Study of Reading, 1984), 23.
2. Rey, H. A. *Curious George Gets a Medal* (New York: Scholastic, Inc., 1957), 31.
3. Ibid., 43–44.
4. Ibid., 39.
5. Ibid.
6. Ibid., 44–46.
7. Clay, Marie M. *Becoming Literate: The Construction of Inner Control* (Auckland, New Zealand: Heinemann Education, 1991), 28.
8. Hiebert, E. H. "Developmental Patterns and Interrelationships of Preschool Children's Print Awareness," *Reading Research Quarterly* 16, (1981), 236–260.
9. Trelease, Jim. *The Read-Aloud Handbook*, 4th ed. (New York: Penguin, 1995), 9.
10. Andersen, Richard C., et al., op. cit., 23
11. Ibid., 117.
12. Ibid., 22–23.
13. Ibid., 23.
14. Whitehurst, G. J., et al. "Accelerating Language Development Through Picture Book Reading," *Developmental Psychology* 24, (1988), 552–559.
15. Jenkins, J. R. and Dixon, R. "Vocabulary Learning," *Contemporary Educational Psychology* 8, (1983), 237–260.

Chapter 4

1. Honig, Bill. *Teaching Our Children to Read: The Role of Skills in a Comprehensive Reading Program* (Thousand Oaks, CA: Corwin Press, 1996), 2.
2. Duff, Christina. "How Whole Language Became a Hot Potato In and Out of Academia," *Wall Street Journal* (Oct. 30, 1996), 1.
3. Groff, Patrick. "Understanding the Issues: Phonics, Statistics and Research," National Right to Read Foundation (1997), 11.
4. Foorman, B. R., et al. "The Role of Instruction in Learning to Read: Preventing Reading Failure in At-Risk Children," *Journal of Educational Psychology* 90 (1998), 37–55.
5. Goodman, Kenneth. *What's Whole About Whole Language?* (Portsmouth, NH: Heinemann, 1986), 38.
6. Chall, Jeanne. "Are Reading Methods Changing Again?" International Dyslexia Association International Conference (formerly The Orton Dyslexia Society), Boston, MA, Nov. 9, 1996.
7. Ibid.
8. Hirsch, E. D. Jr. *The Schools We Need and Why We Don't Have Them* (New York: Doubleday, 1996), 110.
9. Ravitch, D. *The Troubled Crusade: American Education, 1945–1980* (New York: Basic Books, 1983), 63.
10. Goodman, op. cit., 31.
11. Ibid., 24.
12. Ibid., 25.
13. Ibid., 28, 29.
14. Ibid., 29.
15. Duff, op. cit.
16. Adams, Marilyn Jager. *Beginning to Read: Thinking and Learning About Print* (Boston: MIT Press, 1990), 31.
17. Honig, op. cit., 123.
18. Groff, Dr. Patrick. "Parents Take Heed: Phonics Has Not Arrived—Yet," *Right to Read Report* 3, no. 4 (Mar. 1997) 1.
19. Honig, op. cit., 12.
20. Honig, op. cit., 7.
21. *Every Child a Reader: The Report of the California Reading Task Force*, California Department of Education, 1995, 2.
22. Adapted from *Teaching Reading: A Balanced, Comprehensive Approach to Teaching Reading in Prekindergarten Through Grade Three,* California Department of Education, 1996, 4–13.
23. Chall, op. cit.

Chapter 5

1. Adams, Marilyn Jager. *Beginning to Read: Thinking and Learning About Print* (Boston: MIT Press, 1990), 5.

2. Rayner, K. "Understanding Eye Movements in Reading," *Scientific Studies of Reading* 1, no. 4 (1997), 317–339.

3. This research is supported by:

   - Shaywitz, Sally. "Dyslexia," Scientific American 275, no. 5 (Nov. 1996), 100.
   - Torgesen, J. K., et al. "Preventive and Remedial Interventions for Children with Severe Reading Disabilities," *Learning Disabilities: A Multidisciplinary Journal* 5, (1997), 161–179.

4. Adams, op. cit., 105.

5. Ibid., 409, 410.

6. To refer to scholarly work on the psychology of reading, see:

   - Blachman, B., ed. *Foundations of Reading Acquisition and Dyslexia: Implications for Early Intervention* (Mahwah, NJ: Lawrence Erlbaum, 1997).
   - Gough, P. B., Ehri, L. C., and Trieman, R., eds. *Reading Acquisition* (Hillsdale, NJ: Lawrence Erlbaum, 1991).
   - Rieben, L. and Perfetti, C., eds. *Learning to Read: Basic Research and Its Implications* (Hillsdale, NJ: Lawrence Erlbaum, 1991).

7. Adams, op. cit., 410.

8. Ibid., 413.

9. Ibid., 160.

10. Ibid., 148.

11. Ibid., 274.

12. Grossen, Bonnie. "A Summary of NICHD Research on Reading Instruction," (The Plains, VA: National Right to Read Foundation, 1997), 9–12.

13. Chall, Jeanne S. *Stages of Reading Development* (New York: McGraw-Hill, 1983, and Ft. Worth, TX: Harcourt Brace, 1996), 4.

Chapter 6

1. Begley, Sharon. "How to Build a Baby's Brain," Special Issue, Your Child: From Birth to Three, *Newsweek* (Spring/Summer 1997), 31.

2. Ibid., 30.
3. Lynn, Leon. "Helping Children Develop Oral-Language Skills: 10 Activities Teachers and Parents Can Do," *The Harvard Education Letter* 13, no. 4 (July/Aug. 1997), 4.
4. Carle, Eric. *Do You Want to Be My Friend?* (New York: HarperCollins, 1976).
5. Hiebert, E. H. "Developmental Patterns and Interrelationships of Preschool Children's Print Awareness," *Reading Research Quarterly* 16, (1981), 236–260.
6. Martin, Bill, Jr., and Archambault, John. *Chicka Chicka Boom Boom* (New York: Simon and Schuster, Inc., 1989).
7. Carreker, Suzanne. *Reading Readiness* (Bellaire, TX: Neuhaus Education Center, 1992), Letter Recognition section, 1–3.
8. Ibid.
9. Ibid., 4.
10. Binkley, Marilyn R. *Becoming a Nation of Readers: What Parents Can Do*, U.S. Department of Education (March 1988), 10.
11. Ibid.
12. Torgesen, Joseph K., Ph.D. *Phonological Awareness: A Critical Factor in Dyslexia*, a brochure from the Orton Emeritus Series (1995), 7.
13. Ibid., 10–11.
14. Carreker, op. cit., Phonological Awareness section, 2.
15. Ibid., Phonological Awareness section, 15.
16. Ibid., Phonological Awareness section, 1.
17. A teaching strategy known as the "word sort" is a widely used practice. For further discussion on this strategy, see:

    - Henderson, Edmund H. *Learning to Read and Spell: A Child's Knowledge of Word* (DeKalb, IL: Northern Illinois University Press, 1981).
    - Morris, Darrell, "Word Sort: A Categorization Strategy for Improving Word Recognition Ability," *Reading Psychology* 3 (1982), 247–259.
    - Bear, Donald R., et al. *Words Their Way: Word Study for Phonics, Vocabulary, and Spelling* (Upper Saddle River, NJ: Prentice-Hall, 1996).

18. Excerpts from Yopp, Hallie Kay. "Developing Phonemic Awareness in Young Children." *The Reading Teacher* 45(9), 696–703.
19. Adapted from: Bear, et al., op. cit., 81, 139.
20. Yopp, op. cit., 700.
21. Ibid., 701.
22. Ibid.
23. Carreker, op. cit., Phonological Awareness section, 16.
24. Yopp, op. cit., 701–702.

Chapter 7

1. Leonard, Marcia. *My Pal Al* (Brookfield, CT: The Millbrook Press, 1998), 4–22.

2. Oppenheim, Joanne. *Do You Like Cats?* (New York: Bantam Books, 1993), 4–13.

3. Smith, L. A. *The Sunset Pond* (Lyme, NH: Flyleaf Publishing, 1997).

4. Honig, Bill. *Teaching Our Children to Read: The Role of Skills in a Comprehensive Reading Program* (Thousand Oaks, CA: Corwin Press, 1996), 39.

5. Ibid., 39.

6. Share, D. L., and Stanovich, K. E. "Cognitive Processes in Early Reading Development: Accommodating Individual Differences into a Mode of Acquisition." *Issues in Education: Contributions From Educational Psychology.* 1995. I, 1–57.

7. California State Department of Education. *Teaching Reading: A Balanced, Comprehensive Approach to Teaching Reading in Prekindergarten Through Grade Three* (Sacramento, CA: California Department of Education, 1996).

8. Snow, Catherine E., Burns, M. Susan, and Griffin, Peg. *Preventing Reading Difficulties in Young Children* (Washington, DC: National Academy Press, 1998), 80–83.

9. California State Board of Education. *Learning to Read: Two-Day Workshop* (Sacramento, CA: California Department of Education, 1997), glossary.

10. Carreker, Suzanne. *Reading Readiness* (Bellaire, TX: Neuhaus Education Center, 1992), Phonological Awareness section, 11.

11. Ibid., Phonological Awareness section, 11, 12. This is a variation of the activities Suzanne presented.

12. Ibid., Phonological Awareness section, 12.

13. Bear, Donald R., et al. *Words Their Way: Word Study for Phonics, Vocabulary, and Spelling* (Upper Saddle River, NJ: Prentice-Hall, 1996), 172–173.

14. Adapted from Bear, et al., op. cit., 180.

15. Ibid., 181.

Chapter 8

1. Lawson, Robert. *Ben and Me: A New and Astonishing Life of Benjamin Franklin As Written by His Good Mouse Amos* (Boston: Little, Brown & Company, 1939).

2. Forbes, Esther. *Johnny Tremain* (New York: Bantam Doubleday Dell Publishing Group, Inc., 1943).

3. Bear, Donald R., et al. *Words Their Way: Word Study for Phonics, Vocabulary, and Spelling* (Upper Saddle River, NJ: Prentice-Hall, 1996), 279
4. Hopping Frog game was created by Janet Bloodgood, Appalachian State University.
5. Adapted from: Bear, Donald R., et al., op. cit., 191.
6. Ibid., 188.

Chapter 9

1. For more information on the DR-TA approach see:

    - Davidson, J. L., and Wilkerson, B. C. *Directed Reading-Thinking Activities* (Monroe, NY: Trillium Press, 1988).
    - Stauffer, R. G. *Directed Reading Maturity as a Cognitive Process* (New York: Harper & Row, 1969).

2. Ogle, Donna M. "K-W-L: A Teaching Model that Develops Active Reading of Expository Text," *The Reading Teacher* 40 (1986), 564–570.
3. The activity of using a tree and its branches to diagram the root word and word families can be found in many sources, including:

    - Robinson, Sandra. *Origins: Bringing Words to Life* (New York: Teachers and Writers Collaborative 1989), 108.
    - Bear, Donald R., et al. *Words Their Way: Word Study for Phonics, Vocabulary, and Spelling* (Upper Saddle River, NJ: Prentice-Hall, 1996), 328.

4. Activity based on ideas from two sources:

    - Henry, Marcia. "Common Word Roots," presented at the Orton Dyslexia International Conference (Nov. 8, 1996).
    - Sonday, Arlene W. "Introducing Prefixes and Suffixes," presented at the Orton Dyslexia International Conference (Nov. 7–8, 1996).

5. Apple and Bushel game developed by Charlotte Tucker.
6. Adapted from: Bear, et al., op. cit., 81.
7. Ibid., 293, 317.

Chapter 10

1. Lyon, Dr. G. Reid. *Statement Before the Committee on Education and the Workforce* (Washington, DC: U.S. House of Representatives, July 10, 1997), 1.

2. "General Information Packet on Learning Disabilities: Information and Referral Service," National Center for Learning Disabilities, New York, 2.

3. "What a Decade of Research Tells Us About Learning Disabilities in Children and Adults," *NIFL Newsletter*, distributed in the *Roads to Learning* packet of the American Library Association, Chicago, 1997.

4. Wilkins, Angela, Garside, Alice, and Enfield, Mary Lee, Ph.D. *Basic Facts About Dyslexia: What Everyone Ought to Know*, "B" book of the Orton Emeritus Series, International Dyslexia Association, 1993.

5. Richardson, Sylvia O., M.D. *Doctors Ask Questions About Dyslexia: A Review of Medical Research*, "D" book of the Orton Emeritus Series, The International Dyslexia Association, 1994.

6. Shaywitz, Sally E. "Dyslexia," *Scientific American* 275, no. 5 (Nov., 1996), 99.

7. Wingert, Pat and Kantrowitz, Barbara. "Kids Who Can't Learn," *Newsweek* (Oct. 27, 1997), 58.

8. Shalit, Ruth. "Defining Disability Down," *The New Republic* (Aug. 25, 1997), 22.

9. Lyon, G. Reid and Chhabra, Vinita. "The Current State of Science and the Future of Specific Reading Disability," *Mental Retardation and Developmental Disabilities Research Review* 2 (1996), 2–9.

10. Wilkins, et al. op. cit.

11. Coordinated Campaign for Learning Disabilities. "Early Warning Signs of Learning Disabilities," Commonly Asked Questions About Learning Disabilities, press release, The Communications Consortium Media Center, Washington, DC, 1998.

12. Berninger, Virginia, et al. "Educational and Biological Links to Learning Disabilities," *Perspectives* (Newsletter of the International Dyslexia Association) 23, no. 4, (Fall 1997), 10–13.

13. Adapted from a booklet from the Orton Emeritus Series written by Jane Fell Greene, Ed.D. and Louisa Cook Moats, Ed.E. *Testing: Critical Components in the Clinical Identification of Dyslexia*, distributed by the International Dyslexia Association, 1995, 7–12.

14. Chart developed from information contained in the book by Diana Brewster Clark and Joanna Kellogg Uhry, *Dyslexia: Theory & Practice of Remedial Instruction* (Baltimore: York Press, 1995), 147–230.

15. Grossen, Bonnie and Coulter, Gail. "Reading Recovery: An Evaluation of Benefits and Cost," research report, The National Right to Read Foundation, The Plains, VA, 1997, 24.

16. Ibid.

17. Shaywitz, op. cit., 102.

18. Brady, Susan et al. "Perspective on Two Research Reports," *Perspectives* (Newsletter of the International Dyslexia Association), 22, no. 4 (summer 1996).

19. Lyon, op. cit., 10.

20. Ibid., 9.

21. Vail, Priscilla L. *About Dyslexia: Unraveling the Myth* (Rosemont, NJ: Programs for Education, Inc., 1990), 7.

Index

About the Authors

Susan Long Hall is currently president of the Illinois Branch of the International Dyslexia Association. In addition to this position she was appointed to serve on the coordination committee of the Illinois Right to Read Initiative. This initiative, launched by the Illinois State Board of Education, is a five-year effort to improve reading instruction in the state of Illinois. Susan also serves on the boards of The Cove School, a school for learning disabled children, and the Kohl Children's Museum.

Susan became involved in the field of reading when one of her children had difficulty learning to read. She deeply understands the confusion and questions of a parent whose child struggles with the most fundamental academic skill of the elementary school years—reading. Her search to help her child led to a deep passion about the field of reading, and this book.

Susan L. Hall is a graduate of Harvard Graduate School of Business Administration, where she earned an M.B.A., and Lawrence University in Appleton, Wisconsin. She has also pursued additional study in a master's program in education. Previously she was general manager of the executive education business for a financial services firm called The Alcar Group. Her career also includes managing a consulting practice in business plans and shareholder value analysis.

Susan resides in Long Grove, Illinois, with her husband, David, and two children.

Louisa C. Moats currently directs the Washington, D.C., site of a large-scale longitudinal research study on primary classroom instruction, funded by the National Institutes of Child Health and Human Development through the University of Texas at Houston. This project examines how to bring change to early reading instruction in major inner-city schools.

Prior to this assignment, she was a neuropsychology technician, teacher, graduate school instructor, and psychologist specializing in the identification and treatment of learning difficulties. During this time she evaluated over 2,000 children with learning issues and advised their families.

Dr. Moats received her B.A. from Wellesley College, her M.A. from Peabody College of Vanderbilt, and her Ed.D. from Harvard University's Graduate School of Education. She has authored journal articles, book chapters, instructional materials, and workshop materials to support the California Reading Initiative, a major effort to reform early reading instruction. She is widely published in the fields of reading and spelling, and speaks around the country on these subjects. Dr. Moats also serves on the national board of the International Dyslexia Association.

Louisa resides in Washington, D.C., and has one daughter.